D0841356

BLACK BUTTERFLIES

BLACK BUTTERFLIES

A FLOCK ON THE DARK SIDE

JOHN SHIRLEY

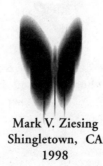

Mark V. Ziesing
Shingletown, CA
1998

BLACK BUTTERFLIES

A Mark V. Ziesing Book

All rights reserved.
Copyright © 1998 by John Shirley

Cover and interior artwork by John Bergin © 1998
Cover design, John Bergin / Custom fonts, Jennifer Dickert
Interior design and Composition by John Snowden

No part of this book may be reproduced or transmitted in any form or by any means, electronic or mechanical—including photocopy, recording, Internet posting, electronic bulletin board—or any other information storage and retrieval system extant or hereafter developed, without permission in writing from the Author or the Author's agent, except by a reviewer who may quote brief passages in a critical article or review to be printed in a magazine or newspaper, or electronically transmitted on radio, television, or in a recognized on-line journal.

All persons, places and organizations in this book—except those clearly in the public domain—are fictitious, and any resemblance that may seem to exist to actual persons, places or organizations living, dead or defunct is purely coincidental. These are works of fiction.

Library of Congress No. 98-060380
ISBN 0-929480-86-4

FIRST EDITION

Mark V. Ziesing, Booksellers | phone & fax: 916.474.1580
PO Box 76 | e-mail: ziesing@bigchair.com
Shingletown, CA 96088 | web: http://www.bigchair.com/ziesing

FOR MY OLD LADY

CONTENTS

Foreword

In the hours past midnight, jet-black butterflies flock into John Shirley's dreams. If he tries to ignore them, if he doesn't sing cold-metal songs to them, the black butterflies slice him with their razorsharp onyx wings. He has to write stories as dark and sharp and cold and beautiful as the butterflies—or they will cut him up from the inside then flutter out to infect the world.

Once written and read, the stories still infect. They rive into your brain and change you in small but unalterable ways. Because of this it is difficult, perhaps impossible, to ever entirely forget a John Shirley story.

This collection brings together some of John Shirley's unforgettable dark stories from the last decade. BLACK BUTTERFLIES is divided into two parts. THIS WORLD offers stories set in the what we call the "real" world—the every day world of the humans thrashing about in dilemma, twisting in obsession; stories from streets and bedrooms and bars and offices peopled with characters whose reality you can never deny or escape—although you may try to.

THAT WORLD comprises the second part of BLACK BUTTERFLIES: tales of the surreal and supernatural, the skewed truth—reaching slightly *beyond* reality...or, perhaps, there is *something* reaching out of that Beyond and grabbing you.

In other introductions to other John Shirley books, you'll find writers who have known him and his work for two decades. They introduce him as the original cyberpunk or an always surprising, constantly amazing progenitor of strange fiction often arising from the chaos of his life.

That's all true, but I never knew the chaos or the punk. The John Shirley I know has, with no small amount of effort, achieved a balance in his life and work. And, unlike others, I first met him through the exquisite nightmares of his dark fiction. Before I ever walked the cyberpunk's fictional future streets and battlegrounds, I knew only the nakedly gruesome, explicitly intense, yet utterly appealing *noir* of his dark side. His stories made me look inward. Like life they are tragic, sometimes cruel, but—also like life—consistently convey a message for us to discover. Invariably Shirley's tales touch a spiritual, and often wryly humorous, resonance by exposing human paradox and exploring the deviations we sometimes call evil. Where there is danger, there is also deliverance.

John Shirley mapped the cyber-wilderness before that terrain was even identified; he creates style before it is acceptable; his dark imaginings are often too extreme for the times in which they are created; he assumes an intelligent reader in an age of "dumbing down;" he writes what he writes regardless of labels in an era typified by niches.

That's why I wanted him to do BLACK BUTTERFLIES— stories from the last dark decade compiled as the arbitrary, but symbolic, millennium approaches. Maybe, finally, the world is ready for John Shirley.

Paula Guran
February, 1998

Sometimes my burden
Is more than I can bear;
It's not dark yet
But it's gettin' there.
                    —BOB DYLAN

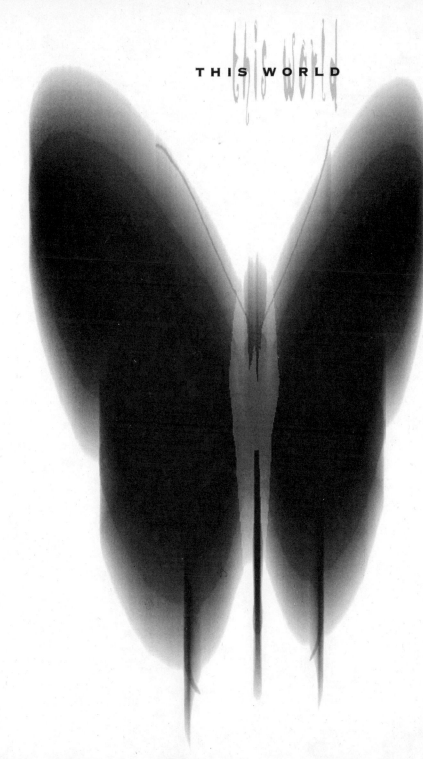

THIS WORLD

"You don't do some guy, even some old guy, them motherfuckers are all NRA nuts, homie; you might think you get some old white dude can't do shit and he dust you up." VJ is telling Reebok this while they stand in the bus shelter, watch people coming and going in the mall parking lot, late afternoon. California spring breeze is blowing trash by, couple of wax cups from Taco Bell.

"He got an AK in his walker?" Reebok jokes. He's out of high school now, still the class joker.

"You laughin', some of those old dudes are strapped big. Some senile motherfucker shot Harold's dog, all the dog do is run up on his porch. They got those M16's, that shit pops off, you canceled."

"So you think...it should be girls?" Reebok ponders, scratching his tag into the clear plastic wall of the kiosk with a house key. Key to his grandma's house. His mama left town with that white dude.

"Girls maybe armed, too. Most of 'em at least got that pepper spray, but you smart, you don't give'm a chance to use it, you take it away, put it in their eyes." VJ nods to himself.

"Can't make her use the fuckin' ATM, she got pepper in her eyes.

"I hear that. I hear that. We just jack the bitch from behind, is all, take her pepper away. Maybe later on, we clock her, too."

"When we do it?" Reebok asks.

"Fuck it. What about that one?"

She knows that Avery loves her. There's no doubt about it. If he says, Barbara, don't call back...that means: Barbara, call back again; Barbara, don't give up. It was there in the catch in his voice. It was heartbreaking, really, how Avery suffered. He *can't* say what he means, not with his witch wife, that witch bitch, nor with Velma looking over his shoulder. Busting his balls, excuse my French. Not letting his manhood emerge. His manhood trapped inside him. Avery should never have let Velma come into the office at all.

When Barbara had been in the office, it was beautiful, they'd share treats, and he'd smile at her in the way that meant, *I want you, even though I can't say so, and you know I do and I know I do: I want you*. It was so precious how all of that was in one smile! That was Avery. But Velma kept him on a leash like he's one of those little dogs with the hair puffed up over their eyes, little brown eyes like Avery's.

Coming out of the mall, Barbara's got the gift for Avery in her straw bag, the Italian peasant's bag she'd bought at the Cost Plus import place, and she's thinking maybe she should have charged the watch, because this was risky, she'd never stolen anything before, almost never, anyway nothing this expensive, and they could be following her out of the mall, waiting till she crossed some legal boundary, and it's not like they'd understand. *Love paid for it*, she could say to them, but they wouldn't understand any more than Velma did. Velma was the one who had pushed Avery into firing her.

Barbara unlocks her car, her hands fumbling. Then she goes all cold in the legs when a man speaks to her, in that sharp tone, and she's sure it's a store cop. She turns, sees it's a black guy, very young, not bad-looking. Wants some money probably. He's going to tell her his car ran out of gas and he just needs gas money, or one of those stories.

"I don't have any change with me," she says. "I don't really believe in giving money to people, it just keeps them on the streets."

"The ho isn't listening," says the taller of the two. How old are they? Maybe twenty. Maybe.

"Lookit here," the other one says, the one with the blue ski jacket, and he opens the jacket and shows his hand on the butt of a gun stuck in the waistband of his jeans. "I said: Get in the car and don't scream, or I shoot you in the spine right here."

In the spine, he says. I shoot you in the spine.

It turns out their names are VJ and Reebok. Reebok keeps talking about making her give him a blowjob. VJ says some pretty mean things about her looks and her age, though she's only thirty-eight and she's only about thirty pounds overweight or so.

VJ says, "One thing at a time. She suck your dick. But just one thing at a time."

Barbara's at the wheel of the Accord, VJ beside her, Reebok in back. He has a gun, too, a kind of oversized pistol with a long black metal box for the bullets. He calls the gun a Mac.

What would it be like to suck his penis? Would it be clean? He seemed clean. She could smell aftershave on them both. It's okay if it's clean.

She wonders why she isn't more scared. Maybe because they seem so ridiculous and amateurish. They don't really know what they're doing. That amateur stuff could make them even more dangerous; an officer had said that on *Cops*.

They almost drive by her bank, so she has to point it out, though she told them which one it was. "There's my bank, if you want me to turn in."

"You better be turnin' in."

She changes lanes, cuts into the lot, kind of abruptly so that somebody honks angrily at her as she cuts them off. Then she glides the Honda Accord up to the ATM.

"You both getting out with me?" she asks as she puts the car in Park.

"You just shut up, ho, and let us work on what we do," VJ says. He looks at Reebok.

"I don't know. We both get out? That might look kinda..."

"Might look..."

"Neither one has to get out," Barbara says, amazed at her own chutzpah "What you do is, you keep a gun on your lap under a coat, you watch me, and if I try to run or yell or anything, you shoot me. No wait—this is stupid! I can just give you the PIN number!"

They look at her with their mouths a little open as she digs through her purse, comes up with her Versateller card and an eyeliner pencil. Writes the number on the back of a receipt, hands it to VJ with the card. "I'll wait here with Reebok. He can keep an eye on me."

"How you know my name?" Reebok says with a whipping in his voice that makes her jump in her seat.

"You don't have to yell. I know your names because you said them to each other."

"Oh." He looked at his partner. "Go own." That's the way the word sounded. *Own.* She guessed it was *Go on.*

VJ starts to get out of the car. Then he turns back, takes the keys out of the car. "Don't try any weird shit, my man got a gun, too."

"I know. I saw it. It's a big one."

He blinks at her in momentary confusion. Then he gets out, goes up to the ATM. He puts the card in—it comes back out. He puts the card in—it comes back out. She rolls down the window.

"Whoa, ho, what you doin'!" Reebok barks at her from the backseat.

"I'm just going to tell him something about the ATM." She sticks her head out the window. "VJ? You've got the card turned the wrong way."

He turns it the right way around. It goes in and stays. He stares at the screen, punches the numbers. Waits.

Barbara's thinking. Aloud she says, "Were you ever in love with anybody, Reebok?"

"What?"

"I'm in love with Avery; he's in love with me. But we can't
see each other much. I see him outside his house sometimes."

"What the fuck you talking about? Shut the fuck up."

VJ comes back scowling, gets into the car.

"There ain't shit in there but forty dollar." He holds up the
two twenties.

"You check the account?" Reebok asks him.

"Forty dollars." He looks hard at Barbara. "You got another
account?"

"No. That was all I have left. I got fired from my job a few
months ago. You know how that is."

"The fuck." He's busy rooting through her purse.

"Just dump it out." she says. "It's hard to find anything
unless you dump it out.

He looks at her hard. He mutters something. Then he
dumps it out on his lap. He finds the checkbook, checks it
against the receipt from the ATM. Same account number. He
doesn't find any credit cards. Any other bank cards.

"You can look through my apartment," she suggests. "It's
not too far away." She looks at Reebok. "We might be more
comfortable there. I have some cold pizza."

"Girl," VJ says with a different, patient tone, as if talking
to an idiot, "you been carjacked. *Carjacked.* We're not eating
your motherfucking pizza. We carjacking."

"We could sell my car for parts," she suggests. "You could
strip it."

"You got any jewelry at your house?"

"You can look, but I haven't got any, no, except junk. All
I've got's a cat. Some cold pizza. I could get some beer."

"The ho's retarded," Reebok says.

"I think I'm the one doing the best thinking here," Barbara
points out. She spreads her hands and adds, "If you want to
rape me, you should do it at my house, where it's safe. If you
want to strip the car we should go do that. But we shouldn't
stay here because it might call attention to us, just sitting in
the parking lot."

VJ looks at Reebok. She can't read the look.

She decides it's time to make the suggestion. "I do know
where there's money. Lots of it. It's in a safe, but we can
get it."

——— ◆ ———

Avery knows it's going to be a good one because his palms are clammy. He's sensitive to things like that. He looks at the clock on his desk. Velma is going to be in here in five minutes, with the outfit he got for her in that shop in Los Angeles, and his willy is already stirring against his thigh, with that sort of core sensation running through it, like a hot wire running back into his testicles, and his palms are clammy and the hair on the back of his neck is standing up, all from trying not to think about her coming through the door of his office with that outfit under her coat. She could be a bitch, and you could take that to the bank, but by *God* there was no one like her when it came to playing those little games that got his blood up. They had it down to, what, maybe twice a month now, and that was just about right. He was almost fifty, and he had to sort of apportion out his energy with this kind of thing. He needed that extra something to prime the pump, and for a woman of forty-five she sure could—

The phone rings. "Beecham Real Estate," Avery says into it.

There's a lady on the other end wants to know about his rental properties. Wonder what kind of underwear *you* got on, he says to her in his mind. Out loud he says, "I can ask Velma to show the place tomorrow morning. It's a great little find...no, this afternoon might be kinda hard..."

The woman goes on and on about her "needs." Her rental needs. While he pretends to listen, Avery fantasizes about getting a line on some little cookie like this, a *young* one, giving her a house to live in at minimal rent in exchange for nookie once in a while. Trouble is, Velma goes over all the rental accounts. She'd notice the discrepancy. There's always a snag and it's always your hag. But Velma is okay. She likes games, likes to do it in the office, in broad daylight. Long as the shades are down.

He remembers that girl in the Philippines when he was in the Navy. He shipped out two days after she said she was pregnant. Like that was an accident, her getting pregnant. But what a tail. That petite golden tail. And he remembers those paper lanterns she got from some Japanese sailor. The shifting colored light on the wall from those paper lanterns,

swinging in the breeze coming through the mango tree while
he worked that golden tail. Man.

Beeping tone tells him he's got another call coming in; he
wriggles off the first call (love to answer your *needs*) and
takes the second call, which is from his lawyer, the
bloodsucking cocksucker. "What you going to charge me for
this call, Heidekker?" Avery asks, looking out the window to
see if Velma's car's in the parking lot. Don't see it. That yellow
Accord, whose car is that? He knows that car, doesn't he?

"No, I'm not charging you for this call," Heidekker says.
"Now listen—"

"I've about had it with you sending me a bill every time
you fart in an elevator with me, pal, I got to tell you."

"Look, I just need you to sign the request for an injunction
because I'm gonna run it over to Judge Chang in about an
hour here—"

"Just scribble my fucking signature on it. Just get it done."
Goddamn it, now Heidekker's got him thinking about Barbara,
and of course his dick starts shriveling up. He tries not to
think about Barbara, it shoots his nerves to hell, seeing her
hang around his house, watching him in the parking lot—

"I'm not empowered, you're going to have to sign. If you
want to give me power of attorney sometime, that might be a
good idea and we could talk about that—"

"No, forget it, forget it, just—" There, that was Velma's Fiat
pulling in. "Just don't come over for half an hour or so. I
won't be in. So, this paper going to do it all?"

"This injunction's all-inclusive—she may not follow you,
watch you, call you, the whole shebang. Can't come within
five hundred yards. There are laws about stalking now, and
we can prosecute her on them if she tries anything cute.
She'll end up doing time. Which might do her good because
they'd send her to a shrink. You change the locks at the
office yet?"

"No, that's tomorrow morning. She might have a key, if
she copied it. Frank says I should be flattered. Hey, not by
the attention I get from this girl, pal."

"Anyway, we'll take care of it. I gotta go, Avery—"

"Hold on now, hold on—" Keep him talking a minute, it
went with the fantasy for Velma to interrupt a business call.

"I gotta talk to you about this bill you sent me for last month, this is right on the edge of outrageous, here, Heidekker—"

"Look, we can go over it item by item, but I'm going to have to charge you for the time it takes to do that—"

The door opens; Velma's taking up most of the door frame, unbuttoning her coat, her long red hair down over the white, freckled shoulders as she slips the coat away: freckles on the white, doughy titties cupped by the black lace corset, those thighs under the crotchless panties maybe a little heavy but when she's wearing crotchless red lace panties, who the fuck cares. Lot of makeup around her deep-set green eyes. Maybe she's got some crow's feet; maybe her butt's beginning to sag. But with the corset holding it all together in black and red lace, with her pink labia winking out from the golden-red bush, who the fuck, who the fuck, who the fuck cares...

"Get back to you later, Heidekker," Avery says into the phone, hanging up.

"I had to have it. I want that woodie in your pants, Av. I was touching myself and thinking about you and I had to have it, I couldn't wait. I want it here and now," she says in that husky voice she does. "Give me that big woodie." She traces her cherry-red Revlon lips with the tip of her tongue.

"It's easy to misunderstand Avery," Barbara's saying. They're in her car, in a corner of the parking lot of Avery's building. I mean, Avery's so gruff. It's really cute how gruff he is. I gave him a stuffed bear once, with a note, it said: 'You're just a big old bear!' The way he talks is very short sometimes, and pretty blue, if you know what I mean, but he's really very, very sweet and sometimes he—"

"There any money in that place?" VJ interrupts, looking through the windshield at the little sienna-colored office building. Kind of place built in the early seventies, with those chunks of rocks on the roof, some insulation fad. "I think you frontin', girl, I don't think there's shit in there."

At least, she thinks, I've graduated from *ho* to *girl*. "He keeps a lot of cash in his safe. I think he's hiding it from the IRS. It was part of some payoff kind of thing for—"

"How much?" Reebok interrupted.

"Maybe fifty, maybe a hundred thousand dollars. It is quite a lot of money, isn't it? I never really thought about it much before..."

"That place kind of rundown, don't look like anybody in there doing that good."

"The recession killed two of the businesses that were there, and it's a little place and Avery's the only one left and he owns the building and he's gonna renovate—he's really just incredibly smart about those things, he always has these great plans for—"

"*Damn* shut the *fuck* up about the man!" Reebok snarled. "Mother*fucker!*"

"Fine, but just remember we can't go in there shooting because I don't want Avery to get hurt—"

"Ho, what the *fuck* you talkin' about—we step where we want, we got the motherfuckin' *guns*—"

"You need me. I know the combination to the safe."

Reebok goes tense in the backseat and shoves his gun at her. "And I know how to use this piece right here, you fuckin' whitetail bitch!"

"Then shoot me," she says, shrugging, surprising herself again. But meaning it. She doesn't care that much, really. Velma has Avery and nothing matters except Avery. That's what people don't understand. Avery belongs to her, and he is the cornerstone, and he is Man and she is Woman, and that's that, and people should understand it. "I really don't care that much," she goes on, shrugging. "Torture me. Kill me. I'm not going to do it unless we do it my way."

The muscles in VJ's jaw bunch up. He points the gun at her face.

She looks into VJ's eyes. "Do it. Kill me. Throw away the money."

VJ looks at her for a full ten seconds. Then he lowers his gun and reaches into the back, and pushes Reebok's gun down.

Right on the desk. He was doing it to her right on the desk, and he was telling her he loved her. He had her legs spread, her bony knees in his big, rough hands, and he had his pants down around his ankles, and there were zits on her thighs, she was wearing some kind of hooker costume, and...

He was telling her he loved her.

Then Avery's head snapped around to look at them, his mouth open and gasping with effort, his face mottled, forehead drippy, and he blinked at them. "She locked the office door..." Kind of blurting it. Then he focused on Barbara and realized she must have copied the keys.

Then—she can see it in his face—he realizes he's standing there with his pants down and his penis in Velma, who's propped on a desk with her legs spread, and two strange black guys are standing behind Barbara staring at him over her shoulder.

"Jesus Christ Mary Mother of God" is what comes out of him next as he pulls out his penis and grabs his pants, and Velma opens her eyes and sees Barbara and Reebok and VJ and screams.

Velma scrambles off the desk, hunching down behind it. Avery hits the silent alarm button, but it won't work; Barbara switched it off.

When Barbara was a little girl in Florida, she witnessed a hurricane. She was staying at her granddad's orange farm. Her grandma kept chickens, and Barbara looked through a knothole in the wall of the storm shelter and saw a chicken spreading its wings and being caught by the wind and the chicken was lifted into the sky and it disappeared up there, in the boiling air. Barbara feels now like there's a big wind behind her, pushing her into the room, only the wind is inside her, and she does what it wants to do, and it's carrying her around the room, like a tornado's whirling, carrying her around and around the desk, and it's howling out of her: *"That's how she traps you, Avery! That's how she did it and she's dressed like a hooker and that's completely right because she is a whore, she's a WHORE who's trapped you with her cunt and she is an evil, evil WHORE!"*

Avery has his pants up and he is seeing Reebok and VJ come into the room and he is reaching into the desk drawer. Barbara is swept up to the desk by the wind feeling, and she *slams* the desk drawer on his hand. *"No."*

Avery yelps with hurt, and when she hears that, something just *lets go* in Barbara; a spillway opens up in her and she thinks, *I forgot what feeling good feels like*. She hasn't felt this good since she was little, before some things started happening to her.

Now she finds herself drawn to the sound that Velma is making: Velma cursing under her breath as she hustles toward the side door to her office, thinking she's going to get to a phone, call 911.

Barbara looks VJ in the eye and says, "Don't let her get away, she's got the money. *Shoot her in the legs.*"

VJ jerks out the gun—and hesitates. Velma's got her hand on the doorknob.

"Barbara, Jeezus Christ!" Avery yells, clutching his swelling hand to his stomach.

"VJ," Reebok says. "Shit. Just grab her."

"No, shoot her in the goddamn legs or we lose the money!" Barbara says, saying it *big*, the voice coming out of her with that storm front behind it.

Then the thunder: the gun in VJ's hand.

Velma screams and Barbara feels another release of good feeling roll through her as pieces of Velma's knees spatter the door and embed in the wall and blood gushes over the carpet. Avery bolts for the door and, feeling like a Greek goddess, Barbara points at him and commands Reebok, "Hurt that traitor with your gun! Hurt him! He's stealing everything that's ours! *Stop him.*"

Reebok seems surprised when the gun in his hand goes off—maybe it was more a squeeze of fear in his fingers than a real decision to shoot—and a hole with little red petals on it like a small red daisy appears on Avery's back, then another—

Avery spins around, howling, mouth agape, eyes like those of a toddler terrified of a barking dog; Avery trying to fend off bullets with his pudgy fingers—she never saw before how pudgy they were—as Barbara reaches over and grabs Reebok's hand and points the gun downward at Avery's penis as his unfastened pants slip down. She pulls the trigger and the tip of his penis disappears—which she saw only that one other time, uncircumcised, with that funny little hose tip on it—

and she shouts, *"Now you're circumcised Avery you traitor fucking that whore you pig!"*

Reebok and Avery scream at the same time almost the same way.

Then she notices Velma sobbing. Barbara crosses the room to Velma, picking up something off the desk as she goes, not really consciously noticing what it is till she's kneeling beside Velma, who's trying to crawl away, and Barbara's driving the paper spike into her neck, one of those spikes your kid makes for you in shop with a little wooden disk, still has some receipts on it getting all bloody as the nail goes *ka-chunk* into her neck three times, four times, and Avery is screaming louder and louder, so VJ turns to him and yells *"Shut the fuck up!"* and makes the top of Avery's head disappear at the same moment that Barbara drives the spike again into Velma *kachunk-boom!*, the nail going in right behind her ear, and Velma suddenly pees herself and stops flopping, right in mid-flop, she stops....

"Oh, *fuck*," Reebok is saying, sobbing as Barbara gets up, moving through a sort of sweet, warm haze as she goes to the corner of the room and points at the cabinet that has the safe hidden in it and says, "Forty-one, thirty-five, and...seven."

It's not until she's in the car, on the road, pulling onto the freeway entrance, that Barbara notices that she peed herself, too, just like Velma. That's funny. She's surprised that she doesn't really care much. She's just been surprised at herself all day. It feels good, its like on *Oprah* those women talking about doing things they never thought they could do, that people said they couldn't do, and how good they felt.

She has to change her skirt, though. She won't chance stopping by her apartment, but she'll send VJ into a Ross or someplace at that new mall out east of town, on the way—she's made up her mind they're going to Nevada, Mexico would be too obvious—and he can get her some clothes for them with some of the money from the safe, almost a hundred thousand dollars....They didn't have to do discount now, they could go to Nordstrom's.

But there was the problem of Reebok. His blubbering. "You'd better quiet him down," she tells VJ softly. "The police are there by now, from all the noise, and they're going to put out an APB and they might have a description of the car from somebody, but I don't think so because no one was around, but even if they don't..." She was aware that she was talking in a rambling, on-and-on way, like she was on diet pills, but it didn't matter, you just had to get it out. You had to get it out eventually. "...even if they don't have a description, they're going to be looking for anything suspicious, and him sobbing and waving a gun around."

"VJ," Reebok says raspily, between gasping sobs, "look what this crazy bitch got us into....Look what she done."

"I got you into a hundred thousand dollars." She shrugs and passes a Ford Taurus. "But I don't think he should get any of the money, VJ," she says. "I had to do half the job for him, and he's going to panic and squeal on us." She likes using that verb from old movies, *squeal.* "I think you should drop him off somewhere then we can go to Nevada and buy a new car for you, VJ, and some new clothes, maybe get you a real gold chain instead of that fake one, and you can have the watch I got in my bag, the watch I got for Avery, and some girls if you want, I don't care. Or you can have me. As much as you want. Then we have to think about some more money. I've been thinking about banks. I read an article about all the mistakes bank robbers make. How they don't move around enough, and all kinds of other mistakes, and I think we could be smarter."

VJ nods numbly.

Reebok looks at him, blinking, gaping. "VJ?"

VJ points at an exit. "That one." The exit's a good choice: Caltrans is doing a lot of construction there, though the workers have all gone home, so there's lots of cover, what with the earthmovers and all the raw wood, to hide what they are doing from people passing on the freeway, and there are places where the earth is dug out, to hide the body. VJ made a smart choice—he's the smart one of the two guys, smarter than she is, she decides, but that doesn't matter, because she is stronger than VJ in a certain way. That's what counts.

She's thinking all this as she pulls off onto South Road exit and onto a utility road, in the country, with the construction between the road and the freeway, and no one around.

She pulls the car up in a good spot. Reebok looks at them and then bursts out of the car and starts running, and she says, "VJ, you know he's going to tell, he's too scared." VJ swallows and nods, and gets out and the gun barks in his hand, and Reebok goes spinning. VJ has to shoot another time before Reebok stops yelling. Barbara, all the while, is watching the wind pinwheeling some trash by, some napkins from a Burger King...just trash blowing by...

Some more yelling. VJ has to shoot Reebok one last time....

She squints into the sky, watches a hawk teetering on an updraft.

VJ is throwing up now. He'll feel better after throwing up. Throwing up always leaves a bad taste in the mouth, though.

She wonders what VJ's penis will taste like. It will probably taste okay. He seems clean.

And VJ's smart, and handsomer than Avery, and much younger, and she knows they belong together, she can feel it. It's cute how VJ tries to hide it, but she can see it in his eyes when he thinks she's not watching: he loves her. He does.

WAR AND PEACE

Butch starts fucking around with the dead girl's body. "Butch," I tell him, real dry, "I'm pretty sure that's not standard police procedure." This, see, was two years ago; the first time I looked at Butch different.

Butch has pulled on the rubber gloves, because when there's blood we watch it real close now. I knew a cop got AIDS from touching a fresh stiff; cop with a cut on his hand turning the dead guy's bloody face for a better look: Boom, an officer's ass shriveling up with HIV. We put on the gloves now.

This stiff is a Chicano girl, big breasted, and she has a little horizontal knife cut about two inches long in the top of her left tit, and there really isn't much blood, I don't know why, most of the bleeding was internal. But somebody has...

Butch says it out loud. "Long thin blade ri-i-ight through the titty and ri-i-ight through her itty-bitty heart."

She's propped up in bed in a motel, wearing a black leather skirt, one red pump, no top, one eye stuck open, the other shut, like a baby doll. There's some ripped clothes lying around.

Butch reaches out and runs the rubber-covered tip of his thumb, real slow and tranquil, along the lip of her wound. Then he pinches a nipple. This is making me nervous. I mean, we're a couple of white cops in the Hispanic neighborhood, shit.

"What the hell, Hank," Butch says to me, grinning. "Let's pump a fuck into her. She's got one more in 'er."

You get into gallows humor, this job, so I grin back and says, "She's still warm and soft."

But he isn't kidding. He starts playing with her titties, even the slashed one, and lifting up her skirt. "You can turn your back if you want, or not, I don't care," he says, his hand on his zipper. I get this feeling he's hoping I won't turn away. "Come on," he says. "She was a fuckin' whore anyway."

"We don't know that, Butch. All we know's a motel manager found a stiff." But he goes on playing with her. "Butch—no fuckin' *way*," I say. "They called her family from the ID in her purse, her fuckin' *mom* might show up and come in and see that shit. 'The white police officers were fucking my dead daughter, Mr. DA! I'm suing the department's ass!' I mean, Christ, are you…" I didn't finish saying it.

He steps back, the same cool grin, but then he catches the tip of his tongue in his teeth like he was just kidding. "Fuckin' with ya. Gotcha didn't I." He walks out past me. But I see him re-arrange his dick in his pants as he went. He has a hard-on.

Believe it or not, I read about it in the papers. No one called me. I'm just coming off vacation but, shit, somebody should've fucking called me. Della, Butch's wife—the wife of my partner, my best friend—turns up dead in the trunk of her own car, and no one calls me.

Now I'm over at Butch's, just being there with him. Making us some coffee. It feels funny, looking at Della's stuff in the kitchen. My own wife Jilian gave Della those dish towels; *Love Our Planet* machine-embroidered on them. Some kind of soybased dye used in them. My wife goes on these spending sprees in Berkeley.

Della not long ago re-did the kitchen, and put everything in its place, and picked out the curtains and the other new gewgaws about two weeks before; spending too much money,

Butch had said. But the kitchen now looks like a picture out of *Ladies' Home Journal*. And then some dirtbag strangled her, and her new kitchen things all seem like placemarkers for her going. *You knew me for years. I babysat your kids. Where am I now?*

I'm just a patrolman, but I see dead people all the time, mostly old people that croak out, and I got to make a report. But this is different: Butch's wife Della, she babysat my kids, made me and my wife dinner. She could be bitchy but Jilian liked her and Ben liked her and Ashley liked her and we were used to her. And some *bug* killed her to make a point, and put her in the trunk of her car. I was glad I wasn't on the detail that found her, after two days...the smell of someone dead two days in a trunk; someone that you fucking went *golfing* with.

I look through the door at Butch sitting on the couch quiet as a mannequin in a store window. Butch wears a yellow golf shirt, and tan Dockers pants, and brown loafers with tassels, and no socks. He has that same butch haircut, going a little gray now, that got him his tag, which he says he wears just because you pretty much never had to comb it. Although I think he wears it because his dad had one, his whole life. His dad was a Marine Corps flyer, stationed right here in Alameda, a real big old hard-ass who shriveled up like a used condom with cancer and died whining. I shouldn't talk about him like that, but I always hated the old fucker.

The Gold Tins are searching the house. Just a routine, but it ticks Butch off. "Treating me like a fucking suspect," he says. "God, Della." Starting to cry again. His eyes are still red from crying for two days. He was talking about Della for hours, what a patient woman she was, how she put up with all kinds of shit being a cop's wife, worrying about him, and it ends up they got her and not him, and how it isn't right. The captain was there for an hour or so of that, yesterday, a hand on Butch's shoulder, sometimes starting to cry himself, and later on the captain tells the reporters from the *Oakland Trib*, "This is genuinely tragic. Officer Behm feels it so deeply. He's got just about the biggest heart of anyone I know." And he talks about Butch's work with the Eagle Scouts and the vocational fair, lots of good stuff he's done.

I tell Butch, "They're looking for stuff that could connect your wife with a killer, like a letter, say—I mean, no offense but they got to consider maybe she had an affair, Butch, and her boyfriend did it. You know?"

He snorts, "Boyfriend. Not Della, not ever." There might be a little contempt in the way he says it. He starts to say something, doesn't say it, then he goes on, "What the fuck is the point of looking for a boyfriend when they got the message painted right on the car?"

Meaning the spraypainted graffiti on the side of her car. They found her car, her body in the trunk, in the Oakland ghetto, right there in gang-banger country, and spraypainted on the side in red was "WAR." And the killers sprayed a little circle around the bumper sticker that said, "OPOBA." Oakland Police Officers Benevolent Association. To let everybody know that *they* knew this was a car belonging to a cop, and the woman was a cop's wife.

For maybe four weeks now, we've been campaigning a "War on Drug Gangs" in Oakland, because of all the drug-related killings, so now, it's figured, their retaliation has begun. Two weeks ago Butch arrested a projects gangster for breaking into a car, and maybe the perp flipped Butch for the target. Who knows, the dirtbag could be related to some big crack gangster. So maybe the gang-bangers start following Butch and decide to hit him where it's easier for them and for a bigger psychological effect on the department. We can get you right in your homes, cops. You can run but you can't hide.

"Thing is, they know the spraypaint could be a fake, Butch," I tell him. "Planted to throw them off. Could be some fucking lunatic who's been watching her for a while, got obsessed with her, maybe somebody she knows."

"I hope so," Butch says, "because then maybe we could nail him. And I could kill him myself." With a catch in his voice.

It's while I'm watching *Jeopardy!*, Jilian's favorite show. All of a sudden, right at the start of Double Jeopardy, I think: *He's a suspect.* After *Jeopardy!*, I'm watching *Wheel of Fortune*. The phrase letters the contestant has, are: _A_ _ _D PE_C_.

Something makes me squirm in the La-Z-Boy while I'm watching this. The contestant starts to fill in the letters. My wife, who's the brainy one, figures it out first. "War and Peace." she says.

"Yeah, that's..." I don't finish what I started saying and she looks at me.

"You okay?"

"Yeah." I'm feeling sick, though.

"I feel weird too," Jilian says. "God, Della was just over here taking care of Ashley and Ben. It was hard explaining it to them, Hank." She starts to sniffle, and I go to the couch and put my arm around her.

"I know. But they're a cop's kids. They know the world a little better than their friends."

She shakes her head, her face getting swollen from crying. Her nose going red on the end, the way it does. "That's maybe the worst part of being a cop's kids."

Another time, I might get a little put off. *The worst part* like it was all bad one way or another. But I'm thinking about War And Peace, and Jilian's attitude is low on the priorities.

I remember Butch, the older kid across the street, helping me with football, soccer, basketball. I was twelve and thirteen, the nerdiest kid with a ball, the Jerry Lewis character and Butch was like my surrogate big brother. Or my dad. He liked to talk about sex with me, looking at those *Playboys*, and that was some heavy duty intimacy for a thirteen-year-old kid, when it came to hanging with a senior. There was a circle-jerk feeling about it, though he never touched me. Makes me embarrassed now.

He took me to the drive-in with him sometimes too, and he'd leave me in the car to watch one of those 60s movies where hippie girls in paisley miniskirts get involved with Hell's Angels and paint flowers on their chests and do a lot of making out to psychedelic music but never quite screw—while Butch went to drink some beer with his football friends in Andy's van. But he always came back and snuck me a can of beer, and told me some incredibly dirty joke and asked me how I liked the sex scenes in the movie and what did I think about who did what to who. He could turn back to thirteen with me, just

like that, though he was about to go into community
college.

I know for sure he strangled Della.

———— ◆ ————

There's no detective work about it. I just know him, and
the "War" thing is like some bullshit from a Mel Gibson movie,
and Butch loves that stuff: Mel Gibson, Clint Eastwood, Bruce
Willis's *Diehard*. He makes fun of it, like all cops do, because
it's such fantasy, but he loves it anyway. Like all cops do.
And thinking about that "War" spraypainted on the car...how
Jilian got a skeptical look when I told her about that. And I
remember Butch, oh, six months before Della was murdered
saying he thought about divorcing her, but he'd still never be
rid of her, there would be alimony fights, and fights over the
house and she knew all his friends and it'd be awkward going
out with people and he finished up by saying, "So I *still*
wouldn't get any peace from her."

People talk about divorcing all the time. It's no big deal.
They fought a fair amount. That's no big deal either. Me and
Jilian fight our share.

War and Peace.

Here's the thing: Butch and I stole some money from the
department. Well really, it was from the bugs. It was money
confiscated from drug dealers and it was a *lot of fucking
money*, see. It was about four hundred eighty grand. We took
it from an evidence locker and covered our tracks clean, but
they could still find out. So, we were sitting on it. We weren't
going to spend it for five years. That was our deal, a blood
oath. No calling attention to yourself. Save it for later. No
matter how broke we got in the meantime. *Don't touch it.*

But suppose Butch is about to go down for killing Della.
If he killed her for sure. Suppose he wants to bargain with
the department. Suppose he shafts me. *Hey Captain, remember
that half a mil that took a hike?*

By about two p.m. the next day I am almost sort of nearly
pretty sure I was wrong. He didn't kill her. You can do that;

it's like one of those rides at Great America where you go in a loop, completely upside down. That's how I feel while I'm following Butch over the bridge into Oakland. Like the bridge is going into a loopdeloop.

And it's the worst thing in the world, somebody you knew all your life turns out to be something *else*. I mean—what's real, then? Nothing. Not a fucking thing. So it can't be right, what I'm thinking about Butch.

I'm officially supposed to be on a Drug Task Force detail in the unmarked car, which basically means watching the basketball court next door to the high school to see if anyone buys or sells, and then I buzz the detectives who get the glory of the collar. But I coop it off. I am following Butch.

Why is he driving into Oakland?

He's on special leave, and he might be going to see a therapist or something, and then I'll feel like a jerk.

He didn't fucking kill her, you asshole.

And the whole time I am mumbling this I am keeping my car back in traffic so Butch doesn't see me follow him.

He drives to San Pablo Avenue, and he cruises a whore. She makes eye contact and points down the road, not knowing he's a cop, and he picks her up. *What the fuck.*

She's a black girl, or maybe what they call a High Yellow wearing an elastic tube-top thing, and that shows her stretch-marked middle, and a short fake-leather skirt. Probably no underwear: if they can't do it all giving head, you cough up a little extra money and they hike up their skirt.

They like to do it in the car. It's easier than keeping a room somewhere—those Pakis who run the weekly-rate hotels wring money out of the whores same as pimps. And it's faster just to do it in the car. They're always thinking ahead to the next trick; to the time they got enough money to go kick it. And the faster they fuck, the faster they get it over with.

They all have their choice spots picked out for getting it done in a car: back parking lots of warehouses; certain kinds of dead end streets; dirt tracks along deserted railroad yards, out next to the dumpster behind Safeway; oh, and parking lots under freeways. The butt-end of the city.

That's where Butch has the pavement princess. They're under a freeway, in a county equipment storage lot. Dull yellow road graders, defunct street cleaning trucks, stuff like that. Butch has some county keys, and he's unlocked the gate.

I watch from across the street, with a piece of fence and a parked truck in between; I'm peering around the truck, through the fence, between a couple of road graders. I can make them out in there. Butch is showing her his badge and she looks royally pissed off. I can read her lips. "Oh, man you mother*fucker*." But it's not a bust. I watch as he makes her bend over his car, spreads her legs, her hands flat and far apart on the trunk, while he checks out her pussy, grinning the whole time, slapping her thighs wider apart with a nightstick he's taken out of the car.

Then he starts shoving the nightstick in her, slapping her ass, pinching her titties, and playing with himself. I can make out what he's saying. "You a *ho* aren'tcha, huh? You a *ho*, right?"

He's having a *good* time. The son of a bitch strangled Della. I can't watch this.

Jilian says, "You shouldn't go, you're not supposed to bug people with too much attention and giving them all kinds of stuff, you're supposed to leave them to feel their grief." She went to a grief workshop when her mom died. She's like that.

"It wasn't my idea!" I tell her. "The fucking fishing trip is his idea! He wants to go!"

So we go, me and Butch. Driving up in his Bronco, he's really pissed off that Stinson made him get permission from the captain to leave town. "Eighteen years on the force and they're treating me like a dirtbag!"

"Hey and you'd be with me the whole time anyway," I say. That was the wrong thing to say somehow. He gave me this *look*.

I don't say anything about how a few days after they found his wife dead he's gleefully rousting prostitutes and playing with their asses. I don't say anything, but I'm thinking about it. How I could tell, watching him play sick games with the whore, he's done this a lot. You hear people talk about how you know somebody for years but you don't really know them.

This case, it's like he's almost not even the sex I thought he was. I mean I don't know *shit* about this guy. And now I'm driving up to a remote mountain lake with him. This is great.

We go to Robins Lake. It's one of those reservoir lakes, a sweetheart arrangement between developers and some senator who swung the dam. Except for a little bit of gas slick around the edges from the outboards and the jet-skis, it's pretty clean, and they stock it with fish. If you go to the north end, the jet-skis they keep at the south end scare the fish up to you.

It's the kind of sunny day that looks friendly and waits till its gets you out in the open and then it pulls out the glare. *Have a headache, buddy.* We rent an aluminum outboard, and since it's the middle of the week we're almost the only guys out on the lake. We both got sailor hats on, folded down like bowls on our heads, and Ray-Bans. Butch's brought a Styrofoam cooler full of Coors Lite. I'm wishing I brought sunscreen for the back of my neck, after just a half hour it's already rasping. I'm asking myself why I'm out on the lake with a murderer.

Because I have to talk to him. Because he's been my more-or-less best friend for, what, fifteen years or so. Because it's inertia, and he asked me.

We fish, either end of the boat, and he doesn't say much. Until finally, "I guess you could see the idea of a fishing trip as kind of weird, now. But I had to get away." I can see sundogs off the lake in his dark glasses.

It's like my lower jaw got real heavy, as I say what I'm supposed to. "People adjust in their own ways. If this keeps you sane, hey, go for it."

He doesn't say anything for a minute. "You think there's anything weird about how they came back last night?"

I feel some hope, then. Maybe it wasn't up to me.

"Buddy, when they don't have a *name*—I mean, okay, they got the gang-bangers lead. But when they don't have a name, or even a description...they fall back on the family. Doesn't mean anything."

"You mean, the 24/24 rule."

"Yeah." The 24/24 rule is that the most important time in a murder investigation are the last twenty-four hours in the victim's life and the first twenty-four hours after the body's found. "So it's been longer than the twenty-four, and they feel like it's getting cold. They clutch at straws."

My lower jaw's *really* heavy now. I can barely force myself to say this horseshit. I'm thinking about his small hands, and figuring he didn't do it with his hands, he did it with a cord or a scarf or something. Thinking he's cute for choosing strangulation so she doesn't bleed all over the place. Only, the gang-bangers pretty much never strangle people. They love guns and knives. Just fucking love them.

I decide I can't sit here like this anymore. It's too quiet out here and I just keep seeing him go through the laundry for just the right scarf and then I see him with the ho.

You have to think things through. That's a rule. You're sorry if you don't think things through.

I come at it from left field. "I mean, shit, even if…if a cop flipped out and killed his wife, the department'd be stupid to push too hard on it."

He stares at me. My mouth goes dry. I open a beer.

I make myself go on, not sure what I'm trying to accomplish, and thinking it might be good to leave the lake early in the afternoon. "I'm just thinking about ol' Detective Stinson's point of view. Or anyway, the captain's." He opens his mouth to say something like *What are you getting at?* and I put in real quick, "See, they could *talk themselves into* thinking you did it." (He did it.) "And the DA could get wind of it and then they got to go through with it. I mean, we know you didn't do it." (He did it. By now he knows I know he did it.) "But you know, if they haven't got a suspect they'll keep turning to look at you and you know how people can kid themselves into shit." (He killed her. We have a picture of Della feeding Ashley with a baby bottle.)

"So what's the point?"

The smell of gas from the outboard is making me ill. "Well…is there anything that could give them the wrong idea? Something they could misunderstand and think it was physical evidence."

He's almost smiling. I'm wishing I could see his eyes behind the Ray-Bans.

"Naw. No I don't think so. I mean, I'm not…"

He doesn't actually say it. *I'm not stupid.*

"You know what?" I stretch, and rub my neck. "This sun is, like, too much for me. Maybe we oughta get back a little early."

He shrugs. He's still not quite smiling. "Hey Hank—there's the money we took."

"We're not even supposed to *talk* about that, man."

"We're out in the middle of a fucking lake, Hank. Just keep that money in mind. You wouldn't want to lose that. And who knows what."

I just nod.

My stomach feels like it's got a bag of sand in it. But I just keep thinking, *You got to think things through.* That's the bottom line, right there.

Stinson's happy. Which is fucked up.

Stinson thinks he's going to make his first detective collar. We're sitting in captain's office. Butch and the captain and Stinson and Mann, the heavyset black guy from Internal Affairs, and me for Butch's moral support.

Stinson disarms Butch, first thing, which freaks everyone out, even the captain, who looks like he's going to object, and then doesn't.

Butch tries to be cool. "You want my Beretta, keep it oiled. I don't want a fucking dust speck in it when I get it back."

I'm groaning inside and thinking, shut the fuck up, Butch.

"What'dya think of Omnichrome, Butch?" asks Stinson, putting Butch's gun on the captain's desk, way out of Butch's reach. Like he's going to start busting caps around the office.

"Stinson you watched too many movies-of-the-week," Mann says. "Butch, you know what Omnichrome is?"

Butch shakes his head. He manages not to swallow.

Mann goes on, "It's this new thing, alternate light source device, picks up stuff you can't see with the naked eye. Foreign matter. The Omnichrome shows up stuff under special wavelengths…"

Stinson can't contain himself. "Like paint specks."

Mann gives him a tired glare. "Like paint specks, yeah. Same color and chemical composition as the ones on the car. Forensics found them on a pair of your shoes."

"Like you get," Stinson says, actually grinning now, "when there's a real fine cloud of spraypaint, and you think you're being real careful not to get any on you, but the stuff is so fine you can't see it settle."

Butch's voice is almost a monotone, carefully flat, as he says, "Spraypaint's mostly all the same composition. And I helped Hank here spraypaint his kid's bike-frame. I think it was red or orange or something."

Everyone turns their heads to look at me.

Jilian doesn't say anything about it till we're halfway to Yosemite in our RV. About two months later. No charges against Butch. The kids are playing with a Gameboy far enough in the back they can't hear us talk over the noise of the engine and the tires, and there's been a silence for about sixty miles before she said it.

"He never was there, helping spraypaint Ashley's bike."

I'm wondering how come what she said makes me feel like I'm the one who killed Della. I say, "You remember that for sure?"

"I thought about it a lot, Hank. I mean, *a lot.* He came over the next day after the bike was dry and she was showing it off, the new paint you put on so drivers could see it better, and she was telling Butch all about it when he and Della..." her voice catches "...when they came over."

Is she, I wonder, going to come out and flat out accuse me of perjuring myself, which I sure as hell did, to protect Butch?

If she does, I'll have to tell her about the money. And I haven't figured out how to tell her about the money yet.

Should I lie to her, and pretend I remember him coming over earlier, some time when she wasn't there, standing there with me when I was using the paint? It sounded too forced. Jilian's smart. I elect to go around it.

"He just figured that's where he got the stuff on his shoes, maybe from some dust that got stirred up or something."

"Oh." She decides to believe it.

I don't say, *You don't really think that Butch could have...!* or some such shit, because I couldn't do that believably.

I just change the subject. Only, it's not really a different
subject. I tell her I'm thinking of joining the Sheriff's
Department, maybe around Santa Cruz, so we could get the
kids away from the Oakland area, all the crime and drugs
and stuff. But I'd never do it if she didn't want to.
She says she'll think about it. It's a big step.
It's a step the fuck away from Butch.

I try to see him enough so he doesn't get nervous, but not
so much it'll make me nervous. It's not that I think he'd kill
me. It's just like spiders. I'm not really scared they're going
to hurt me. I just don't like them crawling around me.
At least spiders are what they're supposed to be.
It's easy to be self righteous. But you got to look at the
whole picture. The kids and Jilian and the money and covering
my ass and the department. No, fuck the department. It's the
fucking money. It's me in the joint with a bunch of dirtbags.
Because, you know, Butch thought it through, himself.
He collected her life insurance, too. It was *way* premeditated.
He'd get the gas chamber like some dirtbag. But his getting
away with it is hard to stand. I hear him say, "You a *ho*,
right?"

One night I go over to his house, after he's been drinking
heavy, and I go up to his bedroom, same room where he
slept next to Della for years and years. He's sacked out, fully
clothed on the bed, his head deep in those blue satin
pillowcases Della picked out. I know him, he won't wake up
after all the beer. I'm standing over Butch, who's snoring
these long contented snores, and I've got his gun in my gloved
hand, and I think maybe I'm going to blow his brains out.
And slip away. Because otherwise the guy'll always have
something over my head. The money. And I just can't fucking
stomach him walking around.
I put the gun muzzle up to his head. But then, at the last
moment, I think it through: if I do it, it might look like suicide.
Which would imply that yeah, he killed Della and so I must've
perjured myself. And making it look like a gang-banger did it
would be a big mess to step into.

Sweat's sticking the gunbutt to my palm. So finally, I take his gun and I put it back in its holster, and I go downstairs. I'll put in my app at the Santa Cruz SD. They got a great benefits package. That's what I'm half thinking about as I walk out to my car.

You got to think things through. That's the bottom line. Hey. They're not going to say shit about perjury.

I go back upstairs, get the gun and I blow his fucking brains across that satin pillowcase.

YOU HEAR WHAT BUDDY AND RAY DID?

What Ray does, sometimes, he runs low, he goes to those jerk-off parlors, those adult bookstores with the booths got the sticky floors, and he hangs out in there, at the corner of the little maze of videopeeps, pretending to be reading those glossy cards on each booth with the pictures of people fucking; those cards show you what video channel for "Virtual Tight" or for, maybe, "Mama's Enema Party"...Ray stands there real casual but watching everyone, till he sees the kind of guy who's maybe got a gold watch, real well fed, crocodile shirt, say Coke-bottle glasses—some guy that doesn't get any ass. So then Ray catches his eye, snags him into a booth, pretends he's gonna suck the guy's dick, but he just sort of plays with it, the dude's pants are down and loose around his ankles and Ray's on his knees coming out with the Hot Talk, all the time his free hand getting into the guy's back pocket, snagging that wallet, says excuse me, I'll be right back, you're makin' me so hot, don't move! Then he cruises on with the wallet...some guys—straight guys, usually—are really expert at this, usually black hetero junkies and crackheads get into that shit…Ray actually learned this because it had been done on *him* when he was just eighteen. Some black guy in a booth started playing with Ray's dick, but he was into Ray's wallet—a big five bucks—and Ray caught on and he said, "You're not ripping me off, motherfucker." And he grabs the guy, but this is a big black junkie and he *grabs Ray's dick and balls*, I'm tellin' you, man! He starts *twisting*, saying, "You fuck with me, you lose 'em," but Ray pries the junkie's fingers off his parts and the junkie bolts out of the place and he yells, "You follow me, you white faggot motherfucker, an' I'll knock you out!" So Ray finds himself standing there between the booths staring after this guy and he realizes his pants are down around his ankles and his dick is hanging out…but he thinks, That could work for me sometime.

——— ◆ ———

Ray's standing on a Larkin Street corner, thinking it's too fucking cold out tonight, maybe he'll try the adult bookstores again. Sometimes he scores that way; other times he maybe only gets five bucks, or nothing at all. Of course, he could let somebody suck his dick for a ten or a twenty, but he just *likes it better* when he rips them off. It's not that getting his dick sucked by some geek really bothers him; it's that ripping them off feels especially *good*. But you could waste hours standing around in those places and the Task Force has been busting hustlers in the booths lately…

"Hey, Butch," Buddy says, coming up to Ray on the corner.

"Don't call me that unless you mean it." Ray says, "and you don't." He's only a quarter Latino, but he's got the rolled-up headband around his head, trying to get the action that wants a Latin Lover.

Buddy's from Texas, long and muscular, tan starting to fade, tattoos, really tight buns; he dances sometimes at the Polk Street Theatre San Francisco's Finest All Male Dancers, but he gets fired every so often for picking up tricks there. He was in some porn, too. Ray keeps trying to get into some porn, but generally he smells a little too ripe; he likes to get loaded and tends to end up sleeping on floors and in places with no showers. "I got somethin' for us," Buddy says. "There's this guy that saw me in one of those Marines movies, I was fucking some real butch Marine guy, he thinks I'm totally tough, but he wants to watch me with somebody else...you know, him watching and shit..."

All of this is, maybe, twenty-four hours before I came on the scene.

Turns out this guy is some kind of computer nerd, into the black-market hacker stuff, too—and he's got a head iron...Buddy knows what a head iron is, because his cousin went ill behind one...but he always wanted to try one...

The dude's place is one of those real nice Noe Valley flats, restored Victorian building, shiny hardwood floors, antiques, modern art paintings, expensive PC with one of those screensaver things wiggling around in tastefully iridescent fractal dancing...first editions of Oscar Wilde...

Trick's name is Charlie; Buddy never could stand a Charlie...anybody who went by Charlie when they could be Charles or even Chuck...Trick's about sixty pounds overweight, hair real short in the arty, almost bald thing, walks kind of pigeon-toed, real nice clothes, good material, gold lambda earlobe ring...WHOA, IS THAT A ROLEX WATCH? Yes, it is, and no, it's not counterfeit. This is looking like potential.

They drink red wine and Ray asks the guy if he's got any cocaine. Charlie sort of leers and says cocaine makes you impotent, don't want you impotent. And some quote from Shakespeare about swords being blunted.

"Take off your pants so I know you're not a cop," Ray says to Charlie.

Buddy gives Ray a look. Oh, yeah, sure, like this lisping, pigeon-footed, Noe Valley fag is a cop. You fucking bet.

But later Buddy figures out that Ray doesn't think the guy is a cop at all; he's just Taking Over. Telling the guy what to do. Laying it down.

The guy has dated some hustlers, knows the laws, knows that a cop is not allowed to take off his pants—so he doesn't argue, he takes off his pants to show he's not Vice, folding the trousers and the underwear neatly on the arm of the antique velvet sofa.

His little dick, hiding under his round white belly, looks like a snail under a boulder that got scared and it's going back into the scrotum, back into the shell.

Well. Maybe it'd be fun to fuck him in the ass.

Buddy asks for the money once the pants are off, and Charlie has it all ready, a hundred cash, more later if everything is good. Fine for starts.

Ray is loading up on the wine. Get what he can while he's here. Ray did some time in Vacaville, see. He's looking around a little too much at all the carefully dusted objecks-dee-art—there's a lot of carved jade stuff that looks like it might be worth money—and Buddy says "So what're you into?"

First, Charlie suggests, just make yourselves at home. Perhaps you'd like to take a shower...together...

He makes it sound like it's part of the partying for them to take a shower and him to watch, which maybe it is but probably it's mostly because they stink.

So they take a shower, soap each other's dicks and asses for Charlie to watch, Charlie's fat little fingers working that snail, coaxing it halfway out of its shell.

Ray and Buddy never did sex together before, they've been mostly, like, friends on the corner, but they're pros by now and Buddy doesn't let his embarrassment show. He kind of likes playing with Ray after a while. Takes him back to a circle jerk when he was eleven.

Half hour later, they're wearing only towels, still a little damp, Charlie's aftershave burning-cold in their pits Charlie has opened a second bottle of this expensive wine *C'est très cher, mai*...he says. Seriously: he said that.

Charlie looks expectant, so Ray and Buddy drop the towels and start full-on going at it. The scene is bothering Buddy a little, so he's not really keeping it up very well his ropy dick is drooping a bit, but it's enough for Charlie who's standing by the bed watching like a dog at a dinner table, grinning conspiratorially, really getting into the fantasy...

Buddy starts to think, We're this trick's video game. It's more than live porn, it's not Ray in control after all, it's Charlie, taking them through levels in one of those games where you go down and down into some cavern hole, and ol' Charlie's

going to win when he spurts his little dinger...then they can
get the fuck out of here, go to Mary's and get a burger or
something and laugh at this fat fuck...

So then Charlie starts getting into the game himself, moving
them around like dolls, reaching between them to personally
guide Buddy's dick into Ray's ass. Stroking their asses while
they go at it, putting Ray's hand on his snail—that's when
Ray says, "You like to do B&D, anything like that?"

Charlie's eyes shine, but he's a little nervous about letting
Ray tie him up, but Ray says, "We'll tie you down to the bed
and we'll fuck *on top of you* like you're the mattress..." And
this gets Charlie so excited he's shaking, but he gets jumpy
when Ray starts to tie his hands to the bedposts with the old
silk neckties, so Ray says "I'll just tie it with a butterfly loop,
not really tied, and you can pull it off when you want, Charlie."

He does tie the guy's left hand just like that, and Charlie's
not looking as close when Ray ties the right hand—Ray puts
an extra knot in it—and Buddy does the ankles, and then
Charlie says, "Go to my dresser drawer, there's an instrument
behind the socks..."

Ray and Buddy figure the "instrument" is a vibrator or a
whip, but it turns out to be the head iron. It looks just like
an old-fashioned barber's electric razor, the kind they use
to shave the nape of your neck, and it probably is the shell
of one, but it was taken apart and they put, like, *gizmos*
inside it, and it's got duct tape holding it together now,
and a little glass cone at the shaving end instead of the
cutting pieces.

"This goes on your head, right?" Ray asks. He plugs the
head iron in and starts to try it on Charlie, but Charlie pulls
back real quick, says:

"No, no, wait, it must go to a precise spot, or it can have
very nasty side effects...one loses control of one's bowels"—
for real, this is just the way the guy talks—"or one may have
a seizure..."

So Charlie has Ray hold a hand mirror over his head. Then
he has Ray put a piece of tape on a certain spot on his head,
stuck in that short hair. That's the spot where the head iron
goes. Then he tells Ray to go ahead...Charlie licking his lips,
breathing shallow, kind of scared and kind of excited...

Ray puts the glass cone of the iron on the tape over the fat guy's spot—forty-five-degree angle—and pushes the *on* switch, and there's a little hum and then the guy's eyes instantly dilate and he moans and he goes rigid and then limp and then rigid and then limp...his dick getting hard and soft, hard and soft, like when somebody mainlines cocaine...

Well, of course, naturally Ray has to try this. Ray, understand, is the kind of guy who used to be into glue and huffing fumes and *just any fucking thing.*

"Now," Charlie is saying, "now, fuck on top of me...fuck...fuck me and fuck on top of me and fuck each other on me...I'm your mattress, do it, fuck on top of me..."

But Ray is ignoring him; he's finding the spot on his own head. A couple of near misses—one time he starts choking for a second—and then, boom, he hits the spot. He gets it. Big ecstasy.

Ray starts trying to fuck Buddy just because he *wants* to.

Buddy pushes him off at first, but then Ray finds the spot on Buddy's head—he gets just the right spot on the first try and he pushes the button and it's like a big wet explosion of GOOD, just plain GOOD pouring out of him. Like you shot him in the head and what came out wasn't blood, it was GOOD.

"Oh fuuuu-*uuuuuuuck!*"

And now it feels good when Ray shoves into him—in this stoned-out place Buddy's in, it'd feel good if you shoved a claw hammer up his butt, claw first. They go at it and they're tripping, they're into some other place, some place that's all penetration and skin-flavored pleasure and waves of maleness that metamorphose into femaleness—

But then it starts to fall apart, kind of fizzing into decay, like an Alka-Seltzer tablet in water; like a flare on the street, bright and then going black...

Buddy starts to imagine what it would be like if his old man could see him with this guy's dick up his butt. His guts crinkle up...

Then Charlie starts yelling he wants another hit, he wants them to do what they said, and Ray gets up off Buddy and suddenly both Ray and Buddy are feeling all wasted and hollow, like they might collapse into themselves, like a cigarette ash that's perfectly shaped till you touch it...

And Buddy feels a kind of icy, gushing rage he never felt before, and he looks at Ray and he can see the same thing in Ray's face. Ray's saying, "Buddy, all the stuff in this place could be our stuff.."

Charlie really starts yelling when he hears that, but he can't get free from that extra knot on his wrist and then Ray is standing over him, making it louder and worse. "You want another hit, here's anothermotherfuckin'hit!" And he starts whacking Charlie around the face with the head iron, making scallop-shaped wounds in him, Charlie screaming and Buddy saying something about the neighbors calling the cops, so Ray stuffs several pairs of dirty socks and underwear in Charlie's mouth—Ray's and Buddy's socks and underwear— and Charlie's screams are muffled and Ray gets up on the bed yelling, "You want us on top of you?!" And he starts jumping onto Charlie, coming down on him with his knees, so Buddy can actually hear Charlie's ribs cracking under Ray's kneecaps...

Buddy's been doing all this to Charlie in his mind same time as Ray does it, it's just like he's doing it when Ray does it, so his rage comes in that way and froths over and after a moment he can think a little and he says, "You kill him, we don't get his ATM number, bro.."

Charlie doesn't want to give up his ATM's PIN number, but of course Ray gets it out of him, also makes him write a bunch of checks and show Ray and Buddy his bankbook. Whoaaaaaaa! Twenty fuckin' grand! Strong! Maybe later they could get him to liquidate some of his stocks and property and shit.

Ray gets so distracted using the corkscrew on Charlie to get the ATM PIN that he almost forgets about the head iron, and Buddy puts some big willpower on the line and hides the thing. He really wants to wreck it, because it scares him, it scares him to feel that high and scares him even worse to feel that *down* afterward, but he can't quite get himself to wreck it. So he puts the head iron in a trapdoor into the attic.

The attic entrance is in the same closet they put Charlie in, in the living room. Charlie's still alive. They figure they're gonna need him. They make Charlie crap a few fumes in the bathroom first, set up a bicycler's sipping bottle he could suck some water out of and tie him into a corner of the closet, really tie him good so he can't bang on the wall to get attention. He looks like he's in the middle of a spiderweb afterward, with that soft white rope they found under the bed, tying him to the hinges and the clothes-hanger pole. Ray wants to pee on the guy, but Buddy won't let him, saying he doesn't want the smell.

Then Ray asks about the head iron, but Buddy puts him off, says let's wait on that till the drugs run out

"What fuckin' drugs?"

"Let's go to the ATM. See what we can get. Charlie ain't doing shit, tied up like one of those guys in a cannibal pot."

"I got your back, man."

First Ray and Buddy do some of Charlie's expensive mail-order crystallized vitamins—they know about rushes and crashes and how to deal with that—and they eat a steak from Charlie's fridge, so they feel some better. The head-iron crash eases out.

And what do they find in Charlie's bedside table? Three guesses. Right, a piece! A .38 revolver that looks like it's never been fired. One box of shells. This is just getting better and better.

Ray stays with Charlie—watching MTV and drinking—while Buddy goes to a check-cashing place with a check from Charlie for a grand. The place calls up for confirmation, and Ray has the portable phone jammed up against one of Charlie's ears and the pistol up against the other. Charlie *approves* that fuckin' check, *pronto*.

Then Ray meets Buddy on the street, by the check-cash place. They divvy a thousand from the check and three hundred from the ATM, and they go on a mission. After midnight, they can get another three hundred dollars from the ATM, and it's almost midnight.

"I still feel kind of weird from that head-iron shit," Ray says. "But, man, that was a fuckin' rush!"

"That thing, I don't trust that shit, we gotta forget that, at least for now, dude. Let's get some good rock, some good ronnie, maybe some pussy…"

"Pussy, yeah, now the man's got an idea," Ray says but Buddy doesn't quite believe it.

About half an hour after midnight, Buddy and Ray come to me. That's right, me.

All they could find was street hubba, it seems, which is pretty much shit cocaine.

"You know Miss Dragon, right?" Ray says. "We got the money. You could get us the good stuff."

I correct him. "That's Dragon Miss, they call her."

Me, I'm terrified of cocaine. Turns me into a hitsucking bug faster'n a vice cop takes a bag. Then I'm gone for a couple of days on a run and I run the wheels off that fucker and then I turn paranoid, which is maybe how…

Well, it's one way people get killed.

So I stick to hashish—which I get from the Dragon Miss— maybe sometimes opium, always some cognac or Johnnie Walker Red. Speed if I need it. And so many vitamins I smell like 'em.

Maybe what I most get off on is the second-story work. One time I popped into this guy's apartment, he's sleeping in the same room, snoring like a chain saw, and there's a wallet on the nightstand, and I snag the wallet and flip it open in the light by the window and see there's a *fucking badge* in the wallet—the guy is a cop. I look over at him and he's still sawing logs, but now I see on the other nightstand there's a fucking .44 lying there like a chunk of pure silver. *This is a cop's bedroom and he's got a loaded .44 next to him and I've got his fucking wallet in my hand!* Now, *that's* a rush!

I took the .44 and the wallet and I took a beer from his fridge, too.

I used to be a writer, one time, plays and journalism. I even did a feature for *Esquire* once. I used to do those readings at coffeehouses that are so chic now, everybody playing beatnik. But then I got into the coke binges, and Louisa…

Well, they found her dead.

And after that, I had to live different. I don't know how to explain better than that. I couldn't go back to writing, but I couldn't be a basehead neither.

But I understand Buddy pretty well. I've known him a shitload of years. On Tenderloin time, anyway. Four years is a long time to know somebody in the Tenderloin.

So I get Buddy talking about what he and Ray did; he's like a free-association machine after he takes a hit on the shitty hubba. During the story Buddy's telling me, Ray is in the bathroom, jerking off by the sound of it. *Whuppawhuppawhuppa.* Some people when they do cocaine, they can't keep their hands off their dicks, which is funny because their dicks don't usually perform for them anymore.

Then Ray comes out of my bathroom looking uglies at Buddy, and Buddy takes the hint and shuts up, and to defuse the situation and just to follow this street and see where it comes out, I tell them, "Let's go see if the Dragon Miss wants your money."

Like I thought: turns out Dragon Miss wants to see this apartment full of antiques and art tchotchkes, and the guy tied up in the closet. "It sounds like just the *best* party, girls...if we can keep the Big Tummies out." She thinks it's cute to call the local cops Big Tummies.

"Neighbors are off on vacation or somethin', nobody gonna call the cops," Ray tells her. "What about the rock?"

She pauses in the doorway of her Japanese-decorated place, framed by the silk hangings, an ancient kendo sword mounted over her head. She's got a long face and eyes like a husky's, and cushy lips. Of course, she's got the big hands and the Adam's apple. One more thing about her eyes, they look startled all the time, like she's surprised by everything, even when she plans it down to dotting the *i*. She talks in that cute, surprised way while she puts a 9mm round in the back of your head.

Now she lets her green-and-gold dragon-figured kimono hang open so we can see both her big silicon tits and her surprisingly large dick. The joint effect, so to speak, always gives me a woodie.

She's got this rich Japanese Houseboy, president of a major airline corp by day, could hire five servants to do the housework—but when he gets out of that limo, his whole style changes on the flight up those carpeted stairs and he comes in with his eyes down and *begs* to be allowed to clean Dragon Missy's toilet. To lovingly arrange her shoes in her closet; to deliver her female hormone pills and cocaine on an antique ivory salver in the morning; to bring her the Xanax and Halcion at night. Waits on her hand and foot, and for his reward she beats his ass. One time I was visiting at the condo he gave her, and since he was going into the kitchen I asked him to take my glass for me and refill it and he said, big outrage, "What, you think I am homosexual?!"

Some phone calls and a cab and bang, we're over at this trick Charlie's house.

"My *goodness*," Dragon Miss says, hanging up her coat, "there's a *man* in the closet!" For a moment there's a flicker of hope in Charlie's eyes (and a flicker of feeling for him in me...just a flicker), but then Dragon Miss hangs up her coat in the same closet, well out of his reach, and, humming a show tune, closes the closet door.

Feet up under her as she sits on the couch like it's hers, Dragon Miss counts the money Ray and Buddy give her, lays out the fine cocaine on the glass-topped coffee table, the flaky chopped-from-rocks stuff that they only dream about on the street. Like a lady putting out the tea things, she sets up the little propane torch, the ether, the baking soda solution, the glass pipe for real freebasing, none of that piss-doorway rockhead bullshit. She puts on a CD of Mozart's *Requiem*. Maybe for Charlie, though he's still alive. Buddy and Ray would rather have the Pet Shop Boys, but there's been a shift in polarity and Dragon Miss is in charge. Maybe I should mention that the Houseboy carries a gun. That's two guns now.

I distract myself from the cocaine prep by looking over the window locks, strategically unlocking a few, shutting off the alarms, mentally totting up the fence value of some of the smaller antiques and the old English silver.

We check on Charlie and his leg looks gangrenous. It's his right leg, maybe to do with the corkscrew wound maybe it's the circulation being cut off, maybe both. He's feverish, squirming in his sweat and stink in the closet (Dragon Miss makes a come-out-of-the-closet joke); he's not quite there, but he mutters some stuff I hear when I'm squatting by him, and some of it makes me sick and some of it makes me flash on ideas.

I'm belting some Johnnie Walker and tripping on how this Charlie's dying and how I don't feel much about it and how the Japanese Houseboy does feel something but it's just fear, and how we're standing around the closet making fun—the others are sucking on the pipe—and it's like that Max Ernst painting of the demons chewing at St. Anthony, and now I'm one of the demons, and I don't remember becoming one. I'm tripping on it, but all the time I'm thinking what I can score on all this.

So then Dragon Miss's friends show up and one of them has royally fucked up: Berenson, this big black guy has brought a bunch of whores with him, two black, two white, one maybe Filipino, and some stoned-out white asshole he met in a sex club who's got a lot of dope money on him. Berenson, funny thing is, gets actual money from the State of California to run a prostitutes' rehabilitation center—and of course he just keeps the money because the guy's a fuckin' pimp! He lays into those bitches with a belt, too. They seem to like it. I can't watch that shit.

I never once hit Louisa.

So all these animals are dancing in the living room breaking the furniture, putting Charlie's smaller stuff in their purses and going through his medicine cabinets and his liquor cabinets and his shoe rack, then checking out his suits, some pretty expensive suits to sell, and they keep coming back to suck on the glass pipes—there's four pipes going now—and sometimes they go to the closet and they kind of *fuck with* Charlie, just sort of...*fuck with him*. He's EveryTrick to them, I guess, and they're getting theirs now. Everybody debates about the best way to drain Charlie's bank account without pulling down too much attention. The air is in layers of smoke, it's got its own ionospheres and tropospheres, and now somebody's got the rap station on the stereo—so far Dragon Miss has kept them from taking the stereo out, which is just common sense—and the

Houseboy is looking *really pale and nervous*. One of the whores is working on Berenson's dick, licking his balls, too, and Berenson's willie is half erect and it's going up, up, slowly, like it's being slowly lifted on a crane, and another whore is on her knees in front of a chair with her head under her girlfriend's skirt licking pussy, and Ray is kind of listlessly fucking a long, skinny white girl with one pump on and the other skinny silver-toenail foot bare and her underwear around an ankle, they're doing it on the rug in front of Charlie's closet, Ray yelling at Charlie to look! look at this, Charlie, but Charlie can't see outside his sick haze.

The doorbell rings and some transsexual prostitutes who work for Dragon Miss come in, so shrill you can hear them over the rap and the laughter, like the high-pitched, whining noisemakers that cut through the bangs and drums of a Chinese New Year's parade. They ooze into the room like they're coming down the runway on the lip-sync stage, invisible microphones in their hands, three of them in pounds of makeup competing for attention. The glass pipes get most of the attention. But these TV whores have got some ronnie with them, brown crystal heroin, and I manage to get a line of that. It puts my head in order so I'm thinking priorities again.

Buddy is in the corner in a real nice chair, looking kind of shrunken in on himself, maybe crashing from cocaine and starting to see consequences in his mind's eye, looking like he's going to panic. I give him the bottle of Johnnie Walker.

Ray is bringing out the head iron. "Y'all ever try this shit?"

I trip on the head iron thing. It's got the heft of a small electric drill. It's like electronic brain drilling, I'm thinking. I'm tempted, but it still scares me. The smell of the vaporized cocaine in the air is tugging at me, and I know I'll never get to business if I get started with cocaine or head irons. I'm feeling rounded out and pleasantly heavy in the dick from the heroin and only a little nauseated. I wonder if Charlie's dead.

Buddy is trying to talk Ray into getting rid of the head iron, but it's too late, the TS whores are already squealing around it, practically spinning on their spike heels to try it...the whole feel of the scene is changing around this head iron...it's putting a weird off-buzz in the air that's like one of those freak waves you hear about that smashes boats...The Dragon Miss frowns at the head iron.

"I don't trust those things, I've heard stories, they are not sympatico with working girls..." she says.

But Ray has already done a head iron hit and is reeling in waves of glory, and the paleness of his rage rises in him and he snarls something at her I can't hear, something about fake fag-bitches, and the Houseboy pulls his gun and Ray pulls *his* gun and Dragon Miss sees that and decides the polarity can shift for a while, and she pushes Houseboy's gun down, tells him to put it away and signals one of the girls. The girl's so fucked up she doesn't even seem to see Ray's gun and she starts playing with his dick, so he lowers the gun but doesn't put it away...The head iron starts to get passed around to everybody...Dragon Miss looks more startled than ever...

One of the queens is giggling on the phone. "You hear what Buddy and Ray did?" So now the thing's leaking at the seams.

I expect Dragon Miss is going to fuck Buddy or one of the younger guys here—I'm old enough to have damage from the New York Dolls—but she takes me by the hand and we go into the biggest bathroom, lock the door. The Houseboy sees this and writhes with jealousy, you can see it in his face. So much for fucking Oriental inscrutability. He doesn't do anything about it—me fucking his mistress right in the next room is more humiliation, which is what he's paying her for, so it all works out.

Till now, Dragon Miss's been watching everybody else's sex in a kind of preparation voyeurism. Now she's ready and probably figures I'm the one most likely to get a hard-on that'll stay, because I've been avoiding the C.

Bathroom's trashed because they've been in here going through it looking for drugs and anything salable. But we clear the junk from the floor and lay down some towels. She's been on the pipe for about an hour, plus did a line or two of the ronnie, so she's as wet as a pretend girl can get.

We do some things with the shower, both kinds. She jets out her ass, and she's a little apologetic when she asks me to pee on her in the tub. But she gets tired of being a dominatrix all the time for the Houseboy. Being a mistress is kind of fun, she says. But.

Then we get down to some serious business. I turn her facedown, I'm taking a drive through her ass, which could be mistaken for a female one, all right, maybe because of the hormone pills, and she's playing with her dick while I jam it to her, and twist one of her arms behind her back and whisper that she's a dirty slut; all of this by request, and it works for me, too. It's like when I fuck a she-male, two parts of me that are usually insulated flood together for a while and that feels good.

I'm careful with her tits, because they're silicone. I cup them gently and do a kind of suction with my palm on the nipple, and this gets her off. She can't come out of her dick, which only gets about two-thirds hard, but there's another kind of orgasm she-males can get, and about the time my knees are getting sore she flaps around in it, like a baby seal getting its head knocked in.

So I let go, and come, too.

Coming, I feel something in me loosen up, and I think about Louisa the night before they found her.

We were on the roof of her place, September evening, having a tar beach picnic, and I'm trying to zing the pigeons with pieces of a broken Mad Dog bottle somebody left, and she's telling me I should call my brother. I feel like her face is prettier and more real in that second because of what she wants me to do; it makes me feel like she maybe really does give a shit, because she wants me to call Dougie and tell him it's okay, that I forgive him for ripping me off, that's what junkies do and I understand that...

I can't do that, but I feel, for a moment, like maybe some of us are going to be all right... *"You got to be part of somebody or you nobody,"* she says. *"You not even real if you can't feel."*

It rhymes; she's pleased with that. "Stop throwing shit at the pigeons," she says. I kiss the back of her neck and cup her tits and she leans back against me...

But now Dragon Miss tells me to wash my dick and go out into the living room with her, it sounds like they're really going off out there, she's got to see how Houseboy's doing...

After we go back out, the whole scene has changed again. The off-buzz saturates the place. The walls are screaming, there's a kind of peak to the noise and tension, two or three arguments going at once, and they're wrestling over the head iron. Two of them, no, shit, *three* of them now, actually fighting, hitting, scratching for the head iron.

Looking around now, I start to get seriously scared because I can see everyone's been doing the head iron *even the Houseboy.* And now there's three guns in view—Berenson's got his out, he's yelling at the Houseboy, and the Houseboy's Japanese skull's showing through the skin of his face with all his straining to control himself, but I can see he's going to lose it. The white asshole Berenson brought is out cold in the corner with his head in a puddle of blood. His wallet's lying next to him like a gutted fish.

Then I see a black whore in a skewed blond wig snag the head iron, because someone dropped it in the fight, and she's got the closet open and she's shoving the head iron against Charlie's head more or less at random, laughing, randomly slimming what's left of his brain, and he's foaming at the mouth and shifting himself and actually breaking some of the ropes with a really gone-off rage and she's laughing and slapping him with the iron, but she puts her hand too near his mouth and Charlie takes off three of her fingers, just as neat as a metal-shop tool, snipping them off with his teeth, and she screams and Berenson—nude, muscular but for that potbelly—Berenson, he sees what Charlie's done and he points the gun and really shakes with relief as he lets go: shoots Charlie four or five times, and the Houseboy gets mad because Berenson's fucking with one of Dragon Miss's assets and he starts shooting Berenson—

Buddy and I make eye contact and we both slide fast into the bedroom. The two other people in the bedroom are out cold, no, wait, one of them is out cold and the other one is dead, looks like a heart attack—and I shout at Buddy over the noise from the next room, the shooting and screaming; and we tip over an antique armoire so it jams the door shut and then we take care of our own business, but I hear the

Dragon Miss stuck on the other side screaming for me to
open the door, open it, they're going to, they're going to, but
then bullet holes punch through the door behind the armoire
and her blood comes through; along with her blood comes
her scent, her perfume, right through the door...

It's the head iron, the glory and the insane rage and misery
that come when you use it; with that thing it's like you get a
lifetime of sin in one blast and then you go straight to Hell,
do not pass Go, all in one minute.

And the head iron's stirring that room up like blender
blades, we can hear it, screaming and laughing and crying in
there, Ray thumping on the door now, Buddy crying because
he wants to help Ray; he tries to move the armoire, but I
won't let him, because they'll all come in with Ray then, and
anyway, I've already made the phone call to 911. Meaning
we got to *get out.*

So I have to half drag Buddy out the window to the fire
escape and up to the roof, and as we go we get a diagonal
glimpse through the window of the living room: here's Ray
with Berenson and two whores, the three of them kicking
Ray, who's probably already dead, but they're kicking him,
kicking him, Berenson's dick wagging with every kick...

A little later we're driving a stolen car, just about a block
away, when the sirens start wailing. I have to laugh. Buddy
starts crying again.

What Charlie whispered when I almost felt something for
him was what was in the false top of the armoire. It was a
locked metal box. I guess Charlie was trying to make a deal...

The dead guy in the bedroom had a BMW key chain and
there were only two Beamers on the street.

So next morning, really burned out, me and Buddy, we're
at a rest stop halfway to Las Vegas, standing behind the maroon
BMW, its trunk gaping, using a tire iron on the box. Takes us
twenty minutes more to finally get the metal box open...

The box contains less than I hoped for but more than I
expected. About thirty grand in cash total and about ten in
loose diamonds. What about safe deposit boxes, Charlie?
Probably had one. But he was one of those guys who liked
to keep some close.

Me and Buddy are doing okay. Cabo San Lucas has a full-on *scene.*

I'm trying to feel those other things again. It helps to think about Louisa. *You got to be part of somebody or you nobody.* I was just so loaded that night. I can't remember. I *can't remember.* I try, for her, but I can't remember: I don't know if I was the one who killed her or not.

ANSWERING MACHINE

Transcription begins:

Darla? Um...Darla?

Yeah Hello, Darla?

It's Georgy.

Yeah look I couldn't talk about this with you, like, in person?

I hope it's okay I just wanna like, leave a message on your machine?

Listen, it wasn't my decision, it wasn't my choice to kill your sister, it was Tush, it was her thing, she goes, "You're such a faggy little wimp."

And she tells me I bitch about people saying I'm faggy, and people just assume gays are wimps—and here I'm acting like a wimp, whining because she was going to put her in that thing and do *that* to her—she was running that whole fucked up trip on me Darla—

And she goes, Tush goes, "Darla's little Tandy wantsa be mutilated let's go all the way...I mean, you know she wants to die...she's, like, tried to commit suicide five times..."

I told her, I go, "Guy if she wanted to commit suicide really Tush she'd be dead by now. It's like it was never serious?"

But she didn't listen. She has that...she has that dominance thing...and it's like...it's so much like her counselor says about her, and she told me what her counselor said like it was such bullshit and I was supposed to agree so I *pretended* to agree but I secretly thought it was true: that she's trying to get out from under something by getting people in shit as deep as she can?

You know?

So I said, "Don't put her in there, don't put her in that..."

I mean, it was at the junkyard after midnight where we go to smoke bongs and sometimes we get some black tar and...you know? And then, when she gets into that place, Tush likes to pretend she's talking to spirits of people who got killed in the bashed up cars and stuff..?

You know?

So I said "Tush, that's—I'm not signing that check, bitch, putting somebody in one of those car compactor things...I mean if she wants to commit suicide she wants it to be painless—"

But Tush goes, "She's totally fuckin' numbed out from the pills I gave her anyway, it's like heavy tuinol and codeine, she won't feel shit, I just wanna see how it looks afterwards..."

Her dad, Tush's dad, he's just the same he's got that same...that same *thing*...

He's, like, an LAPD cop and he used to handcuff Tush...

Anyway they were saying—I swear to God, dude—they were saying that they were going to *put me in there too*, in that machine, if I didn't shut up and then Tush said she heard the spirits of the people killed in the car accidents from all the smashed junkyard cars around us...you know how she goes there and gets stoned and says she talks to the ghosts of people that died in those cars...and the spirits were asking her to put Tandy in the car compactor and I couldn't even cruise with that, serious, and I'm from Venice Beach I mean we've seen it all...we used to set bums on fire but...you don't *know* the bums, right?

And I don't even believe the ghosts told her to do that.
She just wanted to do that. I mean, I know she talks to the
ghosts in the totaled cars but like, they never asked for
anything like that *before*.

I mean, the ghosts—before that night—the ghosts were
always saying shit like, "Would you pray for me? Would you
take the battery out of the car and drop it off the pier because
I think that my spirit is stuck here because of the battery, my
blood got on the battery and the electricity is trapping me
here...and one time one of them asked if we could put some
semen on the car seat so Tush talked me into jerking off on
the car seat and she said she wouldn't watch but then she
jumps out with everybody and starts laughing just when I—

You know what I mean about her? I mean, what a cunt? I
mean *God*.

And like who would listen to those spirits in their right
mind, because last time...last year they told us to do that
paint thinner and make those marks on the ground and then
Duggy-pup, that red-haired guy that used to—? You remember
Duggy. I don't think you were there that night. We made the
marks and then he starts foaming at the mouth and shaking
and he starts clawing his face and saying, "I don't deserve
this face, but only bone, but only bone..." Like, over and
over, it was sickening, "but only bone, but only bone..." So
we had to come up with some explanation at the ER for him
and his Mom sent him to military school but he kept talking
to himself and then he hung himself in the boy's bathroom of
the school but anyway—

About Tush and your sister.

And the trash compactor.

Um....I said...

So I said, "No way are the spirits asking to put her in that
car compactor and I'm not going to stay here so..."

So I just—

I just *left*, I left right outa there, serious—and she woke up
in the thing I guess—your sister woke up in the car compactor,
woke up from being zonked—

Well I'm sure who wouldn't. One time I was zonked out at
a party and this guy started putting ice in my butthole and I
can tell you I fucking woke up from that so...

I'm sorry. I'm so freaked out. I can't think.

Anyway I guess she woke up because...

Because I heard her scream from like a block away?—

I swear to god; I was a block away.

Tush just has that *thing*...that...

I went home and took a sleeping pill and went to sleep and I had this dream

I dreamt...

I had a dream about dead people in car wrecks trying to tell me to call you so...oh wait if this is being recorded it could be used for evidence...

I was—

I was just making all this up...except...Tush has that...

I'm sorry. I'm sorry about your sister. I mean—I just heard about it.

I'm sorry.

I'm sorry.

I can't think.

But...don't keep this tape okay?

Erase this okay, after you listen to this...okay?

Darla?

Are you there listening?

Darla?

Darla?

I gotta—I can't...

I can't think.

I'm gonna hang up.

I'm just...I'm sorry...

I was a block away...

Darla? I'm gonna hang up.

End Transcription. Arresting officer: E. Bloom, Northridge PD.

THE RUBBER SMILE

"Bring up the darkness," said Chambers, absently.

"What?"

"I mean—the *glare,* Schraeder. There's too much glare. Use the filter, I can't make out their expressions with all this brightness on the—yeah. That's okay. Now slow it down a tad..."

Chambers leaned back in his swivel chair to watch the screen of the video editor. On the screen were faces, rows of faces lit ghostly blue. The flickering blue light on those faces was reflected from another kind of screen, a movie screen Chambers couldn't see.

The editing room was dark but for the video screen, and claustrophobic. Schraeder, Chambers's perpetually squinting research assistant, was too long limbed for comfort in here, and he was making it worse with his twitchiness, obviously wanting a smoke. No way Chambers was going to let him smoke in this slightly oversized closet.

Chambers was plump, dark haired, his small blue eyes usually pleasantly quizzical, but sometimes hard as broken bottle glass. He dressed nondescriptly prep, a badge of his seriousness; he sat very still in his swivel chair, but chewed his lower lip when he was deep in thought. He chewed at it now. He was watching a videotape shot with a hidden camera. He'd paid Schraeder to film a typical Saturday night horror-movie audience. He and Schraeder were an audience watching an audience.

Chambers wasn't scared by horror movies. He was scared by horror movie audiences.

He didn't need to see the movie the videotaped audience watched. He knew it by heart. He knew it too well. Researching his paper on audience reaction to film violence for his doctorate in anthropology/media studies, he'd seen a dozen horror films several times apiece.

The video camera panned along the rows, over scores of rapt faces. Schraeder said, "You *sure* these people don't know they're being filmed? Seems to me some of them look right at the camera now and then—"

"You tell me. You're the one who filmed them."

"I could never be sure. Maybe they saw me go into the blind."

"No, Schraeder, Christ." It was two in the morning, they'd been screening the research samples for nine hours, with only one brief break. Chambers was tired and irritable. "No, they're looking around on the screen, trying to spot the slasher as he creeps up on the victims, and sometimes it makes them, you know, seem to look our way. They—hey, freeze it. No, back up, freeze it—*there*. Yeah. Hold it there."

He rubbed his eyes, then leaned forward to peer into the face in the center of the screen. A teenage boy; blond, pimply and thirsty-eyed, his head tilted forward like a football linebacker. "Move in on that blond kid, then run it slow." The editing machine zoomed in tight on the kid's face. Muscles clenched at the corner of the boy's jaw, as if he were ready to bite anything that came in reach. It was a fleeting expression, a half-second of raw belligerence meshed with sheer lust, risen to the surface, briefly expressed, and repressed a moment later. Like a water snake disturbing the surface of a pond and then diving out of sight.

Chambers had seen that ephemeral expression many times. It didn't appear on the big-eyed, doughy-faced girl sitting beside the blond kid, though. She looked as if she *wanted* to enjoy the film—but it sickened her. For her, it was something to be endured. For the boy beside her, it was something to be savored. Chambers glanced at Schraeder and said, "You see the way he keeps shifting on his seat? It corresponds to the penetration, and it's always a forward and back motion, like a thrust of the hips. That's got to be an erotic response."

"You can barely see it. Seems to me, erotic response is hard to prove unless you want to sit beside 'em and risk getting busted for groping his crotch. Can't see a hard-on from here, Doc." Schraeder ran a hand through his stringy black-dyed hair. Twitchily. His hair was crewcut short on one side, shoulder length on the other. He wore a *Pet Sematary: The Movie* T-shirt, and greasy black jeans, rotting tennis shoes. He was a film student, and a habitue of the death-art circuit, a fan of violent film, violent rock bands, violent books, violent performance art. Considering that, it was strange, sometimes, Chambers thought, the way Schraeder clung to a strange ingenuousness on this subject. "I mean," Schraeder went on, "aren't we making too many assumptions here, Doc?"

Doc. Because Chambers was going for his PhD. Something faintly mocking in the nickname Schraeder'd given him.

Chambers glanced at the transcription of the movie's dialogue, with its timing matched against the videotape's time. This audience was forty-two minutes into *Hometown Hell*— and they were watching the fourth on-screen slashing. Forty-two percent of the faces in the audience showed positive involvement, and about thirty-one percent demonstrated subjective identification with the slasher himself, at this point. Another ten minutes on and that figure would up to perhaps forty percent.

"Now I know what you think about the look on that kid's face," Schraeder remarked, "and the erotic response, and forgive me for being the eternal skeptic, but it seems to me he could be looking at the girl's tits and not at the knife going in her throat. You might be mistaking old-fashioned male enjoyment of the naked female bod for—"

"Schraeder, for God's sake, the boy is looking *at the knife and the point of entry.* I've worked out the parallax enough times to support that. Okay? Damn, Schraeder, erotic response or not, at least a third of these people are identifying with the killer and not the victim. That's the bottom line here. The filmmakers know it, too. How many of the ten most recent splatter films included long scenes shot from the killer's viewpoint? Seven out of ten!"

"I dunno, it seems cynical to me, to assume that...Well, I don't like to believe that people—"

"Now we're onto something! You don't like to believe!" Chambers snorted. "Your reluctance to believe in the thing doesn't make it any less true." As he said it, he knew he was overreacting, but Schraeder was challenging the foundation of his thesis, and that thesis was going to be the foundation of his *career.* Starting with a post at the UCLA Film School, with luck. "Well. I'm sorry. I'm tired. Let's blow it off for the night."

Typically doing things backwards, Schraeder turned off the video monitor, fumbled for the light switch. For a few seconds, Chambers was left in darkness. The afterimages of the faces on the blanked screen stayed with him, hung in the air. And melted away when he blinked. But for an instant, just before they'd gone, he'd had a fatigue-induced impression that they'd all turned and looked at him, with that same expression on their faces. Murderous rapture.

Times Square on Saturday night was a mind lit up by psychosis. The dense crowd was dappled with smears of color from neon lettering and neon hieroglyphs and guttering chains of bulbs that rippled in electric vortexes around the marquees. It was a warm night, not yet nine o'clock, and the Forty-Deuce hummed and throbbed. Austere Broadway theaters shared the block with porn houses. On the corners, evangelists bursting with Good News jostled solemn leftist leafletters, and hookers cruised by debutantes who yawned as they waited for taxicabs. A dozen street dealers hawked pseudocoke— "SnoCaine"—and soap chips alleged to be crack, and tobacco-cut marijuana. Scientologists waited like trapdoor spiders at the entrances of their book-lined dens;

their peers, pickpockets, weaved in and out of the shifting crowd. Cops strolled in pairs.

There were long queues at the conventional movie theaters. Chambers stood in one of them, waiting to see a horror-cult favorite, *The Rubber Smile*. It was called *The Rubber Smile* because its slasher wore a horrifyingly ludicrous rubber mask of a man with an impossibly wide grin and protruding eyes.

Under his unseasonal trenchcoat, Chambers carried a tape recorder, a low-noise microphone, and extra cassettes. There were eight people ahead of him in line, mostly teenagers. He watched two thin, whispering boys, one Hispanic and the other a pallid kid wearing a rayon Bon Jovi jacket. They were pulling things from their pockets, comparing them. Rubber masks, waggling obscenely in their hands. The white kid held his own mask up beside his face, mimicking its grin as his friend shook with silent laughter. The Rubber Smile.

Chambers was pleased. It was more substantiation. Grist for the mill. He drew a small spiral notebook from his coat pocket, made a few notes as inconspicuously as possible, concluding: "...Rubber Smile parallel with *Rocky Horror Picture Show* cult in which audience dressed like Mad Scientist transvestite, chanted dialogue with actors..."

Pleased with himself, he put the notebook away, as his turn came to buy a ticket. The next show was at 9:35. He'd take a stroll, come back in half an hour.

He saw them under the Silent Radio billboard, at One Times Square. There were four of them, wearing the Rubber Smile masks and staring up at the board. On it, gold against black, the words THE RUBBER SMILE: PART 2 sailed past, followed by a flat, angular animation of a running man, seen from the side, a knife in his outstretched hand, the animated man turned toward the viewer, growing, approaching gigantically, until the board was filled with the Rubber Smile mask in simplistic electronic caricature. For three seconds, the Rubber Smile leered out at the bustle of Times Square. It was as if he grinned through a vast electronic window, looking at our world from some lunatic's purgatory.

The four Rubber Smiles were looking up at the Silent Radio billboard as if they'd been expecting this. Like priests of some obscure order awaiting a sign from the gods. They were teenager sized and teenager clothed. They slapped palms and laughed when the animated Rubber Smile leered out at them, and then turned away when the Smile was replaced by an advertisement for a musical.

Chambers went to a phone booth and moodily dug for a quarter, dropped it into the slot, punched out Schraeder's number. A click, and then sinister carnival music came onto the line, and Schraeder's recorded voice, "Maybe I'm here, maybe I'm not. Leave a message." *Beep.*

"Schraeder—are you screening calls? Pick up the line, dammit, if you're there—"

Click. "What's up, Doc?"

"Schraeder, uh, I wonder if you could come down to the theater at Forty-third and Broadway, the one on the East Side. I'm going to need another observer. There's a deeper level to this Rubber Smile cult—they're wearing replicas of the mask—"

"Really? During the movie?"

"I—don't know. I saw four of them wearing masks outside."

"Hey, no kidding?" Schraeder seemed almost gratified to hear it. "But hey, this doesn't really fit snugly with your theory, right? I mean, it's all supposed to be subliminal, unconsciously acted out. Nothing so overt as living the role outside the theater with masks."

"It's just another level of acting out. You could extrapolate that some of them might actually—"

"No, that's jumping to conclusions, Doc. If one of them kills after seeing the film it'll be because the dude was pathological from the start. The movie didn't make him that way. I took a class on this stuff. If anything, the film burns off the hostility that could come out in, you know, violence."

"I doubt the films program people for violence, per se, but—"

"Please de-poz-zit five cents for an-nother three minutes."

"I don't know if I can make it down there or not, Doc—" Schraeder began.

"Please de-poz-zit—"

"Dammit." Chambers dropped another nickel in.

"Thank-kew."

"Schraeder, you're the horror buff, you keep up on these

things—you didn't tell me there was a sequel to the *The Rubber Smile*. You know I need it for—"

"There isn't a sequel."

"No, there is. I saw it advertised on that big electronic billboard. It's Part Two."

Schraeder was silent for a moment. "No kidding, huh? Wow."

"You must have missed an issue of the *Gore Gazette* or something. You coming down?"

"I'll be there," Schraeder said, his voice flat. And hung up.

Chambers turned to leave the phone booth. A loud *tink-CRACK* near his ear made him flinch back, convulsively hugging himself. Something stung his cheek. He put his hand to his jaw, felt something warm and wet and sticky. Looked at his fingers. Blood. He turned. The booth's glass had been smashed near his right cheek. There was a spiderweb crack-pattern around an inch-wide hole—and the cracks were superimposed on a face that was on the other side of the glass. A rubbery face with an impossibly wide grin. Its gums and lips painted dark red, bulging eyes luminous yellow, skin sickly pale.

The Rubber Smile tilted its head like a curious dog, and then whirled, moving away. He watched as the boy, wearing a dirty suit-jacket that had bits and pieces of lurid newspaper headlines pinned to it, moved toward the sidewalk crowd, slunk up close to a young woman who wore a black evening gown and ermine stole. She stood hailing a cab, her back to him. He tapped her shoulder: she turned, he made a slashing motion with his fingers at her throat. There was no knife in his hand: he seemed satisfied with her startled shriek, the shock on her face as she saw the mask. She bolted for a taxi. The boy vanished into the crowd.

Chambers left the phone booth and walked slowly toward the movie theater.

Half a block from the theater, Chambers stopped in a bodega and bought Band-Aids. He paused at an optometrist's show window and looked into a mirror below a sign that said: *Are your frames up to date?* The cut on his cheek was a small one, but his hand shook as he stuck the Band-Aid on.

It could have been my eye, he thought. Had the boy tried to break through the glass to get at him? What had he used to break it? Some weapon Chambers hadn't seen.

Something concealed. Something you could carry into a movie theater.

Chambers forced a chuckle. He'd seen one too many cheap horror films. With an effort of will, he turned toward the theater.

It wasn't a humid night, but his shirt stuck to his back and he loosened his collar. The cars seemed to swing their headlight beams at his eyes; the neon lights shared secrets with the red lights on a passing ambulance. He hadn't seen a movie that day, but felt as a man does after a movie—he was seeing things cinematically, as if on the big screen. When he turned his head, it was a panning shot, and everything had the appearance of having been framed through a camera's eyepiece.

Chambers took his place in the ticket holders' line. Waited. Now and then looking over his shoulder. *Maybe the kid intended to kill me.*

It was 9:15. The street growled and honked and muttered. The smell of spiced meat from the sidewalk shishkabob vendor mingled incongruously with the cloying soapy perfume of incense burning from the Black Muslims' tables. Watching a three-card monte hustler barking to attract gamblers, Chambers loosened up, began to enjoy the street action. He found himself watching two boys just ahead. Both wore baseball jackets and jeans; both were Hispanic and long haired. They leaned against a grime-gray brick wall and passed a joint between them.

As the line began to move, Chambers decided that part of his research ought to be interviewing members of the Rubber Smile cult. These two had the masks hanging like kerchiefs from the back pockets of their jeans. Could one of them be the kid who'd smashed the glass beside his face? No, that one had been wearing the weird jacket that made him look like a molting bird of newspaper. But the knot in Chambers's gut came back to him, then, as he stared at the dangling masks. *You're an anthropologist. Talk to the natives.* He took a deep breath, and said, "Say, uh, fellas, I heard there's going to be, um, a sequel to *The Rubber Smile*. Uh—you guys hear anything, you know, about a sequel or, um—?"

It was when he had difficulty talking that Chambers admitted to himself that he was scared. Scared and charged with anger.

"A sequel?" said the taller of the two boys. Blue smoke marking the words. He made that soundless laughter they all seemed to make, his mouth open and nothing coming out, then tilted his head back to stare into the glare-shuttered sky. The other boy nudged the first and said, "Zat duh dude?" He gazed foggily at Chambers.

His friend nodded, once, and said, "Askim can you see his tape recorder, man." He was still peering at the sky.

Chambers stiffened. How did they know about the tape recorder?

"Yeah, *pendajo*," said the one who'd stared skyward, suddenly tilting his head down to smile crookedly at Chambers. "Yeah, there's a spechul midnight cho', man. Sorta sneak preview, you know?"

Chambers nodded mutely.

The other one said, "Yo, Jo-Jo, the line movin'." He added something more in Spanish. The ticket holders' line began to move, a slow two-step pause, two-step dance, like a tentative conga, into the moviehouse odor of popcorn and spilled cola.

As they passed the cashier's booth, Chambers looked at the schedule. There was no mention of a special midnight show.

He hurried in to find a seat near the middle, about four rows from the front. He'd found he could get the best aural spread that way. There wasn't a big crowd for this show—the film was at the end of its second run—and at first no one sat in Chambers's row, or the one behind him.

The theater fell into darkness.

That shouldn't have bothered Chambers. It always gets dark before a movie. Naturally. Of course. So why did it make him cringe down in his seat? The film didn't scare him. He'd seen it four times. The first time it had made him flinch, and look away once or twice. But it never really scared him. It was not a brilliantly made film, or even a very clever one, but it was efficient. The director knew the gimmicks, every cheap trick, and he used them all.

Chambers wriggled in his seat, adjusting the microphone cord inside his coat so that it ran up through his sleeve. The mike was concealed in his right hand, his arm draped casually along the back of one of the chairs. When the opening shot flashed onto the screen, he pressed the record button...

Askim can you see his tape recorder, man.

Someone must have seen him adjust the thing, at some point, well, only a couple of them would know, hopefully.

```
INT: A PROTESTANT CHURCH—DAY.
REVEREND BEST addressing his white,
middle-class congregation. Camera
shoots the scene from behind the
minister. We can't see his face. His
congregation is increasingly shocked
as he speaks.


        REVEREND BEST
...And so I feel that it is the Will of
God. I have no choice. I must resign. I
can no longer preside over a church
that fosters hypocrisy, where church
members permit acts of fornication
between unmarried young people, in open
defiance of the Word of God. I have
implored you again and again to put an
end to this evil, this living obscenity,
and yet it goes on. God will punish
promiscuity with an instrument of His
own choosing...

PUSH IN on TEENAGE GIRL #1, hip and
pretty, trying to keep from laughing as
she sits beside her mother in the
congregation.

                              CUT TO
```

EXT: A DESERTED DIRT ROAD THROUGH
CORNFIELD—NIGHT
The field on both sides of the road
is filled with high stalks of corn.
TEENAGE GIRL #1 walks down the road,
her back to us. Sexy swish of her
ass. She looks furtively around, then
dashes into the field where a red scarf
has been tied to a cornstalk. CAM
FOLLOWS her as she meets TEENAGE BOY
#1 who has made a nest in the corn
with a blanket and crushed stalks. He
produces a pint whisky bottle from
his coat.

                                    CUT TO

INT: REVEREND BEST'S BEDROOM—NIGHT
The minister is alone, sitting on the
bed, his back to CAM. He takes a rubber
mask from a box under the bed, pulls
the mask on. We can't see the mask's
front yet.

                                    CUT TO

THE CORNFIELD
The Boy and Girl in tight embrace, half
undressed, giggling, rolling together
off the blanket, crushing cornstalks.
SHOT FROM ABOVE
The couple on one side of the frame, on
the other something hidden by cornstalk
leafiness is disturbing the stalks of
corn, moving toward the young couple
like a shark through water. Closer and
closer.
(Chambers shifted impatiently in his seat. *Same old devices.
I'm supposed to be tensing with fear now.*)

```
TIGHT ON THE BOY AND GIRL
Laughing, caressing, swigging.
```
(Whoops and catcalls of encouragement from the audience in the theater.)
```
  The girl looks over the boy's
  shoulder, sees the cornstalks part.
  HER POV
  As CAM pushes in TIGHT for a CU of the
  mask, the Rubber Smile's leering face,
  glittering eyes in the eye holes. She
  SCREAMS.
```
(Someone in the audience whispered, just loud enough to be heard, "All *right*. Awesome." And Chambers shivered.)
```
  ON BOY AND GIRL
  As a long butcher's knife sweeps into
  view, flashing down to penetrate both
  the boy and the girl, uniting them with
  steel—
```

Chambers looked away, bored with the Freudian button pushing.

He slumped down in his seat and turned to look at the audience. As his eyes adjusted, he saw that there were only about thirty-five of them. Seven of the thirty-five wore Rubber Smile masks. Their eyes were locked on the screen. In the dim light the masks seemed their real faces. Seven identically leering faces, drinking in the butchery taking place in the eye of the consensus mind.

A group of black girls—unmasked—squealed and covered their eyes, while from the sound track came the *chunk-swick-chunk* of a knife sinking repeatedly into flesh.

Someone said, "They shoulda gone to a motel." A few people laughed at that, and made comments of their own. Later, Chambers would play it all back, and notate the most relevant comments.

Three rows back, a boy about fourteen, with a fox face and scooplike ears, swallowed again and again, his Adam's apple bobbing. His thick glasses reflected fragments of screen images, leached of color depth. Knife flashings, spattering blood and leering rubber lips were reflected where his eyes should have been. Chambers was fascinated with the boy's swallowing. Oral gratification mechanism triggered by screen violence? The wound representing lips?

Chambers watched the audience patiently, noting that with some the loud remarks came during the greatest moments of suspense-stress, simply as a release for accumulated tension. In others, about thirty percent, the noisiness came during the killings, when the Rubber Smile was imaginatively dismembering his victims. These comments amounted to celebrations of the killer's demented sense of humor, or of his cunning ("...they ain't never gonna catch him, sucker's too slick..."), and of his indestructibility ("...this part's cool, they shoot 'im four times, he don't give a fuck..."). This was the percentage of the audience that identified with the killer. For them, the Rubber Smile's motivation was irrelevant and the movie's thin plot an encumbrance. They were waiting for the butchery. They never had to wait for more than twelve minutes; the filmmakers had it down.

Chambers turned to watch the movie for a few minutes, to get his bearings. The police were making their usual futile attempts at locating the killer. A teenage boy tried to tell them that the killer had something to do with the Old Church, and the cops laughed at him. The usual make-the-authority-figures-look-like-bumbling-fools segment.

Meanwhile, the Rubber Smile roams the countryside looking for likely victims. His victims are almost invariably involved in sex, or undressing to prepare for sex.

Chambers was disturbed by an apparent discrepancy in the casting. Something he'd never noticed before somehow. The killings were clearly performed by a number of different people in the latter half of the movie. Their faces were hidden by the masks, but their physiques and brief glimpses of hair-tufts at the masks' lower edges told him that more than one person was acting the part of the killer. *Why?* He could understand one stand-in, or a replacement if the original actor quit, but why so many?

There was another scene showing the parson preaching in the church—he suggested that God Himself had struck down the people murdered in the valley. For the first time, Chambers noticed that several people in the preacher's congregation were nodding in agreement. And with a shock he saw that their physiques, their hair colors, matched the several men playing the Rubber Smile. *Am I supposed to notice this?*

The film cut to a scene in which the audience saw what the killer saw, shared his skulkings through the small town's backyards, into an unlocked house. The camera showed the killer's POV as he stalked a victim slinking slowly up behind a blond lingerie-clad housewife making cocktails beside a kitchen sink...

Chambers looked away when the Rubber Smile drove the knife into the woman's groin. He was losing his objectivity. He should be desensitized to this sort of thing by now. It should be a joke to him, after all his exposure to it. But the Rubber Smile killings were harder to take than the others. Every time he saw them he marveled at how nauseatingly realistic they looked. They'd spent the greater part of their budget on special effects, apparently. It was just too...

Swiiiick-chuk. Splatter.

He was sick to his stomach. It's not real blood, the Rubber Smile was only slashing a bit of fleshlike plastic, releasing fake blood. Maybe it was the efficacy of the sound effects. They were particularly sickening. The sounds of slashing, of blood dripping, juicily amplified.

"Looks amazingly real, doesn't it? Looks and sounds like the real things," said someone close behind him.

Someone speaking directly to Chambers.

Chambers slowly turned, and looked over his shoulder. And froze.

The Rubber Smile sat in the seat behind him. Staring. Grinning.

It's some kid, with the Rubber Smile's mask on Chambers thought. It's not *him.*

"Yeah," Chambers said, hoarsely. "Yeah, it's a little bit too real."

"How can reality be too real? Reality is as real as reality is!" The Rubber Smile giggled, the sort of giggle that belonged to the mask's molded expression.

Something twisted in Chambers's gut. "What?"

"It's real in the minds of the people watching. At *least*. They believe in it when they see it on the screen. You can feel that when you sit with them in the theater. The audience believes—and they get into it."

"Some of them do and some of them don't," Chambers said, turning away. He couldn't bear to look at the mask up close anymore. The way it quivered when the man wearing it spoke. It was a man, not a boy. A fairly educated man. *It's real in the minds of the people watching. At least.* Chambers shook his head. He knew the voice...

Chambers turned in his seat to confront Schraeder—and found him gone. There were only six Rubber Smile masks in the audience now, and they were in the seats they'd occupied all along. They ignored him, or seemed to.

Chambers turned again and pretended to watch the movie, thinking: What was Schraeder *doing?* Is he trying to prove a point? A practical joke? It was an obscenity, Schraeder wearing that mask. He had to be a little crazy. And he'd argued against the idea that the audiences were identifying with the killer. Clearly, Schraeder knew better.

The long minutes passed. Several times, Chambers began to turn around to resume his observation of the audience. But he couldn't do it. He felt sure that they were waiting for him to turn around, planning to do something awful to him, to startle him, to try and terrify him with a trick of some kind. Probably Schraeder had told them what he was doing. That would explain the boy at the phone booth, and the boys in the line who'd known about his tape recorder.

Three more killings passed. Chambers still couldn't turn around. The movie played out its last scene: The police shoot someone in a Rubber Smile mask they believe to be the killer. But when the killer is buried, the minister—the real Rubber Smile—is there at the cemetery, praying "for the tortured soul of this poor, possessed madman." Then he turns away from the grave and grins very, very widely for the camera.

The audience clapped and shouted, then filed out during the credits. Chambers stayed in his seat, he rewound the cassette tape and plugged its small earphone into his left ear. He stopped it twenty minutes back and hit *play*. He adjusted the tone, separated out the bass. Heard someone say, "...the usher been told?" And a reply, "Yeah, now shut up...Schraeder's..." Something inaudible. "Schraeder paid the..." The rest was lost in a squeal of sirens from the sound track.

Chambers slowly took out the earphone and detached the mike cord. He tucked the earphone and the mike in his coat pocket and shakily stood, wondering if he should run, if he could make it to the exit in time.

"Aren't you going to stay for the midnight show?" A voice from the stage. "Don't you want to see the sequel?" It was at that moment, when he saw the man in the Rubber Smile mask on the stage, that Chambers realized that the lights hadn't come up. It was still dark in the theater. Everyone was gone except the six Rubber Smile masks. They were up, sidling between the chairs, moving toward him, in his row and the row behind. One on either side, two behind, and now two in the row in front of him. In a few seconds he was surrounded. "Sit down," said the man on stage, his voice echoing in the nearly empty theater. Feeling numb, Chambers sat, and the six Rubber Smiles sat too, in a ring around him.

Behind them, the projector came to life. Its light stabbed at the screen—showing nothing. Just dead white light, filling the screen. The Rubber Smile on the stage stood silhouetted against that shining whiteness, against the ache of cinematic potential. He wore a long trench coat that didn't go with his black jeans and rotting sneakers.

"Chambers," said the man on stage, voice muffled by the grinning mask. "Chambers, you're a pompous ass. Guys like you make me sick. You think you've got us all statistically, behaviorally analyzed. You think you know what goes on in the minds of the people watching the movie. But Chambers—you ever hear of something called—" he paused to point at the source of the glare "—projection?" He chuckled. "You're projecting on the audience what you feel, deep within yourself. *Your* identification with the killer."

"Bullshit," Chambers blurted. "You're trying to justify your own sick obsessions by claiming they're universal."

"Look at the knife, Chambers..." The Rubber Smile drew a long butcher knife from within his trench coat and held it up in the light from the projector so it flashed fire. "You pretend to be revolted by the use the Smile puts this to—but inside you there's a Rubber Smile that—"

"You lying asshole!" Chambers shouted. He stood up, knuckles white on the back of the seat in front of him. Trembling. "I know your voice, Schraeder! You're one of them, all right, fine. But don't splatter me with it. I've got no part of it. Not inside me, not anywhere."

"Don't you? But you must have known what we've been doing—what we've been *really* doing. You've studied us so close, you must have known—but that ol' denial mechanism works overtime in Doc Chambers. You suppressed it, the knowledge, you don't want to face it, but at the same time you're fascinated, Chambers."

Chambers's mouth was dry as the ash in a burial urn. What knowledge?"

"I was the assistant director on *The Rubber Smile* Chambers. Under a pseudonym—as we all were. The director's in an asylum. Burnt out for good. He couldn't be with us tonight. A drag, huh? But the, ah, gentlemen who played the Rubber Smile are here, Chambers."

And then Chambers remembered where he'd seen the familiar faces among the extras playing the church congregation. He'd seen them standing in line tonight, outside the theater. Two had been Hispanic, two others Caucasian. Two blacks. Once inside the theater, they'd put on the masks...

"Oh, Lord," Chambers muttered.

Behind him, the projector made a rattling sound, and suddenly the movie screen gushed with carnage. The Rubber Smile was butchering the two lovers in the cornfield. Schraeder stood there, a step in front of the scene a close-up of a bubbling wound gigantically superimposed over his trench coat. He was half in the movie's world, half in the real world.

"They sent me to answer your ad for a research assistant, after you called the producer, tried to interview him. He realized you were looking at the thing too closely. I really tried to discourage you from seeing those things, Chambers. I tried to save you. But I suppose I knew you'd notice, sooner or later. I was sure the point would be driven home to you so you couldn't deny it to yourself anymore. You kept coming to the damn movie. Sooner or later you'd realize that the fake blood wasn't fake blood and the fake wounds weren't—"

Chambers gave an incoherent yell, and looked away from the screen.

"Lots of eager young would-be actors and actresses out there, Chambers. Plenty to choose from. We picked the ones who had no living family. No one to search for them. We got our realism in the most practical way. With reality. We got rid of the evidence with our own little cremation facility. Saves money on salaries too. We had a minimal crew. Part of our inner circle, of course. The director recruited them from asylums—particularly the one he was in, before they put him away for good. The whiney little shit went vegetable on us, I'm afraid. A sad end for a creative genius. But it keeps him from talking."

Chambers shook his head slowly, looked up at Schraeder. The Rubber Smile mask. The Rubber Smile wrapped in the red-spattered writhing on the screen. "Creative genius? Is that your excuse? This is *art?*"

"Life is brief and life is cheap, Chambers. And modern life is horror. We transcend that horror by making it into art, yes—but art is not what we're really about. We're a circle of...sensualists, of a sort. Religious sensualists. We do the right drugs, we set the lighting just right—and then we explore our senses, the secret rooms in our own brains, Chambers. It's all done with an exacting ritualism. The ritual staging is very, very important. You wouldn't understand, I'm afraid. We're a very special—"

He was interrupted by a shriek: Chambers had shrieked. Seeing the lightstands, tripod, and large thirty-five-millimeter camera someone had just set up in the aisle to his right.

"I'm the new director, Chambers," Schraeder said proudly. "You're going to have the honor of being in my new film. There *is* going to be a sequel to *The Rubber Smile.* Part Two starts filming tonight. Now."

Chambers acted on instinct. He vaulted over the chair ahead of him, and his knees struck the Smile sitting there. The guy groaned and fell; Chambers tumbled over him, and scrambled to his feet. He evaded a swishing knife, and jumped over the chairs blocking the way to the stage.

Gasping, thinking: The only way to save yourself is to take the offensive.

He jumped onto the stage, entering the projected image, stepping into the movie. He swung his fist at the hideous rubber head turning its death-rictus grin on him. His fist connected, and Schraeder went down. The knife clattered on the stage-deck.

Take the offensive. Save yourself. Take the offensive.

Chambers picked up the knife and stabbed Schraeder, again and again.

He heard screams from the audience. Looking past the blinding glare of the projector, he made out the teenagers tearing off their masks, running up the aisles, away from him, in psychotic panic. Schraeder was their leader, and the ritual had been disrupted.

Chambers looked down at Schraeder, staring at the gashes. He'd done that: he, himself. He shook his head in amazement. He looked at the reddened blade in his hand. The light on the blade, the hot shine of projected light...The movie camera had fallen, lay hidden in shadow...Someone had stopped the movie...There was only the white light of the projector on a blank screen.

Chambers heard shouting from the lobby. Voices shouting with authority. Police. One of the Rubber Smiles running from the theater had probably attracted the attention of a passing cop, maybe blurted something about the killing.

It would be difficult to explain why he'd had to kill Schraeder. They might not believe the stuff about the disguised snuff film...He had no proof. He'd take the rap for Schraeder's death.

Escape. And don't let them see your face as you run. Cover your face.

He started to drop the knife— then realized it'd have his prints on it. Had to take it with him. He tugged the grinning mask off Schraeder's head, and pulled it over his own. The mask smelled of rubber, of childhood Halloweens. Now his tears were making it stick to his cheeks.

He turned to run. A rookie cop burst in; saw the bloodied body on the stage; saw Chambers turn toward him, confused; saw the knife in his hand. The cop ran to the stage.

Chambers raised the knife, to fling it away. To the cop it looked as if he were threatening to use it again. But it was the mask Chambers wore that unnerved the young cop most. It was the mask, he realized later, that made him draw his gun and pull the trigger. Made him shoot Chambers three times.

The young cop had seen that movie only two nights before. It had really scared him. It had given him nightmares.

It was so damned realistic.

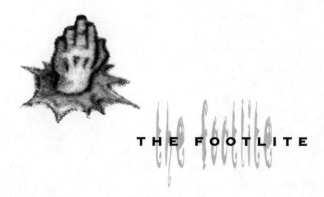

THE FOOTLITE

You know that girl, the one who died from cum? I used to know her, and I know why she did it. I used to see her in a bar near Sunset. It's this bar in East Hollywood, okay, called the Footlite, something to do with a theater that used to be across the street, like back in the 40s and 50s. I guess the theater got turned into a minimall. And this bar doesn't know what it is, it's—this is no shit—it's like a dragqueen straight/bisexual biker bar, okay?, with a selection of hustlers, whores and joyboys, and heterosexuals on the make and guys who aren't sure what they are and don't care, and a core of old gay guys, because the place used to be a flatout gay bar, but now since it's the only bar in the neighborhood it's…Did I mention the crystal? Crystal and Hydro, at least a third of anybody in the bar anytime is on meth of some kind, plus your peppering of junkies. And hormone queens; I always like those jolly Mexican transsexuals, those motherfucking queens know how to have fun. For some people there's nothing left, except two things: fun and courage, and, later on, when the fun is gone, just courage; maybe for everybody, eventually, I don't know.

Now all the queens, and a lot of the girls, who came into the Footlite were really wet for this longhair guy with broad shoulders and a lot of tattoos, his name was DP. I don't know what DP stands for. He'd be standing across from the dartboard most times, never seemed to aim, usually score pretty good. He's half Cherokee so he's got a big, fading tattoo, over his right shoulderblade, of an Indian ritual drum with feathers hanging from it; he's got some other tattoos that he got when he was fifteen, you can't really make out what they are anymore. Pretty fucked up tattoos.

He's only thirty-one, and he's still hardcore; he's one of those guys who never seems to work out, but he's always got muscles. He likes to wear those muscle shirts and swell his chest when he's standing at the end of the bar. And if he gets a hard-on in his tight jeans he grins at you and pats it. That's what he did to me, because he was a hustler, and he knew I was a trick sometimes, but he's not my thing, and the truth is I'm not his thing: he's actually into girls. He's one of those hustlers who gets into letting people suck his dick, or he buttfucks them, but he's imagining something else, and to him it's just easy money for food and drugs. But it could have something to do with his stepdad, how his stepdad, he told me this when he was drunk and wired on hubba once, his stepdad raped him when he was seven. It took him three years to tell anyone, and nobody would prosecute the guy, this being twenty some years ago, so when he was twelve and the guy tried to fuck him again, DP beat the shit out of the guy with a baseball bat, and now he tells tricks, I'll do anything, but if I got to piss on you it costs more, you really got to pay for that, and nobody fucks me in the ass, nobody ever, and if they ever stuck their dick in me when I was, like, asleep or something, that's the last time they'd see their fucking dick, they could say goodbye to that fucker. So nobody tries to fuck him.

DP liked to stand at the end of the bar by the dartboard, and really rooster it up, like when that Bon Jovi song comes on he likes, Here I am again on my own, going down the only road I've ever known, I'm a drifter and I was born to walk alone. Or just about any of those kind of songs, and DP would swell up his chest and his tattoos would sort of spread like peacock feathers and he'd go WOOOOOO and zing that dart.

When Kanya came in, DP's eyes sort of glazed, the way my Dad's used to when he was going to hit somebody.

Kanya pretended not to look at DP.

I was standing at the bar, drinking my calistoga, watching them. I can't drink alcohol anymore, because I had hepatitis twice and anyway I get depressed, and it makes me depressed after I drink. I can't do much of anything anymore, except fuck. But I mean, I'm like, 34, and it's not like I haven't paid my substance dues.

Kanya, she'd gotten sort of fat. Sort of Delta Burke fat, kind of sexy but kind of chunked out. She had this babydoll face but she wore a baseball cap and jeans and this dumpy coat. But also she wore lots of makeup and had her hair done, so you figure that out, I don't fucking know.

Kanya was all sort of jumpy, her head going this way and that, looking any way but at DP, and she'd check herself out in the bar mirror, then go back to her drink, then check herself out in the mirror, then light a cigarette, then thump her fingers to the jukebox, then check herself out in the mirror...

She did that when she was depressed, I remembered, and everything about her seemed fucked up. She looked like she was going to burst into tears but you, really, could have beat her up without making her cry, probably, because she had a stepdad a lot like DP's, only this guy not only fucked her he kicked her ass and put her in the hospital when she was three or four. But she's the kind of girl, anyway, who's got tattoos, but they're of, like, fuzzy bunnies.

You know what you do with little kids, this guy in the joint told me once, you put it in soft and then let it get hard.

I moved over to listen, the way I do, without seeming to, when DP came over in that kind of highstepping strut these guys use to show they're pissed off, and he acted like, hey, we're going to go outside and talk in private, but she didn't want to go.

I don't want you in here, you shouldn't be in here, he said, These people know you were my old lady, they think they can't do anything with me because you're in here, you're gonna cost me money—

They know we broke up and who cares it's a free fucking country and leave me alone, I mean God, DP, I'm not bothering you.

I want your ass out of here, said DP.

My ass goes anywhere it wants. Hi Quinn!

...Just to dismiss DP, Kanya was turning to talk to this big white drag queen, Quinn: really pretty face and a body that looks like a football player from behind.

Kanya was right: nobody cared she was his ex old lady, it had nothing to do with his action, it was just something he did to make himself seem the center of the fucking universe or something. He went back to the dartboard.

Well half of the equation that night, was this: Skull Surfer came in. That's just what I call him, he had this sort of surfer look except he's got these black glovetype things with the fingers cut off them, and some of his tats are kind of more biker or deadhead than surfer. He's really skinny, because he's a speedfreak, face so wasted it's skully. He deals crystal and hydro. I'm not sure which one he sold Kanya, but after they came back from going outside she was checking her makeup twice as often, really tweaking on it, and flirting heavily with Gardner, this big guy who was kind of stupid but otherwise was pretty cute, and then checking out DP to see if it bothered him.

Well then Xandra came in, she's this skinny black drag queen who thinks she's Iman or something and likes boys with broad shoulders and tattoos. She was DP's current old lady, now he was moved out from Kanya, and while DP tended to live with real girls like Kanya, queens—I mean the kind who take hormones and have tit implants—are just basically girls with extra equipment, or you could convince yourself of that if you needed to, and DP needed to because Xandra gave him free rent and food, not to mention blow jobs, and DP needed that because all his hustling money was spent on drugs.

How he got with Xandra was like this: she had this Gypsy roommate. This gay Gypsy guy named Ray, HIV positive but not very sick yet, he'd been okay for a few weeks, but then one day he asked if his family could stay overnight. Well, one night, sure. So they show up and there's twelve of them, no shit: twelve. One old man who kept hacking all night, a couple of younger guys, some wives, bunch of kids, some really weird smelly food. And all of them sleeping on the floor. And you guessed it, they didn't leave the next day. So she's got this family of gypsies in her place with these weasel little kids gawking at her when she puts on her makeup, and to add insult the whole family is asking her, Why do you dress like a woman? Why did you start doing that? Don't you want to stop? I mean, it's not enough that they're camping their family of twelve people in her dinky one-plus bedroom apartment but then they start giving her shit about her sexuality. And how was she supposed to work, she couldn't bring tricks there anymore with these bratty screaming kids watching her every move, so she had to do her work in their cars, which doesn't pay as well, and you're more likely to get busted and the tricks get all paranoid and can't cum and they act like you ripped them off.

But it was finally too much when two of her money orders, that she kept instead of a bank account, these money orders disappeared, almost four hundred dollars, and the twelve gypsies are looking at her with big innocent eyes, like, us? These are the people who're sending their little kids to the grocery store to fucking steal all their food every day. Like they didn't steal the money orders! She tries taking Ray aside, telling him they have to go, he says hey this is my family.

So Xandra goes storming out, and over to the Footlite and starts crying to DP about these people she can't get out of her apartment. DP looks interested when she talks about the money she had put aside: he had no idea she was such a good wage earner. I mean, all Kanya gets is SSI checks and food stamps and housing subsidy in a hotel.

Xandra's not telling this to DP by mistake: almost every night the bouncer tells him to "take it outside" with some guy he's in an imaginary beef with, sometimes there's a fight and sometimes not. He gets in a mood and looks for shit.

So DP goes over there and gets all wired up on speed and when Xandra sends Ray and the two other Gypsy men out to talk to him, DP starts taking off his belt and smacking it on the ground, saying get out, get out, get those people out, I don't want to have to kick ass but then again I might like it. The younger, hairier of the two Gypsy guys, he takes off his belt, he starts smacking it on the ground, they do this sort of back and forth thing like you see in one of those PBS shows about ape territory rituals, Gypsy makes a move at DP, DP backpeddles, then starts cursing, snarling, whacking his belt on the ground, coming at the Gypsy guy saying he was going to beat his ass like a bitch, and the Gypsy guy saying I beat you like I beat my kids you punk faggot, but neither one of them wanting to really get in close and do it—and then the landlord and the cops came, and there was a lot of attempt at Community Policing mediation and a lot of back and forth accusations, but it ended up the cops did a kind of on the spot judicial action, and they and the Landlord basically kicked the gypsies out.

It had never occurred to Xandra to call the cops. And it was them and not DP who kicked the gypsies out really. But Xandra gave DP the credit and he was king of the hill and she asked him to stay the night to make sure they didn't try to sneak back and he did and she sucked his dick half the night while he poofed hubba. He has a hard time coming, even when he's straight, but I guess he did, eventually, and that sort of cinched it, because Kanya hadn't been able to make him cum for awhile.

So he was spending part of his time with Xandra so Kanya got pissed and kicked him out and he moved in with Xandra completely and she said, Baby, you ain't never got to work again, because I'm your wife and I'll do for you.

A few weeks later and it's now, that night, at the Footlite, and Kanya looks like she's gained weight. I heard her say, "I mean, I'm not trying to be funny, but if he's, like, so much into girls, why'd he move in with a fucking drag queen, I mean that could be, you know, construed as, like, kind of fluffy. And then he's all, Bitch get out of the bar, and I'm like, bite me, and he's all, you're getting in the way of my action, and that's so childish, but you know what? I think he just wanted to talk to me, he keeps looking at me, I don't think it has anything to do with that girl that's gotta shave, he just wants me back but he can't figure out how to do it, and it's not like she's ever gonna be half as good a fuck as me, she doesn't even give head as good as I could, I was the only one could ever get him to cum, could I have another margarita?"

Maybe she wasn't wrong, because I watched DP real close, and he kept looking at her, like Kanya was something out of place. But love? It was more like she was an asset that wasn't in his wallet where it should be and he couldn't figure out how to get it back into his wallet.

Then Toothless Tom came over and was staring at DP; Tom is this fag deadhead guy missing his front teeth, he had a lot of bracelets and long dirty hair and tiedye shirt and he looked like he'd like to ask DP if he could go outside somewhere and suck his dick, but he couldn't afford it, and that staring gave DP his excuse, he's going:

What the fuck you looking at motherfucker.

Tom said: nothing, I wasn't looking at you.

You got something to say to me?

No. What you come at me like that for, I didn't say shit to you. You're tweakin' man.

You saying I'm tweaking?

I didn't say that.

You sure as fuck did.

Leave me alone, man, I ain't bothering you.

You're saying what to me?

What?

You're saying WHAT to me?

Sure I said "what" to you—

So you're fucking with me.

What?

Now you're really fucking with me Toothless—

You call me Toothless?

I didn't say that. You're the one tweakin.

That's disrespect bigtime calling me Toothless.

I didn't say shit to you. Fuck you, you want to give me shit, let's do it. Let's go.

...they're doing that back and forth thing, not quite engaging, while the CD jukebox plays Madonna, a song about "Spank Me" or something.

The bouncer comes over, real casual, looking REAL bored, says: I got just three words for you, "take it outside".

DP says to Tom, Come on, motherfucker, you heard him,
let's go.

After you, man. Fine. Let's go.

...but there's a little catch in Tom's voice, he's no fighter.

They went outside, though, DP going with big "I'm taking
a motherfucker outside" strides, his chest puffed out, that
extra bounce in his soles, and he was looking at Kanya as he
went, to see if she's watching this.

Tom followed outside with his shoulder's hunched. Nobody
worried about those two—they figured nothing much was
going to happen. There was more of the same kind of back
and forthing and display talk outside, like:

You were fucking looking at me like you had something
to say and then you tell me I'm tweakin—

I didn't tell you shit but if you want to go, then let's go,
let's do it, but I didn't do—

Well all right, come on, let's do it—

You come on, motherfucker, you start, I ain't taking the
first shot, let's do it—

I'm not that way, I don't take the first one—

I ain't going to jail for fucking you up—

Now that's a fucking joke, Well fuck you, tell me when
you're ready pussy.

...Then DP came back into the Footlite, sneering, his walk
saying: he backed down.

He looked at Kanya as he walked past her. She looked
pleased because she knew he put on this whole show for
her. She's got control of the dynamic.

But then the dynamic changes; the polarity shifts; Good
Queen Xandra came in right then. DP's meal ticket.

DP wanted a hit of something and he wanted a drink and
he wanted them now. He kissed Xandra up, and curled his
arm around her and now he was really full-on NOT looking
at Kanya.

Kanya was checking her makeup about three hundred
times.

(I remember when she showed me the scar on her stomach.
It almost killed me, the way stepdad hit me, and they had to
operate and I don't wanta be funny but there was this crazy
guy in the hospital who had cut off his balls with a razor and

he was, like in love with-me, and he used to ask to see the
scar, but then they put him in another room, and I used to
ask my girlfriend to pretend to be him when we went up in
the fort in the vacant lot and we'd take off our underwear
and once she had some of that jelly with fruit and she put it
on my pussy, I didn't even have hair, I think I was ten, and
she licked it and she licked the scar—After that operation I
couldn't feel much below the waist because of stepdad
smashed up some nerves or something and it's like if you
touch me it's pins and needles so sometimes I like people to
bite me so I can feel something in my legs, I had some bruises
on my legs, could I have another margarita?)

DP got the money out of Xandra and went outside with
Skull Surfer again and then came back with his head every so
often making little involuntary bobbing motions and ordered
a Bud and a shot of Cuervo, and then he let Xandra rub his
crotch—it was hard for me to pay attention now because I
was getting hustled by this ugly queen with skewed
cheekbones from a bad operation, her nose carved too small
like Michael Jackson; anyway she was trying to hustle me,
she was reaching over and stroking my crotch just like Xandra
with DP, like synchronicity, and she asked me point blank:
Do you like boy-pussy?

I remembered Quinn saying about this same ugly queen
once: Girl, look at that face, she is toh up pitiful.

I didn't want to give up my barstool. The ugly queen
ordered a drink and then the bartender went: $3.50 please...

And the queen went, I don't have it. Maybe hoping I'd
pay, but I looked away and the bartender got pissed at her:
What am I supposed to do, pour that vodka out now? You
can get 86'd that way, Miss Thing.

Sure I'm Miss Thing, she said, because I don't Miss a Thing.

What'd you say?

I said I'm sorry I don't have the money. I'll bring it in next
time.

She started working on me again, bartender could see I'm
annoyed, said to her, You keep hustling my customers I'll 86
you out of here.

I'm not hustling. (To me:) Was I hustling?

I kind of thought you were, yeah, I said.

I wasn't. But could you bump me some money, I'm broke.

I gave her five bucks so she'd leave me alone, because I didn't want to start some stupid beef and because I wanted to watch Kanya because...

Because that's what I do.

Kanya was checking herself out in the mirror—why doesn't she fucking wear a dress if she's going to be a vain female?—and DP was talking to Skull Surfer, both of them a mile a minute and not hearing each other, like two tapedecks turned toward each other, blasting.

Xandra kissed on DP, that's what it's like: kissing on him, and he sort of let it happen, not getting into it till he notices Kanya watching then he gives Xandra a big soulkiss. Then she whispers something to him and shakes her ass a little and goes out the door—and stops, goes back to the lady's room, fixes her makeup, then goes back out the door again. She's going to Santa Monica to catch a date and make some more money.

Then Kanya suddenly makes some kind of move, and I follow, pretending I'm picking a song on the CD jukebox; she goes like a dart to DP carrying a double tequila and gives it to him, says she thought he could use a drink after having that guy dogging on his thigh and all.

DP might've gotten pissed off but he just laughed and drank some tequila and stopped her as she started to walk away. Which is what she was hoping for.

Hey, what?

I don't know, what?

You doggin me?

You been hanging out with too many niggers, talking like that, he said.

You're weird to be a racist, a fucking Indian.

Indians got good reasons to be racist.

Then she starts to go again, and he says, If you want something, let's go, let's do it.

Almost the same way he talks about a fistfight but he's talking about fucking.

She shrugs and looks around, shrugs again, looks at herself in the mirror. Shrugs.

If you want.

So they leave together and I follow them. They're both pretty fucked up and don't notice me.

But I couldn't follow them into the building. He'd have kicked the shit out of me if I'd tried that.

The rest of it I know from her black hooker roommate: That they went to bed and he said, Let's have one more good fuck, I know you want it.

You fucking pig, she said. But they did it, and she almost got him to cum too, I guess she had to practically dislocate her jaw, but then he had to finish with his hand, shooting his load on her chest.

Then he got up almost immediately and got dressed.

Where the fuck you going? she asked.

My old lady's waiting for me, she got my hubba.

I could get you some.

Bullshit you're, like, broke all the time. I'll see you around. You had your last one. You wanted a last one you had it. I'm cruising on.

And he left her, and she was sitting there sort of hyperventilating, her room mate said. So, yeah: she was way, way more into him than she ever let on.

So then she does something she hasn't done in two years since her sister died of HIV from the needle: she gets a hypo, gets it from her roommate. Her roommate says, Girl, you don't have nothin, what you going to shoot?

Kanya draws off some of his cum from her chest and she shoots it up, right in her mainline, this big glop of semen, okay?, into her veins...

And then she went into convulsions and she died of a bloodclot, later, in the hospital.

I saw her in the hospital before she died. She was in a coma. I reached under the blanket and squeezed her leg real hard, enough to hurt.

She didn't move. And I'm, like, crying. Sort of.

CRAM

Gino and Telly were already half an hour late and the BART train was just now leaving the last station in Oakland. The train gave out a soft squeal as it started out of the station, snaking into the underground tube for the trip across the bay to the Embarcadero. "It don't matter, dude," Telly was saying, "Geisenbaum don't give a fuck which fuckin' bike messengers are there, long as somebody's there to take out the first packages." Telly was lean, muscular, tanned, longhair tied in three pony tails. He wore a sleeveless Coil tee he'd bought from a scalper at the concert, and surfer shorts. He didn't like having a tan on his arms; all that sun in August, biking the waterfront. Didn't like it because he thought it blurred his tattoos. But wore the short sleeves so the tats could be seen.

"Yeah, Telly, but if he's got a morning rush floodin' packages, we'll get our asses fired."

Gino could talk acceptable bike-messenger but he was a night school grad student in Modern Lit, postmodern specialities, when he had the tuition, and he'd pulled a 3.8 with almost no effort at UC Berkeley, majoring in English Lit, minor in Philosophy, and it didn't come exactly naturally to him. Working with guys like Telly was philosophically satisfying, it was Working Class, and it gave Gino a sense of meshing with the genetic core of humanity, the people who'd rejected him in high school. The ones who knew how to be really into whatever they were into.

Gino only had the one tat, the Maori pattern around his wrist like a bracelet. Enough to give him credibility with the Tellys, not enough to prevent his getting tenure someday.

Telly had his bike with him on the subway car; Gino's bike was locked up at Geisenbaum's. Telly'd picked up some glares pushing the glossy black, sticker-swatched mountain bike into the crowded train car. It was the last car, where you could bring a bike, but this car was packed and so was every other car for the peak of morning rush hour, and whatever the rules the question in this metal and glass and plastic box asserted itself physically: the bike's pedals jammed into the ankles of the thirtyish probably-a-lawyer lady in grey pants-suit standing across from Telly; its handlebars forced a heavyset, heavybreathing man in a red jogging outfit to hold his gut in. Telly usually said "Hope nobody farts, bro'," when it was like this but, mercifully, hadn't said it so far. He and Gino had got seats when two people got off at the downtown Oakland stop; Telly leaning on the bicycle seat, and in the swaying press of people looming around them they felt agreeably hidden away though they could smell the exact proportions of sweat mixed with perfume and deodorant around them, and Gino knew for a fact that the lady in lavender with the big hair, standing next to his left knee, had a yeast infection. Her crotch smelled like a bakery on fire.

"Big shit, if he fires us," Telly was saying, tugging on a tuft of goatee. "How many messenger services we can work for? Hella bikin' out there, bro'."

Gino leaned back a little to peer through the swaying forest of fabric and torsos, thinking about losing his job, at the same time trying to define what was always so odd about the light here, in the crossbay tunnel; maybe because they were beneath the bay, beneath sand and silt and sharks and ships and a sheath of rock and concrete, there genuinely was not a trace of light here except the artificial light.

His gaze settled on a black security guard squeezed in the access passage to back door of car, guy at least a hundred pounds overweight, with a long silvery cop's flashlight propped on one shoulder like a sentry with his rifle. Beside the fat black guy was a woman in the same kind of Brinks uniform; a roundfaced, otherwise skinny black security guard, with badly conked hair, and she had a flashlight too. Both of them standing, wedged together. They weren't guards for BART, why'd they need a flashlight at this hour, working downtown? Maybe they were coming off-shift from an all nighter in the East Bay. They looked tired enough. And their expressions said they were underpaid.

"I like working for Geisenbaum," Gino said at last, "he pays fifty cents an hour more than most of 'em."

Telly ducked his head to acknowledge a baseline truth. "We gettin' there, dude." He looked at his Zippy the Pinhead watch; then reached down and absently flicked his thumbnail up the spokes on his bicycle wheel, the faint twang almost lost in the metallic hiss-and-rumble of the BART train as it strobed past tunnel lights. He continued the motion up the spokes and past the wheel to flick, finally, the ring in his lower lip and the one through his nose; sounds you couldn't hear. He was peacock proud of his tattoos and his piercings. Glanced at the twining red-and-blue-green Chinese dragon on his forearm as he raised it to look again at Zippy's gloves, repeating: "We gettin' there—"

He broke off, lifting his head, listening like a dog at a whistle pitched too high for everyone else. Then Gino felt it too: a cross-wave of vibration, a shivering of the car that didn't harmonize with the faint vibration of the plastic seats, the metal floor. And then the train braked; it braked with a suddenness that rattled vertebrae like dominos, and everyone became rodeo cowboys in their seats, and then darkness, profound darkness like when he'd toured a cavern and the State Park guide had switched off the lights so they could experience geological absolutes; and then a scream of metal that sounded almost apologetic and a sizzle of breaking glass and he lost his seat entirely as the world pitched him over its shoulder. And direction, as a thing-in-itself, was uncreated: and Gino had a new relationship to gravity. Bodies pummeled him and people wailed and sirened, so loudly, from so deeply, Gino could feel the twisting weight of their bodies in the sound.

After that a cymbal crashed against the side of his head and he heard Telly screaming like a baby and the sound got very faint and distant and vanished in the silence.

———◆———

When Gino came to, it was to a cold wetness on his right side and wet warmth on the other. His thoughts were almost immediately clear and he was surprised at his own comforting detachment.

He knew with a knifelike certainty that there had been an earthquake.

He knew he was lying atop a wet stack of bodies in the darkness and in blood and seawater and a thin scum of sewage from ruptured viscera.

He knew it had been a big earthquake and they were halfway across the bay and under thousands of tons of water, and no one would ever, ever rescue them.

He knew he'd been hit in the head and knocked out and something was still breaking in his head, but he was sure, somehow, that it had only just happened, no more than a minute had passed. Maybe it was the energy in the screams and the flailing around him. It was the energy of a fresh catastrophe.

The screaming, though, came to him filtered through a buzzing in his head; he was fairly sure that one of his eardrums had burst. There was pain in that ear, but it seemed unreal. That surprised him, too, in an insular kind of way: pain ought to be the realest thing of all. But mere pain had no rank here. Both fear and pain were subordinate to the seeking cone of perception, the exploratory probe of a terminating life. Two of his senses, smell and taste, had mostly shut down; he knew this meant that the rest of his senses would shut down. That the oozing chill in one corner of his skull was spreading, would shut him down.

These realizations were not articulated for Gino: they were experienced the way one experiences the cold surface of a concrete wall under the fingers.

Because he didn't know what else to do, he tried to look
around.

There was no light.

Experimentally, he tried to move. It didn't hurt more to
move than to lay still. He began to crawl. A hand flapped in
his face; fingernails, probably a woman's, dug into his cheek,
and he pulled his head back, in reflex, but otherwise ignored
it, kept moving.

Sometimes the wailing ebbed and there was only a vocal
rasping, a murmuring, like the sounds of an unseen flock of
birds. Then the wailing would resume. One sound was equal
to another.

Gino turned, and his eyes cleared, and he saw that now
there was a little light, yellowish light from below mostly,
and a faint sheen of red light from the sides, and after what
might have been a full minute of looking he knew that the
yellow light was from the rear of the car which was now
directly below him. The BART tunnel had curled like a
bent-finger, knuckled under to the buckling of the earth's
crust, to a wedge of strata jammed upward, sheer as a
seismographic spike; horizontal had become vertical and
everyone was pressed down into the tin can of the car by
bodyweight and by slowly-increasing water and by mud
coming in through widening seams of metal and by thickening
blood. And more bodies had come in from the second to last
car, gravitationally forced through the shattered door, packing,
cramming this lower car so full there were only a few
crawl-spaces left...Yet there were apertures, wet and ready
places, that seemed to be there for him, for this moment, for
whatever remained to Gino...

The bodies under him in that moment were rearranged by
the dynamics of suffering, and parted legs and tilted torsos
shifted at angles to create a kind of wriggling shaft, a space
letting more light through, and down which blood and piss
and brown scum and seawater trickled, in no hurry, like a
spring oozing from a muddy hillside; a living crevice...

...a living crevice...

...maybe fifty feet deep and at the bottom of it he saw
parts of the Security Guards, the lady perhaps alive, seeming
to wriggle with life but maybe just shaken by the twitchings

around her, the man split open, you could see the yellow fat
through the ruptured belly, a mock layer cake of exposed fat
and intestinal tissue garnished by a splintered rib; and
somehow the flashlight had been turned on, maybe by one
of the hands groping from the layers of people, and the
flashlight's butt had slipped into the fat man's gouged open
belly, which quivered with the movement of struggling bodies,
shimmying the light up the shaft of bodies (was that a rainbow
in a spill of piss and seawater?) and playing over faces, some
of them alive and staring with a disbelief almost identical to
the staring dead (but for the randomly tracking eyes) and
some profoundly identified with hurt and some trying to claw
their way out and too stupid for despair.

There was a man whose interior had been pressed out
through his mouth and he was choking on his own throat,
and died as Gino watched.

About two layers of people down from the top, a hand
thrust out into the crevice; there was a tattoo of a flying pig
on the brown and streaming wrist of that hand. It was Telly's
hand.

Gino reached down and tugged and thought the arm was
going to come free, torn away, but after a short, wet slide it
resisted, and he knew it was still attached by a ribbon of
flesh; he knew with a spiraling assurance that Telly was dead.

*Dude, I'm gonna sing in a rock band, my cousin he's got
this anti-racist skinhead industrial band going and his singer's
leaving and he says if I shave my head I could join and I said
what the fuck, it grows back. I don't know, though, I might be
able to get on this tv show instead, there's this show called
LIFE STRAIGHT UP that's gonna be on this new channel that's
gonna compete with MTV and they follow YOU around and
film whatever you do except you got to live with these people
they pick and they wanted a bike messenger but maybe, you
know, I could be in both things, the band and the—*

Telly's ambitions. Gino's ambitions. *Yeah, Jane, you're
right, you can't teach fulltime and write novels too, not great
ones, but I can do one and then the other. It starts with the
day gig, you know? I thought maybe if I got a
professorship...but, I don't know, that's like years in grad, and
it sucks up a lot of creative energy, all those papers, but, shit,*

carpe diem, I gotta go for it now, I blew the last scholarship but I think I can get another and maybe I could do both...and...

...and I'm gonna get a website...

I tell you that? That I'm gonna get a—

One of the red lights fizzled and went out. Someone was shouting, "Okay, folks, those...uh, those of us who are...who can move okay, we uh, listen we got to...we got to...to organize, we got to move toward the door, a few of us and...and try to get down the tunnel, there might be a way through..."

An aftershock shimmied through them. Metal like rubber. Another window not far below and to the right burst in the aftershock and Gino could see it in the light from the remaining red emergency light. The lady in lavender with big hair was being pressed by the weight of bodies above her, forced through the ragged gap in the glass like one of those kid's molds that shaped playdough forced through a little patterned hole and he could see her living flesh pressed into the outline of the hole in the glass. The woman's scream was one note, one very high and incredulous EEEEEEEEEEEEEEEEEEEEEEEEEEEEEEEEEEEEEEEEEEEEEEE—

"What we gotta do is, not panic—"

Someone laughed. Gino was vaguely aware, and almost surprised, that someone was FUCKING on the top of the pile, just a few feet away.

"—there's always a chance and there could be a way through, it might...uh....it might not be as bad as it seems..."

More laughter. Male, Gino thought.

"I...I can't get this door open and if, please, if we could...if we could push some of the...those who didn't make it, if we could push them...push them out a window...we...please, hurry because, um, I'm...there's blood and water and it's coming up to my...I'm wedged down here and there are too many people on me to move so if someone could just move to the...the sound of my...hello? If someone could...uh, the water is...buh wabuh ess...wabuh us—hey! I...wabugh ess..."

More laughter.

...EEEEEEE. Then that scream stopped, and the red light by the window went out too. Someone else screamed that they were drowning, please help them.

Gino could feel the coldness in his head spreading. There wasn't much time left. The heart of all life was underneath, beating in the crevice, the living crevice. Very deliberately, Gino plunged into the crevice, headfirst.

He liked the way it felt, as he went down. Like it was a throat and his body was a dick. He thought: That's really how it feels.

Then he hit the bottom of the shaft, and was plunged under the surface of the mingled liquids there, salty and shitty, and he squirmed around, holding his breath, till he got his legs under him, and stood up on someone's dead face and on someone else's—what? an arm?—and felt another, vertical crevice in the jigsaw of bodies open in front of him, warm and wet and suffering, and it was just what he was probing for, so he pulled off his clothes, all of them, and then he forced himself into the crevice in the canyon of bodies, headfirst, and squirmed immediately forward, and thought it serendipitous how the blood and the other liquids had become lubricants here, and how remarkably easy to move it was, so long as he stayed more or less horizontal, and how there were pockets of air to breathe, as he was still above most of the seawater, and how marvelously indifferent he felt when someone in psychotic agony sank their teeth in his shoulder and sawed at it, how it felt rather good, in fact, and merely felt cold when he tore himself away from it, losing a chunk of shoulder, and forced himself into a steaming gap which he realized was the gut of a human being, he was actually worming through the center of a living person, the wound flesh tight as sex around him, the smell hideous, but they didn't seem to feel it: he could feel the crooked end of their halved spine scraping along his own backbone. Sometimes he heard voices, whispers, mutters, weeping, rising and falling as a whole as if by some consensual signal; other times it was echoingly silent. Or maybe it was just his hearing shutting off, at intervals. He could taste nothing, smell little, and he was grateful for that, but his skin was exquisitely alive, and he realized he had a hard-on and he dragged it, furrowing it along the bodies, the wet fabric and flesh, and humped now and then, and squirmed

onward, remembering maggots he'd seen in a sealed jelly
jar that had so outraged his father, nineteen years earlier,
and nosing wormlike through darkness, then realizing that
he was had found his way to two full, bloody-wet breasts,
a woman below him, was oozing himself over her from
her head toward her feet, and she was alive and put her
arms around him, and tried to force his face into her crotch,
but then he'd found another woman, this one turned the
other way, and he felt her hand on his cock guiding it into
her, as the weight of bodies around them increased with
another aftershock, a shift of the subway car, and pressed
down on them so they could scarcely breath, and somehow
he knew, he understood with what might have been the
telepathy of human minds under incredible pressurization,
that she wanted to copulate with him because it was the
most life-confirming thing she could do, at that moment,
with her body, she couldn't get out and this was all that
was left, this praying with the body one person into another,
each thrust of her hips and his cock saying I am here, I
was here, I am alive, I was alive, this is alive, you
acknowledge me more deeply than in the puniness of talk
and hand-holding and kissing, you acknowledge in me the
reproductive impulse that connects to life, you fuck your
way toward that recognition, you come into me, you come
into me, I'm here, I'm alive, I was alive, I was, I am, I was,
I am...was...was...The pressure increasing, no more
breathing, no more air, oxygen starvation forcing their
minds from their bodies, entwining to rise together, wet,
locked together, in life, in death...he ejaculated into the
void of death.

WHAT WOULD YOU DO FOR LOVE?

Later, when he was thinking about what it would be like to take a bullet in the head, Darry found that, even then, he couldn't blame Marla. He thought: Marla was only one part death.

Three parts of her were something else. Somewhere in her was a kind of mythic terrarium, where she kept another Marla, a little mental doll that moved with the power of imagination through a clean landscape, a place where neither fear nor pain could take root.

He taught high school, American Lit. He met Marla in the El Loro High School parking lot when she came to pick up her niece.

———— ◆ ————

He stood on the front steps in front of the school office, beneath the flagpole; not wanting to stay, not wanting to go home to Bette. It was almost winter in El Loro, but it was Central California and the trees had shed only an outer skirt of leaves; the sky showed blue through fissures in the smears

of number-two penciled clouds. His name was Darius; he
went by Darry, and didn't like that much either. He stood in
a wind that smelled faintly of leafy decay, watching Marla get
out of the car.

Marla's niece, Cecily, was a pretty girl; except for the weak
chin. He thought of Cecily as a student who sometimes tried.
She wore baggy overalls, one strap deliberately left hanging,
and a Pearl Jam t-shirt. Her hair was teased over to one side;
there was a touch of irony about the coif. When Cecily saw
her Aunt Marla coming to get her, instead of her Mom, she
got a look on her face he knew from a thousand displays of
adolescent embarrassment: Oh Gawd, not her.

But Darry felt a bittersweet tightness the first time he
saw Marla. She wore a taut leopard-print blouse, black
vinyl skirt not-too-short; a black butterfly tattooed on one
ankle; around the other a charm bracelet. Her lips were
full, voluptuous with shiny burgundy lipstick, but her mouth
seemed not quite wide enough. Her nose was small, her
eyes were a goldflake green; it was only later that he saw
one eye was just a little higher than the other. Her hair
was an unnatural shade of blonde, cut close like a Roaring
'20s flapper, and you were *supposed* to notice that it was
an unnatural blonde; and her earrings were little silhouettes
of Queen Nefertiti. There was a half faded tattoo of an
ankh on her forearm. And her feet were packed into almost
vertically elevated spike heels. They looked at least a size
too small.

"You like to look *close!*" Jan said, stepping up beside him,
smiling to show she was Just Kidding. Jan taught computer
science to juniors.

Darry realized that Jan had caught him staring at one of
his students' female relatives. And with his mouth open, just
a little.

He shut his mouth with an almost audible snap, jerking
his gaze from Marla, who was standing on the school steps
with Cecily. "Well, she's...striking."

He smiled, hoping she took the remark and the smile as
condescension toward the woman in the leopard-print top;
the woman who wore black onyx beads, he saw now, glancing
back at her; who was looking past Cecily, back at him.

Snap. Look back at Jan. She was a small, tidy woman with mousy brown hair; narrow in the shoulders and broad in the hips. She had large, pretty brown eyes; she wore contacts to give her best feature its best shot. He hoped she wouldn't press another behavioristic computer-model questionnaire on him. She had a fetish for computer-modeling behavior with artificial-life analogs. But she was saying, "Oh most definitely, she's a prize. I can almost read her rap sheet from here."

"Now that could be a little uncharitable, Jan."

"I guess. I feel like I knew her from gym class at my own high school. She reminds me of the one who put pepper in my brassiere. How's your Bette?"

"Bette's...she's good." Someday he was going to learn how to talk about his wife to people without it sounding like she was dying of something. She wasn't dying. She was just sort of housebound. Sort of. His looming sense of their mutual decline was almost certainly exaggerated. They were only in their forties. True, American Association of Retired People had sent her a sample newsletter, because she was two years older than him and had popped up on some AARP databank; but he hadn't got one yet. Not yet.

"How's sophomore English?" Jan asked.

He managed to stare at his shoes and not Cecily's aunt. He had heard Cecily say, moments before: *Oh no it's my Aunt Marla oh Gawd she's so...*

So...what?

He managed, "'How's sophomore English?'...um, in one word: apocalyptic."

Jan laughed. "I'd call you melodramatic except I know better. Try juniors and computer science." She'd been married once. The guy had just disappeared one day. Story was, she'd had a single, apologetic postcard from Florida and no other word, for years. And there was a rumor she was quietly rich from designing computer software and didn't need to work here at all. With modern kids, teaching for the love of it had always seemed incomprehensible to Darry.

He knew she had a crush on him. He could feel it like something sticky under his shoe. Sometimes he was tempted. She seemed willing; she seemed sympathetic but he wasn't sure what she was sympathetic about. What did she know about his marriage?

"Sophomore English, sophomore science—both oxymorons."

"But keep in mind—"

"I know: our teachers thought we were a hopeless generation, too. Et cetera. Sure."

She sang softly. "'Why can't they be like weeee were, perfect in every way'..."

"You have to pretend not to remember that musical, so it doesn't date you!"

She laughed. He watched Cecily argue with her Aunt Marla. *"What are you so embarrassed about, girl? Just get in the car..."*

Jan was murmuring, "Well...I guess..." She was trying to think of something else to say, to keep him here. She'd prod him about the computer modeling questionnaire, and would he fill out another. But school was out and there were no meetings for once and he could go home; see his dog, avoid his wife. Marla was taking the reluctant Cecily to her Mom's car. The aunt looked only ten years older than the niece. There was some story or other behind that, he thought.

He said: "Well—papers to correct—"

"Me, too."

But as he started to turn away she thought of something. "You still writing that book?"

"Oh—perennially."

"If you sold it, would you quit teaching?"

He'd asked himself that a dozen times but he said, "Not a chance. I don't jump without a parachute. I'd quit if I got a half million dollar advance but—" He paused to chuckle. "I don't think it's that kind of novel. I think it's maybe a three-thousand-dollar-advance novel. Or maybe a 'paid in contributor's copies' university press novel."

"Your mistake is getting literary. Not enough shootings." She looked at him, then looked away. "Or enough sex."

"You're...probably right. I'm afraid this is more like a *Lucky Jim* for secondary school."

"Uh oh—anybody I know on the faculty get brutally caricatured?"

"Wha-a-at? Me? Write about anybody I know?" Darry winked. "Give me some credit."

She gave a brittle little laugh. He thought he needed another excuse to leave; he could tell her he had to feed his dog. But that would seem like no priority at all to her: he'd heard her say she didn't like animals. He didn't trust people who didn't have pets.

Inexorably, she said, "I do have one more questionnaire for you—"

"You know, those questions are getting a little personal."

"Sorry. Computer modeling knows no boundaries. I mean it is, you know, behavioristic. But it's all very anonymous and 'hypothetical person number 39' and..."

"Am I number 39? I'll do one more for you, tomorrow. Well..." He glanced at his watch. "Whuh-oh."

"Me, too!" she said chirpily, just a flutter of regret, and backed away, smiling goodbye, then hurried off, briefcase swinging.

Darry saw Marla looking at him as she maneuvered to get out of the stunningly-illegal red-zone parking spot she'd picked, between two smallish handicapped-student shuttles. She backed her car...right into his Mitsubishi. Both cars rocked. She made a big show of grimacing.

He smiled sympathetically and his heart leapt as he walked over to the car and looked at the bumpers. She got out and looked too.

"Eek! Is that your car?"

"Uhhh—"

"I know it is, actually." She talked fast, which didn't sound right with the mild Texas accent, at first. "Cecily told me right before I backed into it. 'That's my English teacher's car and he's watching so don't—' And, you know, wham! And not even a bam and thank-you-ma'am!"

"Gawd, Marla!" Cecily said, with exquisite misery, getting out.

"It's your fault, girl," Marla said, shaking her head slowly at Cecily as she spoke. "You got me all tense saying—" She did a little mimicry of Cecily saying: "'He's watching so don't back into it'. And then of course I get tense and I—"

"It's okay, really, there's no damage done," Darry interrupted.

"She scratched your bumper, Mr. Bentworth," Cecily said, rolling her eyes.

Marla was looking at his wedding ring. She looked up into his face. "Really? 'Cause see, I don't have any insurance—"

"Ooh big surprise there," Cecily said.

"—and I don't know how I'd—"

"Seriously. It's okay."

Marla cocked her head and the mimicry this time was of a you're-my-knight-in-shining-armor look; an irony meant to show real gratitude.

"Well, thanks. I owe you one. For true."

He hadn't noticed her fingernails before. They were the same color as her lipstick and shiny as a beetle's wing, about an inch too long, long enough to curl a little, and on each one there was a little quartermoon of spangle.

"Can we go, Marla?"

"I don't even know the man's name! Ex-cuse me!"

Cecily gave a sigh; he heard the sigh at least half a dozen times a day from various kids. *The world on my shoulders is more than heavy, it's flawed, and it's all I've got.* "This is Mr. Bentworth, Marla."

He shook her small hand; the long nails reminded him of seashells in his palm. "Darry Bentworth."

"Darry?"

He shrugged. "It's short for Darius. My old man was into Hellenic history." He almost added: Actually that gives the impression that Darius was Greek whereas, in fact, he...

Stopped himself in time.

Cecily was looking anxiously at passing teenagers and pulling her aunt by the arm. "I think I'm being summoned to the car, Mr. Bentworth...Darry...but I do, I owe you one!"

She waved with the tips of her fingers, her curved nails, and they got into the car and after backing and filling four or five times, they got out of the spot and drove down the street, only about ten miles an hour past the speed limit.

———— ◆ ————

Bette was still in her nightgown and pink slippers.

He heard the TV when he came up the walk to the condo.

What was it, Rosie O'Donnell? Rikki Lake? It was a talk show of some kind. Then it abruptly cut off and he knew she'd seen his shadow on the window shade as he stepped onto the front porch. When he came in she was poring over bills on the coffee table.

He debated telling her he knew she hadn't been working on bills, she'd been watching TV, and she'd switched it off as he'd arrived to make it look as if she wasn't just watching TV all day. But he knew where that would end.

He stood in the archway between the dining area and the living room, looking at her. Seeing her, in that moment, as if seeing a stranger. He felt almost that he'd intruded in someone else's house.

She looked up from the phone bills. "Oh hi. I didn't hear you come in."

Uh-huh. "Hi."

"You okay?"

"Why wouldn't I be?"

"You look funny."

"You're pretty funny-lookin' yourself." He smiled so she'd know it was a joke.

She looked back at the bills. He wondered how her calves got so big and so white. Her cheeks were round and white and heavy. She'd remembered to put on those half-glasses she wore for reading as she pretended to squint at the bills. Her long black hair was stringy, its washing at least a day late.

Think how you're perceiving her, he told himself guiltily. It isn't fair. It's your mood. And she's not at her best.

The ashtray beside her was brimming with cigarette butts.

Irma, their miniature collie, lying at Bette's feet, woke up when he came near the sofa. She leapt up to stand on her hind legs, put her front paws on his knee, gazing raptly up at him. He laughed, reached down and grabbed her nose and shook it, making her snuffle.

"She's been flirting with that dog next door again," Bette said, smiling at Irma.

He sat on the arm of the couch, petting the dog. "Didn't you tell her she's been spayed?"

"She's ready to party anyway, I guess. I don't know where she gets the hormones. Today she ran down the walk after the postman—and she's always been nice to him, he's never been scared of her, but I was afraid he was going to mace her."

"Why?"

"She jumped up and grabbed a cardboard box that had some kind of sausage sample in it, right out of his bag!"

They laughed, and he patted Irma. "You're the lady pirate, Irma."

For a moment there was a warmth between him and Bette; the dog was the medium for it. He thought: We relate to each other through the dog or not at all...

He got up and went into the kitchen, opened the refrigerator. It was amazing how something so stiff and crispy as celery could become as limp and droopy as one of Dali's watches, hanging over the edge of the metal fridge tray. There were some moldy pickles; lonesome condiments; two cartons of half eaten Chinese food that'd been there for two weeks. Nothing else.

"I'm sorry," she called from the living room. "I forgot to shop."

"You forgot?" He closed the fridge door.

"Yup."

He went to the door, looked through the dining area at her, still on the couch in the living room. "You've forgotten for a month. I always do it or we order out."

"It hasn't been a month."

"Yeah it has. Want to go over some receipts together?"

"Not necessary, Inspector Clouseau. I'm sure I must have..."

"Bette—you haven't gone out in a month. I've even taken the garbage out." He thought: Don't say it. But he took the leap. "Does the word agoraphobia speak to us at all?"

She stared at him. "You're saying I'm mentally ill because I've been a little depressed and haven't gone out much?"

"Depressed? Agoraphobia is not depressed, it's a step beyond it. It's fear of going outside. And it's not in the mental illness category. It's just neurotic. But you could get a little therapy or Prozac or something."

"Now you've gone from Inspector Clouseau to Dr. Kildare."

"God. No one remembers Dr. Kildare."

"You spend too much time around high school students."

"Yeah, well, that I won't argue with."

"You know what, I could take a shower, put on my special nightie—"

"Don't put yourself out."

He regretted it as soon as he said it.

Her face crinkled up. "You're right. You're right." She made gulping sounds as she cried, her head bowed; her hair drooping. "You're right I'm just...I'm a lump. I'm a fucking lump. I'm neurotic and scared and I'm a lump. You should leave me." The crying went into a higher gear.

He wanted to go to her and tell her it wasn't so, but he was too angry and he was surprised at how angry he was. It wasn't like this was unusual or anything.

"Look—just...calm down. Have some of that calming tea, watch one of your shows, I'm going to the grocery store, get us some stuff. I'll make some soup, you'll feel better."

It was a way of trying to make up to her for provoking her to tears and then not comforting her. And he was hungry.

"No, I'll go."

But he knew if he waited for her to go, she'd make excuses and then it'd be ten p.m. and she still wouldn't have gone and there'd be no dinner and they'd both be in foul, low-blood-sugar moods and it'd escalate into a huge fight.

As he went into the bedroom and changed his clothes, he thought: I ought to be able to do something more to help her.

But there was something between him and what he knew he should do to help her, and he couldn't see what it was and he couldn't get past it. It was like one of the force fields in a science fiction movie. He felt a burning when he tried to cross it, to get to her, and he knew the burning was all in him.

"I can't even have a baby, I just have bloody pieces of baby," she sobbed.

He didn't want her to talk about the series of miscarriages. He very badly didn't want her to talk about it.

"Hon—just...take it easy. I'll be back. Bring you some ice cream."

Just what she needed. Ice cream.

Oh come on, he thought, as he went out the front door. She's only fifty pounds or so overweight. Some people at the

mall, you couldn't believe they could get into a car to get
there.

He stopped at his little blue Mitsubishi and looked at his
condo. It was attached to the other condos, same shape and
color, a deep red brown that was supposed to look foresty
somehow, and there were little leafless trees in front of it;
the little trees were the same size as TV antennas and almost
the same shape. People had stopped using TV antennas, he
thought, so the antennas had disguised themselves as trees
for survival.

He got into the car and drove to the mall.

—— ◆ ——

"El Loro means 'The parrot'," the bartender told Buck.

"No shit." Buck ran his hand over his bristling jaw. Two
days short of a shave, he thought. "I wonder why they'd call
it after fuckin' *parrots*. Parrots don't come from California."
He drank some more of his rum and coke.

"People let their parrots get out and they get wild and we
end up with quite a few wild parrots. Maybe named after
that, some of them local wild parrots. The town is only about
thirty years old, see."

It was one of those Howard Johnson's bars attached to the
Howard Johnson's restaurant, which was attached to the
Howard Johnson's motel where Buck was staying. Usually
nobody was ever in those bars except for traveling salesmen,
fat and sullen.

But sometimes you could get some pussy there: somebody's
runaway wife, or whatever. They go right to the motel bar
from their room.

Buck liked the Howard Johnson's because you didn't even
have to leave the motel to get your food. The less you had to
leave, the more you could leave when you didn't have to.
Good to remember. Crimebuster tip.

In the joint, in Vacaville, they'd loved it when he'd say "I
gotta crimebuster tip for ya" and then he'd tell them how to
slip the cops.

Of course the inevitable question would come up.

Why you here, if you so smart motherfucker?

Because, he'd said, every time, assholes like you need my help. It's charity, why I'm here.

Usually got a laugh. A motherfucker was laughing with you he wasn't sticking a piece of tape-handle shit-metal in your back.

The bartender, here, he was an old guy, kind of guy who lived to get away to Vegas when he could.

"You in town looking for work?" the old guy asked.

"No. Why?"

No particular belligerence in the way Buck said it, but the bartender could tell Buck didn't like the question about work. It implied more, unspoken questions, like: *Where do you get your money, and what have you been doing recently, and are those jailhouse tattoos on your wrist?*

"I don't know," the bartender was saying, "there's some work at the motherboard plant, lot of people come here to try and get some of that..."

"What's a motherfucking motherboard?"

The bartender tossed his head the way some people did instead of laughing. "A computer part."

"Oh, sure, that's right. No, me, I work in construction." Last job he'd had, ten years before, that'd been construction. He'd got seven hundred dollars for the company's truck and tools, when he left. "No, I came to town to pick something up belongs to me."

"Get you another rum and coke?"

"Nope."

Buck was looking out the window. A cop was rolling by. The cruiser went on, two small-town cops with their dicks in their hands.

Buck decided to go back to his room, look through the phone book.

———— ◆ ————

The Muzak was playing the "left the cake out in the rain" song, and there was a sale on Lunchables on aisle 3. Darry was trying to remember what else they needed at the house. Dog food? Probably. Ice cream? Definitely.

Then Marla came wheeling fast around a corner of the aisle and ran her cart broadside into his.

"Oh my God—twice in one day! It must be destiny!" She laughed and he had to laugh too. She saw he'd changed his clothes, he was wearing an *X-Files* t-shirt one of his students had given him, only because it had been clean, and she burst out, "Where'd you get that tee! I haven't got that one. I thought I had all the *X-Files* t-shirts!"

"Umm—one of my students gave it to me. He's kind of a fanboy or something..."

"Oh you're a fan of the show too, oh my god, that's so— what's your sign?"

He blinked. Had he said he was a fan of the show? He'd seen one episode of the show, which had seemed pretentious to him—pretending it wasn't ordinary TV when it was—and...

And he said...

"Oh yeah I love the show, never miss it." He hoped he sounded sincere. Uh—my sign is...Scorpio." Actually his sign was Libra, but Scorpio sounded sexier.

"Oh...my...god I knew you had to be a Scorp...So am I! I could see all those Scorp fires in you, seriously, I mean I know how that sounds, but it was just like you were one of those gas fireplaces."

"Uhh...Hell, yes, my gas is burning, you bet. Especially after the school cafeteria."

She laughed. Her cart contained Lunchables, a half gallon of tequila, chicken wings with a packet of barbecue sauce, pork rinds, Doritos...

"You know what I don't have anybody to talk about the *X-Files* with..."

...Oscar Mayer franks, white bread, a 12 pack of Budweiser...

"Well—one of these days we should—"

What was he doing?

"How about now!"

"Um—" He felt like a crevice had opened up in the tile floor of the supermarket and he was pitching into free fall, as he said, "What the hell, yeah."

Something in him knew: It was happening so fast.

He found himself following her to the checkout. She was saying something about having to drop off all this stuff and did he have anything to drop off and he said no, don't worry about it.

In the parking lot he thought he saw Jan, she of the questionnaires, sitting in her minivan, watching him as he walked out with Marla. So, let her look.

In a kind of dream, Darry drove behind Marla's car—her sister's car—to a flaking white crackerbox house between two enormous pine trees; there was a silt of red needles on its roof.

He parked well back from the house, at an angle, as she drove into the driveway; she ran over the wheel of an overturned bicycle. She carried the bulging bags to the house, one in each arm, with no visible effort.

He thought: I should have carried them in for her. But he was hoping Cecily wouldn't see him out here, let alone in the house.

A police car cruised slowly by, and the crewcut young cop riding shotgun looked at him. Darry became uncomfortably aware that he was parked crooked, rear end of his car sticking out into the street.

But the cops cruised on, slowing in front of Cecily's house but not stopping. They turned the corner and were gone and then Marla came running up from the house, grinning. She'd left the two bags leaning on the front door.

"I don't have a key and my sister's gone and Cecily's gone, but they'll be back soon so I guess the stuff'll be okay." All this as she opened the door and got in. "Well, let's go!"

They went. She seemed unaware of the bike wheel crimped under the car . He decided to say nothing about it.

They drove to the town's main drag, Silbido Avenue, and he turned right and immediately regretted it, thinking someone who knew his wife was sure to see him on this street. But then, who knew Bette, anymore?

"Um—where we going?" he asked, smiling, trying to make a joke of his vertiginous uncertainty.

"I should've brought the tequila. Well, let's go where we can have some drinks. Any ol' place. You know what, I don't watch X-Files all that much, really, some of them kind of

bore me, I just like the alien ones. My favorite show is
Sightings."

"*Sightings*. UFOs, right?"

"Oh yeah UFOs bigtime, man, but for real, and they also
have, you know, ghosts and bigfoot."

"And the ghost of bigfoot?"

"I didn't see that one. They had this one where they showed
a crop circle getting made, this light was flying around over a
field and this crop circle appeared..."

He'd read about it. The film had been analyzed and it was
a hoax. And he thought about telling her this. But he could
see her cleavage, from where he was sitting.

"Oh I know," he said. "That was mind blowing. You'd
think the president would say something about all this. Flying
saucers. I mean, it's evidence."

"Oh exactly, I'm so glad you think so. I really think I was,
you know, from there, in my last life."

"From...?"

"Another planet. Well, I think it was Mars because, see,
Mars used to be this really green planet thousands and
thousands of years ago but then they had a catastrophe? And
what they had there, you see, was an Egyptian civilization,
and they brought it to Egypt, but see the first pyramids and
sphinxes, they were on Mars. That's why I've got this Egyptian
jewelry, because really it's my connection to Mars."

"Yeah? How about this place? I mean, for a drink. 'Shady
Corners Bar and Grill...' Most places that say 'Grill' don't
have a grill though..."

"Whatever. And they had a catastrophe on Mars? And the
people all went underground...and all that's left is that Face
on Mars thing...But, see, I was one of those people in a past
life..."

"Did you have, uh, hypno-regression, whatsit, to find out?"

"No. I don't think so..."

They got out of the car and he looked around at what the
neighborhood was like, and he checked twice to make sure
he'd locked the car doors. She was already on her way into
the bar.

He followed her in. It was dim inside. There was a juke
with colored lights in it. The place had a collection of beer

signs on the rafters. There was a lifesize cardboard cut-out of
a sunnily-smiling Dallas Cowboys Cheerleader in a bikini;
the bikini was made of Budweiser labels. There were no
windows that he could see. Only one customer; an old man—
a shaking, sunken faced barfly—sat at one end of the bar,
talking to himself or maybe to the TV set tuned to an afternoon
talk show. Darry felt a twinge of guilt, seeing the talk show.
Knowing Bette was probably watching the same show, right
now.

"Um…two margaritas," he told the lady bartender. She was
about fifty and wore a remarkably short skirt, gold-mesh hose,
and had a bell of yellow hair. Her swooping eyebrows were
cartoonishly inked in.

"We don't do margaritas, honey," she said, as Marla put on
a song from a solo album by Stevie whats-her-name from
Fleetwood Mac.

"Tequila-up for me!" Marla yelled, punching more buttons
on the juke.

"Ummm…for me too," he said.

They sat in a booth and drank and Marla told him a
rambling story about why she'd left Texas. A boyfriend she'd
been with five or six years: he'd abused her, knocked her
around, and he sold her big screen TV one day when she
was at work, and he talked her into ripping off her boss and
got her fired, but it was a sucky job anyway, working in one
of those little glass booths at a gas station. But it wasn't so
much that kind of thing. If she just knew where he was going
to be on Christmas eve and on her birthday because on your
birthday a person should, you know…

Darry agreed with her completely. She'd done the right
thing, going to live with her sister to get away from the guy.
Sounded like an abusive jerk.

"Oh he wasn't so bad, some ways."

And she told him about the dreams that had informed her
she was a reincarnated alien princess, and he acted as if it
were entirely believable, and they danced, and he drank
several more tequilas, and he'd begun to get the spins halfway
through "Hotel California" and then he'd run to the bathroom
and when he came out she handed him some little white
pills and said these'll fix you up and for some reason he took

them and, after the glass of water she made him drink, he
surprised himself by drinking more tequila...

They talked about favorite bands, and then the pills hit
him, and his blood came up into his ears into a kind of roaring
high tide, and the beer signs seemed to be grinning
conspiratorially at him, and then she was pulling his arm and
he was throwing a twenty and a ten at the bartender and
then they were in the car, and the car blurred into the grubby
little office of the Happy Now Plenty Motel, which was run—
and apparently named—by some Vietnamese people who
scowled a lot when he and Marla signed in, and she astonished
him, as they went into the equally grubby little motel room,
by referring to the people in the motel office as "fucking
slopes, excuse my language", but then they were kissing on
the bed and his hard-on was like an open pocketknife blade
under his pants...

...then she jumped up and turned on the wall mounted TV
and he was surprised, once more, to see they had a
pornography channel here, that this was an adult motel, and
she was laughing at the girl blowing the black guy, "little cunt
polishes that nigger's knob like she had a lot of practice" and
he felt he ought to say something about these racist remarks,
enough was enough, but then she had given him more small
white pills and another tequila from the liquor store...

...and then he was throwing up again in the little bathroom
and in a fit of giddiness deliberately aimed a stream of vomit
at the cockroach on the floor and he had to spend ten minutes
cleaning it up with a towel which he felt compelled to get rid
of so he threw the soiled towel out the bathroom window
into the airspace and then he had to rinse out his mouth with
the Lavoris that was on the bathroom shelf which had to be
the single worst tasting mouthwash in the history of oral
hygiene and then...

...then she was pounding on the door and saying she really
had to pee but...

...as he was going out the bathroom door, thinking that
his head felt like a beach ball with dozens of little race cars
spinning around on its inner surface, she said, "You don't
have to leave while I pee, we can talk. We don't need to
stand on ceremony...You know what, why I think I started

doggin' on you, because you remind me of this English teacher I had when I was in ninth grade, I wanted to fuck him bad, but he wouldn't even talk about it, but he was so cute..."

And he stood awkwardly, hands in pockets, trying to look out the little bathroom window, rather than stare at her as she talked on and tried to pee, with her red lace panties down around her ankles, sitting on the toilet smoking a cigarette, and he thought: *We just met...she's the aunt of one of my fifth period kids...*

Then she said, "I can't pee yet...come here..." And she took his hand and pulled him down beside her and put his hand between her legs and he gasped and she said, "Rub to help me...help me pee...rub to..." And almost immediately he felt a warm aromatic stream twining his palm, his wrist, ticking onto the porcelain, and she pulled him close and peed into the toilet and on his arm and kissed him on the mouth; she tasted of cigarettes and tequila.

She dropped the cigarette into the metal trashcan, and pulled him to stand in front of her and drew his dick from his pants and laughed when it jumped springily at her and then her mouth was on him, he could see lipstick on it, and she was still peeing, and he almost came that way, but in a few minutes she had led him into the other room and he was on his back, his hand still wet, and she was straddling him, with her skirt still on, her panties in one hand, a cigarette—when had she gotten another cigarette?—in the other hand and she pushed the panties into his mouth as she bounced on his dick and he clawed her blouse down so he could weigh her breasts in his palms and she said, "Pinch the nipples, pinch 'em, pinch 'em, come on...shit, pinch 'em, yeah..." And on her breasts were tattoos above each nipple: *sweet* and *sour*. There was a name in the cleavage, two letters curving down one tit *BU* and two more curving up the other *CK* and then he came in her and he felt sick and wanted her to get off him and she just laughed and kept rocking on him and—maybe it was the pills—he stayed hard and then...

Can't remember...can't remember...

He first thought about Bette and how late it was when David Letterman came on the little TV.

"Eleven o clock..." he muttered, seeing Letterman.

Marla was sitting up beside him, eating the Chinese food she'd sent out for. Sweet and Sour pork. He hadn't been able to eat any of it. She was wearing the panties now, and the leopard pattern blouse. He could still taste the panties.

She put the Chinese food on a cigarette-burned lamp table by the bed, under a lamp shaped like a glass swan. She lit a cigarette. Marlboro Lights. "You haven't said much for, hell, hours," she said, reaching for the channel changer. There was an old cigarette burn on the channel changer. "David Letterman, I just don't git him. Let's see what else is on. Oh, Jay Leno, I like him..."

"Yeah, he's..."

Eleven o'clock. Bette would be looking out the window.

Good. Looking out the window was almost as good as going out the door.

"You should have somea that Chinese food, slopey little fucks did it up good."

He winced. "What's up with this racist stuff, Marla?"

"Ooh, is that not politically connected?"

"You mean—politically correct?"

She turned a look on him that would have set him on fire if he'd been doused with gasoline.

"I guess you think I'm just a stupid kinda bimbo?"

"What? No! I mean—if you have some prejudices, everybody gets, you know, conditioned somewhere..."

"Conditioned. Con-ditioned. Somewhere. 'She's conditioned somewhere'. You saying I'm white trash? My Mama was a racist?"

"Um—no, I'm just...hey, forget it. I have my kneejerk responses to stuff, you know. I mean, the irony is that my objection to racist comments is a reflex of my class status...It's itself, um, 'classist' and..."

The look she gave him now would have set him on fire without the gasoline.

You dumb shit, he told himself. Patronizing fuck.

"I'm sorry," he began, "I'm just...babbling. Drunk. Still drunk. Those pills—first they get me high, then, you know, confused."

"You don't know what drunk is, faggot." She got the fifth of tequila they'd sent out for and poured him four fingers. "Go for it."

"I don't wanna throw up again."

"You're past throwing up. Listen to Mama Marla, she knows."

He drank about half the tumbler. His stomach burned. He laughed. She drank the rest.

A thumping came on the door. Marla sat up straight. She was like a cat hearing the call for dinner; looking around to see where it came from.

"Marla?" A low voice from the door.

Darry felt a long, shimmering chill.

"Marla!"

She was up and he was standing, the room spinning, and only then did he realize he had on the *X-Files* shirt but no pants, his scrotum slapping against his thigh. He looked around blearily for his pants, thinking maybe it was just her sister's husband. Obviously she did this sort of thing all the time and they had to fetch her home...And everyone would hear about it from the disgusted Cecily...

Marla was talking sweetly through the cracked-open door, the brass chain locked over it. "I'll meet you downstairs, baby..." Deep basso mumbles and rumbles from whoever was out there. "No baby...I wasn't running from you, I just needed some, you know, breathing space. Didn't you get my note?" More mumbles. The word *bullshit*. Rumbles. "...no I meant it, I was coming back..."

Darry had found his pants and was pulling them on but it was the wrong leg and they faced backwards so he had to start over.

"...No baby, I'll be right down because someone might— Buck, baby, don't be stupid..."

Buck. *BU* on one tit, *CK* on the other.

Each of Darry's blood cells iced over individually.

"No, baby, you'll attract—"

Then the door gave out a thud and the chain snapped and flew across the room and Marla was sliding backwards across the floor on her butt and the door was slamming and Buck was there, big tattooed guy with his hair shaved off on the sides and long on top, little pony tail. His lower lip hung a little bit too far. He wore a guinea tee and oversized jeans and Nikes. He was looking at Darry with his mouth open, looking more stunned than angry. But his hand went behind him.

Marla shot to her feet and went to him, hands raised in front of her. "No you'll get 'em all over us—"

He straight-armed her so she flew with her feet six inches over the floor, smacked into the bathroom door and slid down it.

She sat there panting. Darry realized that she was aroused. "Okay, baby…okay, baby…"

He reached behind him again and drew the gun out, slowly. It was a .45 automatic, blue steel.

"Hey, no problem, I didn't know she was your girl, I'm outta here…" Darry said, desperately sorting words in the hope of coming up with the combination that wouldn't set him off.

As he spoke, he walked past Buck, his neck prickling, and got all the way to the door.

"He's the kind of guy, might call the police, Buck," she said. "That's why I wanted to meet you downstairs, he might get 'em down on us—"

Darry turned to stare at her. Had she really said that? He jerked at the door handle

Darry felt a big hand on the back of his trousers, flew backwards, off his feet, flung to the floor much the way Marla had been. Found he was sitting on his ass, his back against the bed.

"You get some good pussy, you punk-ass motherfucker?" Buck asked, his voice a rasp. His expression unchanging. Sort of flat, vaguely curious.

"Um—no we just—"

"He's so full of shit. He did me hard, Buck."

Darry gaped at Marla.

She went on, chattering happily, hugging her knees against herself like a Campfire Girl at a sleep-over. "But he was such a fag about it, I had to lead him along by the dick and he let me sit on him…"

Buck laughed. "You rode him like a donkey?"

"Shit yeah!"

They both laughed. Then, almost affectionately, Buck turned and grabbed her by the hair and pulled her to her feet and back-handed her, knocking her back to the floor.

She was weeping now, weeping happily. "I deserve that.
Running out on you and fucking this asshole. I do."

"You deserve a lot worse."

Darry began to see the depth and width of it. He jumped
up and stumbled to the window, tried to yell for help. "Hey!
Somebody call the police! Hey—!"

He heard her small footsteps behind him and heard a crash
through a sudden burning in his scalp and he fell through
the sensation, fell backwards, onto the bed. At the end of a
tunnel very far away he saw her standing over him with a
broken table lamp in her hands. "That's my girl," Buck was
saying, as the tunnel shut down, and Darry lost consciousness.

———— ◆ ————

He heard them talking for awhile, before he really completely
came to. His hands were tied behind him with lamp cord. He
couldn't feel his fingers. There was something jammed in his
mouth: his own salty socks. He kept still and listened.

"For real, you're right over there in the Howard Johnson's?"

"For real. One block down the fuckin' street."

"We almost went to that one! But I think the cheap fag
wanted to save money."

"You like assholes like this? Full-of-themselves assholes
with Ph.D.s and shit?"

"Lord no, baby, you know I don't. I just wanted to go out
and I didn't want nobody like you because it would just, you
know, make me want you. You went to my sister's house?"

"Yeah, she saw you leave with some asshole. She thought
you was going to the motel strip. I ask a few people and,
guess what, you stand right out. 'Yeah that little slut's over in
that shit hole right there, I seen her go in.'"

"Well I guess I surely do stand out! It's not like I was
hiding that much, baby, don't you git that? If I wanted to hide
from you, would I come to my sister's..."

"You got any more of that speed?"

"Right here, darlin'." He heard her rummaging in her purse.
"Here you go...I mean, baby darlin' if I wanted really to get
away from you would I go to my sister's? Like I didn't know
you wouldn't look there?"

"Stupid little cunt you should've picked some place closer. Drove my ass three nights getting here."

"You drove all that way? But you see there, now I know what you'd do for love, to come out here and get me..."

"I start to come onto this speed I'll show you what I'll do for love you stray bitchin' dick dogging whore."

"Say that again." Her voice husky with arousal.

"You heard me. Dick dogging whore...turn your ass over..."

"Just don't break nothing please baby..." The sounds of slapping and her grunt of tearful happiness as he sodomized her.

Darry tried to wriggle around, get to the door, but he felt Buck fishing for him, felt callused fingers on his scalp, twisting his hair, jerking him to sit up, and then Buck was banging Darry's head on the wall beside the bed with one hand, while slamming himself into Marla, another fuck and a slam, a fuck and a slam, Darry trying to pull loose but kitten-helpless, a fuck and a slam, Buck's fingers around her throat from behind, jerking her back onto his dick with that hand, the other slamming Darry on the wall, Darry starting to swallow the socks, realizing he was going to choke to death like this, a fuck and a *slam.* "How's that feel, you two bitches, both of you bitches, how's that, how's that—"

That's when the door opened and shut and Darry heard Buck shout "What the fuck—?" And Buck let go of him, Darry rolling onto his back to see the police—

It wasn't the police. It was...

Jan? The computer science teacher from school. Was here. In the room with him.

"Hi, Darry." Jan had a snub nose .38 in her hand. She held it very steadily.

"You know this bitch? This your old lady?" Marla asked, with real wonder. She had separated from Buck; the two of them turned to look at the door; she reached down and pulled the socks from Darry's mouth. He gasped, and found his voice.

"Jan—run for the—" He gagged, and tried again. "—the cops!"

Jan shook her head. "I don't think you really want the cops to find you like this...Your wife would have to hear about it and everyone else too..." She was still in her school work clothes. She was smiling, very gently.

Marla and Buck were naked, on the bed. Buck made a grab for the .45, but Jan was already scooping it up and stepping back from him. She pointed the .38 at his chest as Buck got ready to lunge at her.

"I took those classes for women—the ones where they teach you to be aggressive, to fight thieves and the like," she said, looking him in the eye. "They taught me to aim and to shoot. I really will shoot. And there's no reason for that to happen unless you insist. You're not going to jail..."

Buck sat back on the bed. "You his sister or what?"

"I'm a friend. I knew he was getting into trouble. He was due for it. Exactly due. I've been following him since the supermarket, when I saw him leave with her. I've sort of been expecting her...Can you stand up, Darius?"

"Uhhh...I think...oh shit my head hurts." A sob escaped him. Blood trickled hot on the side of his head.

"You see? He's such a sucky little shit," Marla said.

Buck laughed. "He is that, ain't he?"

Darry felt a rising fury. He pictured getting loose, getting the extra gun, shooting them both.

He wobbled over to Jan and turned his back to her. "You take off these wires?"

"No—turn your back to the bed. Marla? Would you do the honors?"

Marla looked at Buck. "Go ahead, darlin'," Buck said, grinning.

Marla untied Darry and feeling came painfully back into his hands. But they continued to hurt and so did his head and all his muscles. His heart was hammering; his stomach lurched. He wanted to throw up. But he managed to get his clothes back on; one of the most painful things he ever had to do. He found his wallet; they hadn't emptied it yet.

"We'll get you checked for a concussion," Jan said. "You got your wallet? Good...Come on..."

"You in love with him, huh," Marla said, lying back on the bed, eyes wide.

"That's right."

"I like that. That's romantic. See what she's doing for love, baby? I'd do that. I'd do way more than that."

Buck put his arms around her and said nothing, just watching the other two balefully, like a half tamed lion, as they backed toward the door.

"I need some money," Buck said. "He took some pussy off my woman."

"No," Darry said. "You took it out of me already."

"Best to leave everyone feeling equitable, Darry," Jan said. She handed Darry the smaller gun. She reached into a skirt pocket, pulled out five twenties. Darry realized she'd had the money ready for something like this.

The guy hammers my head against the wall and we're going to pay him too.

She tossed the money on the bed. Darry suddenly became aware of the agreeable weight of the gun in his hand. He came close to shooting. His fingers tightened.

But the fury was dissolving. *I like that. That's romantic.*

Buck looked at him and knew that Darry was thinking about shooting. "You one lucky motherfucker," Buck said. "I was going to kill your punk ass," deliberately pushing Darry.

Darry turned away and Buck smiled.

Jan ejected the clip from the .45, checked for bullets in the chamber, tossed it back to Buck.

Darry looked at her. "You're going to give him the gun?"

"He can't fire it now. He can get a new clip. Those things are expensive. I respect guns. I respect these two, really. Except he shouldn't be beating that girl up."

"I know I shouldn't," Buck said, evenly. But without sorrow.

"He knows he shouldn't," Marla said, nodding. Without judgment.

Darry couldn't stand it anymore. He lurched out the door. Jan came after him and closed the door behind her. As they went down the stairs she took the .38 from him and discreetly put it in her purse and they got into the minivan.

He retched in the minivan, as they drove to her place, but nothing came out.

"Was it the models?" He asked, after he was done retching. "You did that detailed a computer model of...of my behavior...my life?"

"Yes. I knew you'd get in with someone like that. And that she'd have someone like Buck. I modeled most of it—roughly what'd happen. So many variables, it's hard to be sure. It might not've happened. But I'm right about 63% of the time, computer modeling; projecting from personality with behavioral spreadsheets and probability ratios, weighing in primary environmental factors."

This kind of talk, just now, was ungraspable for him. All he understood at the moment were things like *I was going to kill your punk ass.*

"I called your wife, just before I came in, and said I heard you were the victim of a hit and run, and you weren't hurt bad, just stunned and wandering around, but I thought I knew where you were and I was going to get you to a doctor. She was interested but not, you know, frantic."

"Jesus. What a story. You should be the writer, not me."

"I'm taking you to my place to clean you up, then you go home to her, but...Do you want me to tell you what you should do then?"

"What the hell. You just saved my 'punk ass'."

"That's the Darius I love. Well—you should divorce your wife, but see to it she has therapy first. She doesn't want to be married to you. I got her to do the questionnaires too."

"No, come on."

"Oh yes. Came to the house. Had to, to get your model right—you weren't detailed or honest enough. I used to bring her treats. Pastries and lattés. Told her not to tell you...She'll have a series of crushes on therapists and then she'll find someone amenable. She'll lose weight, too. She wants to be as free of you as you are of her..."

"Really?"

"Fifty-nine percent probability. And then you should...You sure you want me to go on?"

"Yeah. It takes my mind off the way my head feels."

"You should live with me for awhile and see if you're ready to be serious with me. We'll be traveling. We're going on one of those cruises to Alaska first. I always wanted to see Alaska."

"Cruises?"

"We're quitting our jobs."

"We are?"

"I only stayed there for you."

"You're kidding."

"Nope. Not kidding. I don't need to work. I don't really like teaching all that much. I've got 680,000 dollars in the bank. Plus another half million in shares. Software royalties."

"You're shitting me."

"That's such a revolting expression."

"Sorry...Alaska? All this sounds..."

"Like I'm as crazy as Marla in my way. Not really. Only a little. But we're such a good fit, you and I. Now me, I want, um, to take care of someone, very completely take care of them, and you, well, you really, really like to be taken care of. You're quite...passive, honestly. Deep down. You want excitement but you don't want to...to be the leader in getting there."

He didn't like that. He didn't really admit that it was true till about five months later...

...when during the day they watched an iceberg shuddering parts of itself into the sea, shattering in the spring wind: Temporary gems of ice falling, splashing in evanescent transparent lace.

And Jan's lace...

Her lace was black, in their little ship's cabin, at night: Narrow shoulders, wide hips: *holy shit, she fucks like a goddess!*

...and only then could Darry admit that it was true...when Jan was bouncing on his dick, and he asked her to stuff her panties into his mouth.

If you think this Universe is bad,
you should see some of the others.
—Philip K. Dick

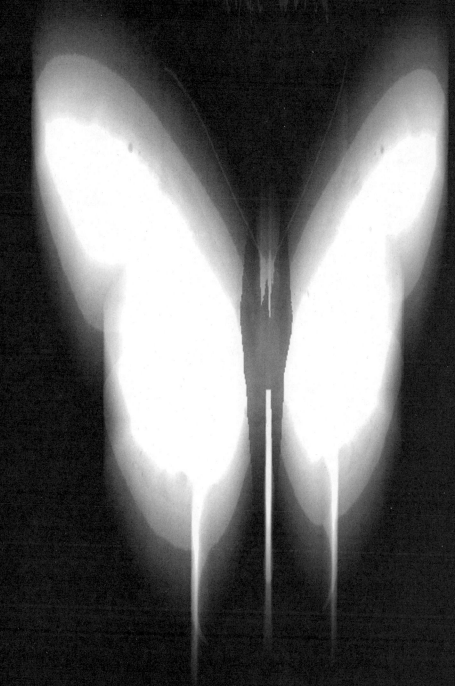

THAT WORLD

DELIA AND THE DINNER PARTY

Delia watched from the upstairs window as the guests arrived. Two cars of them, one couple per car, about ten minutes apart. There would be four guests here tonight, for her parents' dinner party.

"There will be six adults," said the Telling Boy.

She nodded. She went to the top of the stairs to watch the last couple come in.

"Hey, you guys made it!" Delia's daddy said, greeting the man with a handshake.

"How's it going, Jack?" the man said.

"Kinda weird until, oh, maybe two months ago now. I had to get a new agent—picked up on somebody good through Robert Longo—started selling paintings again. Three today to a collector in Chicago."

"That's great," the man said. Delia thought his name was Henry something. He was a balding man in horn rim glasses and a turtleneck sweater; he was much taller than her short, thick-tummied daddy. He was a man who wrote restaurant reviews, she knew. She'd seen him before. And his plump, nervously friendly wife, Lucy, in her neat dove gray and blue pantsuit. She was older than the others.

"She plays mother to Henry," the Telling Boy said. The Telling Boy wasn't consulting his book yet. He was talking off the cuff. He had the little book, which looked like one of those gold-spined Golden Wonder books for kids, tucked under his arm. He stood there, stiff and formal in his jammies, six feet tall and wearing those jammies with the booties, wherever did he find them so big...?

The Telling Boy didn't look like a boy. He looked like an old man, in fact, tall and bent a little and age spotted and hooded eyed and sunken cheeked and gray haired. But the old man was called the Telling Boy anyway. You got used to it.

"I wish I had a cigarette," the Telling Boy said wistfully, as he did rather often.

She had tried giving him cigarettes, but he couldn't really touch things in the world, and he could only look at them longingly.

"Who's that spying on us up there?" Lucy said impishly, waggling a finger in cutesy accusation up at Delia.

Mama looked up at Delia and smiled wearily. Mama had dark hollows under her eyes and thinning hennaed hair and a special padded bra because one of her bosoms had been taken away by the cancer.

"Come on down and say hi, Delia," she said, with a resignation that was heard as a certain flatness in her voice.

Another flatness came into Daddy's eyes when he saw her up there. They didn't like her to watch them in secret. Her daddy had gotten mad, very mad, when he found Delia hiding under the kitchen table watching him, and realized she'd been watching him silently for a full hour as he puttered around the kitchen, taking bites from things in the fridge and putting them back, reading the comics pages, picking his nose, calling a woman Delia didn't know on the phone, talking to her in a funny, hushed tone of voice....

Delia came down and said hi. Everyone sat around in the living room, listening to The Gypsy Kings on the record player, drinking aperitifs, admiring Daddy's paintings on the wall and Delia's dress. The other guests, the Crenshaws, smiled at

Delia at first as if they meant it, but the smiles got more strained, after a while, as they always did, because she didn't respond. Mrs. Crenshaw was a tall and thin and very elegant black lady, skin more like creamy cocoa than black; she wore a tight red gown that showed a lot of cleavage, kind of dressy compared to the others. She used to be a model, Delia had heard Daddy say, and had appeared in lots of ads in *Ebony.* Her husband, Buddy Crenshaw, was a white man, shorter than his wife and stocky, with a neat little gray beard and a bald spot on the back of his head. He was talking about trying Rogaine for the bald spot, Rogaine was the baldness cure that he had helped promote, and what a rip-off it was because it hadn't worked for him and it was really expensive, and how he was going to do another promotional campaign for it. No one thought this was funny. And they talked about the parking around here, on these steep streets in San Francisco, and how hard it was on a Saturday night because they were near North Beach, but how nice a neighborhood, at least, to drive around in looking for parking, because you could "look at all the lovely Victorians."

The black lady, whom they called Andy even though that's really a man's name, tried to talk to Delia a little, and laughed when Delia told her how old she was.

"You're certainly a big girl for five years old," the Andy lady said, smiling indulgently, thinking Delia was joking. "Did you do a Rip Van Winkle sort of thing?"

"She's almost eleven," Daddy said, with a faint disgust in his voice. "She likes to pretend she's five. She believes it, too."

Mama gave Daddy a quick look of reproach. He was supposed to make light of all that, and he'd made it worse. Delia glanced through the door into the dining room and saw the Telling Boy there in his blue and white jammies, sitting awkwardly on the edge of the dining room table. How dirty the jammies looked in this light. They had something like mold on them in the crotch.

No one else looked at the Telling Boy. Even though he was staring at them. He looked at Delia and held up the book, tapped it. She nodded. Her mother frowned at her, puzzled and vaguely angry.

Dinner. Andy and Buddy were talking about having seen
Nureyev's new ballet. Nureyev was choreographing, they said,
instead of dancing now, and both Andy and Buddy chuckled
over Nureyev's choreography. "He's really not a Renaissance
man, should have stuck to dancing, but his ineptitude is taken
as brashness and progressivity," Buddy said glibly, and
everyone snorted and said, "God, Buddy, you're right, ballet
critics are blind where Nureyev is concerned, they've all shared
vodka with him."

Talk like that. Delia was glad when her mother said she
didn't have to stay for dessert. "A little girl who doesn't like
dessert?" Lucy chirped. "My goodness, where did you get this
one? Mars?"

Daddy almost said, No, but sometimes we wonder...

But he got a warning look from Mama and didn't say it.
And he looked at Mama in a way that said, *I told you this was
a bad idea. We shouldn't try to have dinners here in the house.*

Delia knew her parents very well. Thanks to the Telling
Boy, she knew them better than they knew themselves.

Delia went upstairs, supposedly to watch the Disney
channel on her TV and go to bed, and the others went into
the living room again for coffee and the expensive imported
cookies that Mama was using as dessert.

The Telling Boy was waiting there, of course.

The old man dressed like a little boy for bed.

With the book open, waiting for her.

She had a feeling like a snake of excitement biting its own
tail off. Its jaws, chewing slowly, were dread.

Today, Delia saw, the book was called *Delia and the
Dinner Party*.

Delia turned out the lights.

The Telling Boy began to read, even though it was dark.
A gentle light from the book lit his dry gray mouth as he
read. The lips moved like a puppet's mouth. In a voice that
was old but not grandfatherly, he read:

"Delia was a little girl, or maybe not so little. If you think
five years old is little, then she was little. But maybe you are not
yet five years old—and then she might be a big girl to you."

Delia thought: I've been five ever since the first time the
Telling Boy came to explain things to me.

"One day Delia's parents had some people over for a dinner party. Delia didn't feel like talking to them, even though her parents wanted her to. Delia was a sad little girl. She didn't have any friends except a boy who lived in the attic.

"After Delia went to bed, she thought and thought to herself 'Maybe I can make friends with these people after all,' she said 'I'll ask my friend the Telling Boy.' So she went upstairs and asked her friend the Telling Boy. He was a very wise little boy who wore wonderful magic jammies and could talk to all the little creatures who lived in the attic. 'Delia,' he said, 'I don't know if you can be friends with these people, or your parents either. The only way to be sure is to go see them again and try to decide.' So Delia went along with the Telling Boy into the Looking Tunnel..."

The Telling Boy tucked the little book under his arm, and gestured to say, After you. They walked toward the corner of the room that was nearest to the living room downstairs, and the lines of wall edges that met in the corner seemed to extend themselves into a new depth, a reach that extended beyond the wall and became a dusty road stretching into darkness. They walked into the corner and down the road. In the sky were stars and spiders, both glittering. There were cobwebby rafters up there, and there were clouds. There was a cockroach crawling along the horned moon. The place smelled of dust and mildew.

And then, on the road up ahead, was the living room. It was a box. A room-sized box glowing gently in one of its corners from the light of its table lamp.

They walked up to the nearest wall of the translucent box, and looked through at the dinner party. She could see them; they couldn't see her.

Daddy had broken out the Chivas. They sat sipping their liquor—Lucy taking hers in coffee, becoming much more nervously giggly—and Daddy was drinking his on the rocks.

Delia and the Telling Boy could hear what was being said, though it was a little muffled. "I love that dress," Lucy was saying to Andy. "It's so assertive and...I wish I could wear something like that but I'd look silly. I mean, you look wonderful...."

"They seem very nice," Delia said. "Andy liked that. She's smiling."

"Let's go over here and see what Lucy really said," the Telling Boy suggested.

Delia followed him around the corner, and saw the same scene played again, with the Telling Boy translating the dialogue. He read from his little book: "'I love that dress,' Lucy said with a well-disguised sarcasm. 'Black people are always ready to overdress, aren't they? I suppose if you were a black man instead you'd have a big gold chain with a clock on it so I should be happy for small blessings. All my senses are assaulted by your skintight red satin dress with the neckline that plunges to your navel. I could never embarrass myself that way.'"

But Delia hardly heard what the Telling Boy was reading; she was watching, wretchedly fascinated, the Telling Boy's visual translation.

In her bedroom she had a book she'd been given when she was three. It was called *The Magic Kids,* and it was about someone who learns that their neighbor kids are elves in disguise. And it had a special cover on it with a little plastic see-through panel holding a picture of the Magic Kids. When you looked at the illustration straight on they looked like ordinary kids; when you tilted the book and looked at an angle, the picture shifted and revealed the little boy and girl as elves with wings and pointed ears.

The living room box that the Telling Boy had shown her was something like that. When you stood on one side and looked in, you saw the people in the room as they looked "normally." When you went around the corner and looked, seeing it from another angle, the image shifted and you saw what the box really held.

Mama and Daddy and Buddy and Andy and Lucy and Henry.

Monsters. Skin stripped away, red meat and blue white bone exposed and nastily wet, teeth bared, fingers boneless and ropelike, barbed tentacles; black tongues three feet long that whipped out like the tongues of lizards, tubular tongues with lamprey-mouth tips. Bodies overgrown in some limbs, unnaturally tapered in others.

Her Dad—she knew him by his clothes, they all wore their human clothes—had a second face on the side of his head that was snapping its jaws at Mama like a vicious little dog barely kept leashed. Mama's head was triple faced; the one facing Daddy was angry and frightened, one of its eyes had been gnawed away....Skinless dwarfish faces oozing pus and blood...

Their genitals were repugnantly exposed, their clothes gone crotchless; Daddy's penis was a two-headed lizard thing that hissed and twitched and then convulsed with sickness, vomited sticky white fluid that fell sizzling to the floor....Mama's vagina was a big hairy spider on its back with its belly cut open, waving its bristly legs.

Delia looked away, her stomach twitching like a fly in a web....

The Telling Boy had prepared her for this. He had been showing her things for many years now. He had given her glimpses. But never so clearly.

It's just a story in his little book, she told herself. That's really all it is, in the end.

She watched the Lucy thing and the Andy thing; the Lucy thing lashing out with its finger tentacles, slashing at the Andy thing's face, scoring it with bloody grooves. The Andy thing recoiled. *I love that dress. It's so assertive...I wish I could wear something like that...*

Delia was seeing the hideous underside of the conversation. The truth. Or so the Telling Boy told her.

The Telling Boy said, "Let's go look on the other side again."

They went around the corner. It was both a relief to see them human again, and disturbing. Knowing what was just one flicker behind the facade.

Daddy was saying, "How are things at the agency?"

"Kind of a bore, lately," Buddy said. "Getting to be a routine. You wouldn't think it would be the same-old same-old at an ad agency, since we're constantly having new accounts, doing creative work, but—"

"Hey, I could believe it," Daddy said a little pityingly. "You uh..." He picked up his glass, smiled smugly as he sipped. "You find time to work on that novel you were telling me about?"

"The novel? Sure, bits and pieces." Buddy's smile was false.
"It's growing slowly but surely."

Lucy was unusually quiet.

The Telling Boy opened his book and read the translation.

"'How are things at the agency? Are you bored out of your
head with the same old rip-off manipulations of the public,
the same old scams to sell unnecessary junk? Are you writing
that novel you used to talk about? I doubt it. You're not, are
you? You're not that creative. Not like me. I'm an artist. I
make my living as an artist, and not a commercial artist either.
An abstract artist. Artists are better than other people. So stay
in your place, you little weasel, I'm the celebrity in this house,
I'm the artist, not you, your best hope is to follow me around
like a puppy dog, looking up to me....'"

"Was that what Daddy was saying?" Delia mused. "I don't
know what he means by some of that stuff. Rip-off
manipulations. What does an ad agency do anyway?"

"They make TV and radio commercials," the Telling Boy
explained.

"Oh."

"I'm sorry. I don't mean to go over your head. Sometimes
it's difficult to put things in terms a five-year-old girl can
understand."

Delia was tempted to argue about being a five-year-old.
She knew she wasn't really. But the Telling Boy didn't like
her to talk about that.

They peered around the corner long enough to see that
the Daddy monster was standing over the Buddy monster, its
tongue sucking out one of the Buddy monster's eyes; the
Buddy monster was on its back, its arms and legs in the air
like a dog surrendering a fight. The Daddy monster's penis
shot sizzling white fluid onto the Buddy monster's exposed
belly, so that he writhed in pain....

*You find time to work on that novel you were telling me
about?*

Delia's stomach lurched again, and they looked back at
the other side where Lucy was saying, "I guess I'll go outside
and have a smoke."

"Oh, you can smoke in here," Daddy said, "if it doesn't
bother anyone else..." He looked questioningly at the others.

Andy said, a little stiffly, "No. It's okay. The occasional ambient smoke doesn't bother my asthma much."

The Telling Boy opened his book and read the translation. "And Andy replied, 'You may as well—you've already been offensive to me. Why not torment me some more? You disgust me.'"

Delia knew what she would see if she looked around the corner: the Andy monster chewing at some exposed place on the Lucy monster.

"Why don't you have your cigarette in the kitchen," Mama said, "while I'm giving you that sauté recipe you asked for?"

"If it's all right. That'd be nice," Lucy said, smiling icily at Andy. She got up and followed Mama out of the box. Gone from sight.

"I'm glad she left the room to smoke," the Telling Boy said, sadly, "I sure would like a cigarette." He turned to Delia and said, "If you ever grow up, don't start smoking. You never quite get over it even after you quit."

"Did you die because of smoking?" Delia asked him.

"They said it was lung cancer brought on by cigarettes," the old man in the jammies said. "And that was part of it. But it was also because my wife wanted me to die, so I didn't try to fight it. I was hoping she'd feel guilty, afterwards."

Delia nodded. She understood. She'd learned a lot about people from the Telling Boy.

Buddy was talking over something called stock options with Henry. "They are both pretending they know about stock options," the Telling Boy said. "But they don't know anything about them. They are bragging to one another by pretending to know about the stock market. Do you want me to read the—?" He started to open the book.

"No," Delia said. She was watching her dad. He had gone with Andy to help her pick out a CD.

"Let me give you the benefit of my vast good taste, Andy," Daddy said, jokingly.

The Telling Boy read his interpretation from *Delia and the Dinner Party.*

"'Let's go over here,' Daddy said, 'where I can flirt with you and you can flirt with me without anyone noticing.'"

"Oh no," Delia said. "He wouldn't do that."

Feeling really sick now, like she was going to cave in.

"You saw the monster," the Telling Boy said. "He might do anything. A creature like that."

They were flirting with one another. The woman was pretending to push him out of the way with a sideways shove of a hip so she could get to the rack of CDs, both of them giggling. Daddy picked out James Brown, the woman laughing at him, saying he'll be playing rap records next; she picked out Bartok's string quartets, and whispered teasingly, "James Brown, that's an example of that big, hard organ of good taste of yours?"

"If you want an example of *that*—" he said, laughing. "I know a motel—"

"Oh, listen to him! Stop!" She laughed.

"Seriously—what I would like to do is show you a painting in my studio—I just feel like you could relate to it—"

"Oh, it's let me show you my etchings now!"

They both laughed, but she went along with him, downstairs, to his basement studio. Andy just calling casually to her husband that she'd be right back. He waved and nodded, scarcely looking up from his conversation. No wonder he was losing her, Delia thought.

Delia felt cold. She looked around. Darkness, except for the translucent box that contained the living room. She thought she saw a shiny blue black beetle the size of a wheelbarrow crawling along upside down through a hole in the sky. She shivered.

"I wish I'd brought a coat," she said.

"I wish I had a cigarette," the Telling Boy said grumpily.

"He's not going to do that thing with her in the studio, is he?" Delia asked.

"Do you want to see?"

She hugged herself. "No."

"It's what happens next in the book."

She looked at her shoes. "All right."

He turned and walked off into the shadows. She followed him. Something scuttled out of their way. And then he was descending, walking down into the dusty and infinite floor, down an invisible staircase. It looked like he was sinking into the ground. Delia was used to this, too. She stepped down into the floor, where it looked solid but wasn't, and found the steps with a probing foot.

The basement studio was another translucent box, in another shadow gallery. It was shaped rectangularly, and had pipes pierced through it. There was a stack of paintings and a table of paints and a big wooden stand that held a twenty-foot-wide painting. She had seen it before; an abstraction that hinted of iris shapes and orchids and parting folds of red velvet. Daddy was pointing to one side of it, saying something about organic and inorganic shapes, and then he took Andy's hand and led her to the other side of the long painting. And didn't let go of her hand. Turned to her with a you understand, don't you? look.

"It's beautiful." she said.

The Telling Boy said. "Come and see." He led Delia around the corner, where the image shifted.

The monsters were writhing against one another, copulating and rending, Daddy's hideous animal penis smashing itself with suicidal fervor into the creature's vagina...a vagina that was a sucking spiral of wet flesh lined with tiny flechettes, oozing coagulated blood: the mouth of an oversized leech. The two skinless creatures making sounds like lard in a garbage disposal, like fluid in a tubercular chest, like a record being played backwards; gnashing at one another with random sets of teeth erupting from their chests; the woman's breasts were the teats of dogs; her butt convulsively spat feces, and his belched masses of clinging, squirming pinworms. They licked at each other's effluvia with their long black tubular tongues, licking and sucking, feeding, grinding, clawing. Not enjoying this, just doing it because they had to, for some reason.

The painting was changed too. It was revealed as an enormous, grotesquely photo-realistic image of a huge woman's vagina, spread open and nauseatingly displayed.

Gagging, Delia looked at the dusty, infinite floor and yelled, *"Daddy stop it stop it stop it stop it get away from her stop it!"*

She ran around the other side of the box, the side where her Daddy looked human, where he was simply kissing the Andy lady. And Delia began to bang on the translucent wall, yelling, *"Stop it stop being monsters with her!"*

Daddy looked up. Not toward Delia but up toward her room.

"What is that girl doing up there?" he muttered. "Yelling that kind of shit. The therapist told us to let her act out and not to make a big deal, but, goddamn it, she has to learn sometime—"

He was heading for the stairs. The Andy lady, breathing harshly, turned with embarrassment to pretend to look at the painting.

The Telling Boy said, "We'd better go back to your room. He expects to find you there."

"Do we have time?"

"I don't know."

They hurried back the way they'd come. Found the stairs, walked up through a ceiling, hurried back along the shadow corridor of the Looking Tunnel toward the entry corner of her room. She could hear Daddy walking up the stairs to her room. She could see his silhouette, over there, off in the distance. Coming angrily. Losing his temper. Reaching the door.

No. She wanted to get there first, before he found her missing.

She saw her room at the end of the Looking Tunnel, where three lines converged. It was a box, translucent and far away, with another box glowing in it in one corner: the TV. In her room. Daddy was storming around, looking under the bed, slamming open the closet door, looking to see where she was hiding; on TV, Donald Duck was making enraged sore throat noises as he chased a mischievous chipmunk around his cartoon fishing cabin.

Delia stood on the verge of the room, looking at her daddy poking through the closet.

"Go on, while he's not looking," the Telling Boy said.

She stepped through. Her daddy heard the noise and turned. "Where the hell have you been hiding? Damn it, Delia—I'm sick of this bullshit. This kind of acting out. You're too old to play these little games. You're not five, you're eleven, and this is five-year-old stuff—not talking to anyone, staring at everyone like they're insulting you, screaming at us from up in your room and then hiding when I—"

Mama was coming in. "What's going on?"

"Daddy," Delia said, "why were you being monsters with that woman in the basement?"

He blinked at her. "What?"

"Rubbing on her body and kissing and all that. That Andy lady."

Mama turned to stare at him. He worked up a convincing look of outrage. "Goddamn it, Delia, now you've gone too far—making up this bullshit—"

"You were downstairs with her," Mama was saying. "You were."

"We were looking at my new painting—" Daddy yelled. Covering up by making a big noise of it. His skin was fizzing. Bubbling. Fizzing. Foam coming out on his skin. And then his skin sloughed off him in patches, carried away on the yellow mucky bubbles of the fuzzing. Mama was hissing at him, "God, this is humiliating, you and that woman at a dinner party, for God's sake—"

And Mama was fizzing too. Her skin bubbling. Melting away. The monsters from anatomy charts—mixed up anatomy charts—were coming out, right there in front of Delia, without the Looking Tunnel or the Telling Boy. One of Mama's eyes popping out with centipedes. The big spider moving with horrible slow rippling motions under her dress at her crotch, pushing its way out. Daddy's penis fighting to get loose. The little ugly extra faces growing on their heads. Ropy fingers. Muscles and bone and tendons exposed and trimmed like something you saw hung on a hook in the back of the meat section in Safeway.

Both of them snarling at one another; making gibbery, sputtery noises; snapping many sets of jaws.

Delia finally screamed. A scream that had waited six years to come out.

They turned to her, angry at the noise she was making, coming at her. Red, oozing, snarling, snapping.

She felt a papery hand on her wrist, pulling her back.

Back through the wall. Into the safety of the Looking Tunnel.

She turned and saw that the Telling Boy had his hand on her wrist. And she could feel his hand.

"I can feel you," she said.

"That's why," he said, pointing at the translucent wall.

She turned and looked into her room. Saw her mother and father, as humans, bending over her. Over Delia lying on her bed. Lying there staring. Not moving. Breathing, but nothing more.

Her dad still angry, not believing this. Mama telling him to shut up. Seeing that the catatonia was real.

Delia and the Telling Boy turned away, walked back into the Looking Tunnel. As they went, the Telling Boy read from his little book.

"And Delia saw, then, for sure, that she could not be friends with anyone else but the boy in the attic. So she went to live with him, and lived happily ever after. The End."

P E A R L D O L L

It was one of those nights that releases trapped odors. The August heat steamed the reek of rotten fast-food grease and urine from the alley behind the Fatburger place on Santa Monica Boulevard. It made the smog seem to coagulate in the air, so a breeze that should have been a relief reeked of benzene and monoxides and ozone. The heat brought out the deepest layers of human sourness from the tramps slouching in the doorways. When you passed the discos, it summoned the hidden tincture of animal glands in the perfume of the fantastically coiffed ladies who stepped out of white limos, the underscent of lab-animal suffering and caustic chemicals in the cologne worn by their golden-chained escorts. It seemed to emphasize the cyanide and carcinogenic tars in cigarette smoke: it cooked the sewage under the streets...

And the semen left over in your pussy, or so Candy thought.

She'd douched after that creep Guido had come in her, but she couldn't quite get it all out, imagined she could smell it cooking and curdling in her...

It's too fucking hot.

She was walking down Santa Monica Boulevard, wishing she hadn't worn pumps, wondering if maybe there were some flats in the trunk of her car she could put on.

Sometimes you can't remember a dream—until later on. When something calls it up. Prompts it from the back of your head somewhere. She was passing a boutique, tight stripped-back leather skirts and tops for women in the window. Standing in front of it were these two skinny blond hustlers. One was wearing a Levi's jacket with some sort of rock-band emblem on the back. And she heard that one talk about the Face Eater. "It's no shit, Face Eater got Butterbuns and Darla, got both of 'em, put 'em on a pentagram thing and tied 'em down and ate their fuckin' faces, man—"

"Bullshit," the other guy squeaked.

"No, for real, dude!"

For real? She'd always thought the Face Eater was something in a movie or...but now that she thought about it, she remembered seeing some headlines...Some sick "Night Stalker" type in Hollywood who...She didn't even want to think about it. She glanced at the hustler as she passed to see if the guy was, like, serious or what. He looked serious...And then she saw the window reflection, and it made her stomach jump like a scared cat. Because it was something she'd seen in a dream. A dream about Frank. The snarling, toothy, bloody mouth superimposed over a girl's face. Took her a full two seconds to realize it was a reflection of the rock-band logo—a wide-open shark's mouth—superimposed by reflection against the face of a mannequin in the store window. She'd seen that in a dream, hadn't she? A dream about Frank? Frank...She tried to remember...and couldn't quite.

Hurrying past the store, she glanced up at a different mannequin in another store window—and thought she saw another reflected face, this time superimposed over the mannequin's crotch...

Frank's face. She turned and looked for the source of the reflection. He wasn't there.

Big surprise. He couldn't be there. Frank was dead.

She took a long, ragged breath, and walked on. Think about something else.

She passed the black dude with the badly conked hair who was selling his phony sensimilla, which was just California pot dusted with PCP, and her feet hurt, and she still couldn't make up her mind what bar to go to...when she saw Frank. For real this time.

God damn it, Frank, you're dead.

She stopped in front of Bleeding Heart Records, under the big animated bleeding-heart logo, neon blood dripping on her head, and stared down the street at Frank Cormanstadt, and said, "Oh I'm sure. I mean is this too weird or what?" to herself. Bleeding Heart Records was open, it's open late, and Metallica was smacking the air from the record-store speakers. She guessed it was one of those Arthur Koestler synchronicity things her spacey brother Buster talked about because they're talking about the dead on the song—and here comes Frank.

Okay, so he's not dead. After all, she never saw his body, never heard it from anyone but people on the street. But it just felt so right she never questioned it. I mean, everyone was expecting Frank to die, from one thing or another, right? Drugs or drinking and driving or something. AIDS, maybe, from some whore.

But Frank was coming down the street wearing a kind of David Byrne oversize suit, forties-type thing, blocky with padding, his long curly black hair dancing over those cubistic shoulders, his black eyes glittering with neon, the hollows of his cheekbones pooling shadows. He smiled as he saw her, a smile like a squiggle from a can of white Day-Glo spray paint.

She was going to ignore him. Just cross the street. If he wasn't dead, then he'd ditched her. He hadn't tried to contact her, he'd swept her under the rug, or under some girl's skirt...

Under some girl's skirt
Like a pile of dirt

If she got that band started with Sachet and Ellen she'd use those lyrics. If they let her sing.

Ignore him. Cross the street.

But she lingered, mad at herself for it, checking herself out in the glass of the record-store window. The little ponytail on top of her head like a water-fountain splash up there, kind of Valley Girlish, she thought now, but the neoprene shortpants and the skin-tight neoprene imitation snakeskin bikini top and the heels, they were killer, they ought to make Frank suffer.

As she'd suffered. How long had it been? (He was about twenty yards from her. There was still time to cross the street.) Six weeks? No, more like ten weeks. After three weeks of it, she'd heard he was dead. After five weeks—including two weeks getting drunk every day as a kind of endless wake for her dead Frank—meeting that mulatto dude in the Dead Monkey and getting it off with him, the whole thing another kind of drinking, really; and then the Skateboard Nazi, a skinhead jerk with a lot of tattoos. But his intensity had done something for her. Until he'd pushed his skateboard down on her face while he...

And then Lonny, three days with Lonny, surprised he didn't just split the next morning.

But he'd had to go back East to see his parents. Called once.

Last night with Greaser Guido hardly counted. But Lonny...

Come on, get real, that wasn't going to happen. Lonny was like, a real prep type. And she was a bit relieved (Frank was about ten feet away—just time to dash across the street if she went now) that it hadn't happened with Lonny; it was too soon after Frank...

Frank and that bitch Pearldoll.

I mean, what kind of name is Pearldoll?

"Hi," Frank said. and it was too late to cross the street.

"Hi," she said. Saying it so it'd sting him, she hoped. *Hi.*

The sounds of the street, all those Saturday night cruisers, those lowriders in their chopped convertibles and Beverly Hills kids in their Mustang convertibles and those bored celebs in their limos, all of it a thousand miles away, somehow, when Frank stood there looking at her, talking softly...

Telling her he was sorry. A lot of weird shit had come down. He had been out of touch with everyone, even his agent. So you know it's serious.

"What kind of weird shit?" she asked.

"I was really sick," he said. "From...an OD. And Pearldoll—she died."

Her heart jumped. She was a little ashamed when she recognized the provenance of the sensation. "She died? You were doing up shit together and she OD'd?"

"No. No, I was alone, afterwards, when I OD'd."

"So you OD'd because she died?" She said it accusingly. Though she knew she should be nice about it, because his old girlfriend had died; I mean, oh wow, death was pretty heavy shit.

But she couldn't help it. That tone.

"No. I...No, she died and...Well, I don't know, maybe. But, you know, I wasn't even thinking about Pearl, I was going with you then, and, you know, I guess I, like, hadn't seen Pearldoll in like—"

"Come on, you were always thinking about her." Comparing *me* to her, Candy thought.

And thinking: I could always feel Pearldoll there, in the background, feeling like if she came around he'd leave me in a second. Well, he lived with her for three years, when he had that TV series on HBO, but when that fell apart and there was no more money, Pearldoll just *cruised on*, just left him, which should have told him what kind of cunt she was, but *no*...

"No," Frank was saying, "I wasn't thinking about her when I OD'd. I wasn't thinking about girls. I was thinking about acting. I guess Joey thought I was dead, I mean I guess I *was* dead, but they revived me, you know, got my heart started again, and I guess they didn't tell anyone..." He shrugged, with elegant dismissal. Life and death, a shrug.

He was so cool, the asshole.

"You mad at me?" he asked.

"What do you think? What's it been? Ten weeks? You haven't been in the hospital all this time."

"Yes I have. But not the...not that kind."

She stared at him. "Oh Jesus. They put you in the—? A fifty-seven fifty?" The *mental* hospital.

He nodded. Milking it, though she didn't realize it at the time.

"Oh shit, honey," she said, taking his hands in hers.

Then she broke away. "You still could've called me from the ward."

"I was on all these meds...I could barely remember my name. And then when they let me use the phone I was, like, making crazy calls to the FBI and shit, didn't know what I was fucking doing, so they wouldn't let me use the phone after that...I'm lucky they let me out."

"Oh."

Feeling like the one in the wrong, now. How did he do it? Always leave her feeling like it was *her* that had screwed up.

"You wanna get a drink with me?" he asked.

Wham bam thank you ma'am.

An old, old David Bowie tune playing on the sound system of Booty's. A mostly gay club, where Hollywood Kidz hung out, a lot of fag-hags and a few guys hoping to cop some X or some blow or something.

Candy and Frank stood at the bar, Candy drinking a seabreeze, Frank with his eternal margarita. He was talking, and she was nodding, but only half listening at first. It was hard to make out with the disco banging away—now it was Jody Watley—and, anyway, her mind had taken a step back from him. Was looking him over. What was it that looked different? The suit? All bulky like that. Just heavier and...clumsy when he moved.

She thought she knew what it was. Meds. He was still on meds. Some antidepressant or maybe even Stelazine.

Don't embarrass him by saying anything about it.

She was thinking pityingly about him, which invariably led to thinking tenderly about him, when he said, "It was really weird, how Pearldoll died."

God damn him. He was going to talk about her.

She remembered when she first realized how Pearldoll was always going to be there. She was at the Anticlub with Frank, their second date, they were, like, making out in the corner, walking everywhere holding on to each other, it was really close and sweet—and then Pearldoll walked up. And he changed. Just like that. Kind of froze up. Pulled away a little. "Hi, Frankie," Pearldoll said, like some torch singer in some old gangster movie. *Hiya, Frankieboy.* But real smug, too. Pearldoll was a cruelly pretty, painfully petite girl, half Japanese and half Swedish, her parents some kind of MDA-dealing hippies. Pearldoll smiling like the Mona Lisa at Candy. Condescendingly. Obviously an ex of Frank's. The look said, You might have him, but he's always mine. Just check him out if you don't believe me!

And it was true. Frank looked slack-mouthed after Pearldoll, gawked at her as she walked away.

"Okay, Frank," Candy had asked him, that night. "How long did you go with her?"

"Uh—kind of obvious, huh? About—couple years."

"Pretty serious."

"Yeah. Pretty serious."

"What happened?"

"I don't know. She's kind of schizy. I got freaked out one night when she said we should do a death pact."

"A *what?*"

"That we should commit suicide together to declare, I don't know, ultimate love or something."

"I think, guy, you're kind of better off without her. I mean, death pacts? Or *what?*"

"Yeah. I'm better off without her. For sure."

But every time he saw Pearldoll in the clubs, he had that gawky longing in his face. And she had that smug knowledge about her. And now she was dead and he was *still* thinking about her.

"Okay," Candy said, now. Tonight, in this hot, sweaty, loud club. They had to yell their conversation in each other's ear over the music. "So how did she die?"

"Sacrificed."

"What?"

"She was into Espiritu."

"What the fuck is that?"

"Espiritu Bebida. It's some Spanish cult from...Cuba or someplace. Like Santaria. Kind of an offshoot of it."

"I thought you said she was Japanese and...and Danish or something."

"Her roommate was Hispanic, got her into it. Pearldoll hated Japanese stuff, 'cause she hated her mom. She was into Latin stuff."

"Half Japanese, half whatever, Norwegian or something—"

"Swedish."

"Half Swedish—but into Spanish stuff. I never noticed her maracas."

He grinned. "She had some."

"So her roommate sacrificed her?"

"No, her roommate killed herself about two weeks before that. The police talk like Pearldoll was murdered by someone. They even hassled me about it. But she wasn't murdered. She did it to herself. Killed herself. Which is weird, how Japanese that is, like hara-kiri—kind of funny."

"Oh hilarious."

"She killed herself in an Espiritu suicide ritual."

"I told you she was fucked up. And it wasn't just jealousy." Candy looked around at the club, suddenly conscious that it was crowded and noisy and choked with cigarette smoke. A fat girl wearing too much makeup was trying to shove past her to get at the bar. Candy said, "This party sucks."

"It's not a party, just the usual crowd on—"

"That was from a song, 'This Party Sucks.' You *have* been put away."

"You wanna get out of here? Go to my place?"

"Your place?"

"Not mine. Where I'm staying."

"I better not." But hoping he'd talk her into it.

"Come on. I won't make moves on you. I just want to listen to records and talk. Let's fortify first." And he ordered two double Cuervo Golds. And then two more. She was wobbling on her heels when they finally got out, giggling and gasping, onto the sidewalk, and he guided them back to her car, seemed to know where it was without asking. Probably spotted it earlier.

Frank seemed hardly even drunk. He drove her up into the Hollywood Hills, one of those old bungalows built split-level into the hillside. The little porch kind of overgrown with shrubs and bird-of-paradise and morning glory, their blossoms closed and wrinkly for the night, like girls with their legs crossed, labia folded away...

Inside, air-conditioned shadows. Santa Fe-style furniture.

"Awesome view," Candy said. She stood in the dark living room, at the picture window, looking over the tapestry of light, electric blue and sulphur yellow, that was Los Angeles. The night sky was dark violet, somehow, and an eternal stream of cars swept in rivers of headlight glow along the boulevards.

She stood in a deep rug, enjoying its feel on her toes, holding her pumps in one hand; one of Frank's cigarettes, a Sherman, dangled in the other.

Suddenly music, The Cult's "Sonic Temple," was playing from somewhere. He'd put on a CD. "I thought you didn't like this band," she said.

"I like 'em, now," he said, coming up behind her.

She could feel the heat from her cigarette on her knuckles; she could feel heat from Frank as he stepped up behind her. Put his arms around her waist. She could feel a rod of warmth at his crotch, pressing against the crack of her ass.

"Forget it," she said.

"It was you," he said. "I realized that when I was in the hospital. You were the one. The only one."

"Frank, don't—" But she wanted to hear more. To cover the doubts. His story about the hospital had come out too rehearsed. But playing it back in her head again, it sounded reasonable. Sort of. She turned around, knowing she shouldn't. "I still don't think—"

But then he was kissing her, hard, had his arms around her. It felt like he was around her and up under her. That was how it felt to her, with men, when it felt really good. Around you and coming up under you. Protecting and coming *into* you at the same time. He wasn't actually in her yet, but she could feel it pushing, straining at his pants, and there was an answering rush of oozing melt in her pussy...

"You...goddamned..." she tried to say. And then his tongue was in her mouth and it was like plugging into an electrical socket, the current was flowing. He felt different now, to her; he felt bigger and sometimes his tongue felt like it was—

Wait. He was carrying her in his arms.

She couldn't believe it. He wasn't that strong. She looked around and saw he was carrying her up a flight of stairs, which was even harder to do, and then he had toted her effortlessly into a bedroom. There were candles lit here. Blue and red candles. Nice. Romantic.

He put her gracefully on the bed, which was bare but for a sheet, and knelt beside her, kissing and groping. Only now, mixed in with the excitement, there was an anxiety, a feeling that someone was watching them...

Whose house was this? Not his. Some sicko voyeur, maybe, some flake he'd met in the nut house, watching them from a two-way mirror?

He was peeling her clothes off her, she was nude almost before she knew it, and he had taken off his coat and shoes but still had his pants on, how rude, but there was a certain excitement to that, too, a feeling that he was out of control with lust for her, wanted her that badly...

And then he was on top of her, wriggling into her. She was looking dreamily over his shoulder at the candlelight. Her eyes adjusting, the dark room coming gradually into focus. Little dolls, figures made of cornhusks and straw and rags, and a ceramic Mother of Mary but a Mary with the muzzle of a dog, and on a wall someone had painted a slogan or something, ornate in red letters. She could only make out a couple of words.

Hermano demonio...consagrar...

Spanish.

Panic surging, she looked around, seemed to see Pearldoll everywhere now. Saw her face in the folds of the curtain, in the curl of candlesmoke, in the shadows gathered on the ceiling.

Candy yelled hoarsely, tried to push Frank away. His cock in her no longer felt like a connection—it felt like an intrusion. "This is *her* place isn't it! Pearldoll's house! You pig! I don't want to be here—"

"Chill out. She left it to me."

God. Maybe he *did* kill her. Maybe he was a murderer. Maybe he was into this Espiritu stuff. Maybe he had sacrificed her.

She managed to pull her hips away from him, turning under him to crawl away. Saw the sheet for the first time clearly. There was a pentagram, painted on it, in red, and some Spanish words. And a brown stain.

"I'm glad you turned over," came the voice from his mouth. "I want you from behind like a dog."

It was not his voice.

He was holding her down with arms that were just too strong; they were like metal bars; she felt like a rabbit in a cage that was too small for it, and then he was entering her from behind—god damn him, this was rape—and it hurt, and now he was shifting his cock, putting it up her ass— "Oh you bastard you *shit!*"

"What's the matter, sweet Candy?"

Not his voice?

She heard his clothes ripping. He had both his hands clamped down on her wrists, his knees on the bed, so how could he be ripping his clothes? There must be someone else in the room helping him. Maybe she wasn't dead. Candy hadn't heard anything about it on the news. Maybe Pearldoll wasn't dead, maybe she was here and they were going to sacrifice her on this pentagram—

And then she saw the woman's hands closing on her forearms. Those little white fingers with their oxblood nails. Pearldoll's. Digging into her forearms from behind. Then moving up to her breasts, digging into them with her nails, hurting, piercing, blood running over her nipples. A scream caught in Candy's throat.

They were taking her together. Pearldoll had hidden herself up here—must be lying close beside him.

Candy squirmed, trying to turn around to spit in the bitch's face. Frank held her down. and Candy only managed a glimpse over her shoulder. Saw only Frank's face, laughing without sound, something weirdly faggy in it. Maybe he was a repressed gay and that's why he was raping her up the ass and, God, they were going to kill her—

Panic went off, burned like a Fourth of July sparkler in her, and she thrashed and screamed at them, tried to see Pearldoll so she could kick her, could only see Pearldoll's arms, fingers clawing at her eyes. Tried to wriggle free, it was hurting more and more and more..

The red candle on the little blue Santa Fe-style end table beside the bed had been burning awhile, was pooled with quivery molten candle wax. Candy shot a hand out, grabbed the candle, flung its hot wax over her shoulder into the grinning bastard's eyes...

He shrieked with a sound like a cat under a car's tire, and his grip loosened for a moment, Pearldoll's, too. Candy wrenched loose, clawed free of them.

Scrambled around to face them, looking for something to throw.

Froze.

Frank's clothes lay in tatters beside the bed. There were two of them, facing Candy—two of them there, nude. The light made it seem...No. It wasn't the light.

There was only one. Made of two. Frank's head and shoulders and arms. And *her* arms, growing out of his torso, down under his arms. Pearldoll's arms and hands looking too small on Frank's body, making Candy think of Buster's Revelle model of a Tyrannosaurus.

He had no dick. He had no cock. He had a...

"No way," Candy said. "No fucking way."

It was Pearldoll's face. (Where was the door?) Pearldoll's face in his crotch, instead of his genitals. (Find something to throw.) Pearldoll's giggling, rabid-animal face.

Looking out from Frank's crotch, Pearldoll opened her mouth. Frank's cock came out of her mouth instead of a tongue. *She had his cock for her tongue.*

Frank opened his mouth, and then she saw that he had two tongues, one smaller and pinker than his own. Her voice came out of his mouth. Her voice mixed with his. "Want you. Always wanted you. Frank said you wouldn't share." Taunting. "Frank wouldn't kill you. Wouldn't hurt you. Bitch. Bitch. Brother Devil gave Frank to me and me to Frank and you, now. Bitch, bitch, bitch—"

Candy sprinted for the door. White fingers with oxblood nails closed on her wrist, jerked her off-balance so she fell facedown, skidding. The air knocked out of her.

Pearldoll's voice chanted in Spanish. A wave of weakness washed over Candy. A sweet, warm weakness. A weakness that soothed and murmured comforting lies. She was limp, like that time she'd taken three ludes, like a jellyfish, and someone was dragging her to the white sheet with the red pentagram...

It felt nice, being dragged that way. Like the rug was a big tongue licking her whole body, warm and wet. *Stoned. Stoned on something. Magic or drugs or both. Fight it.*

There was no fighting it. Not even when Frank straddled her and she saw Pearldoll's face descending toward hers, filling her vision, a pretty Japanese-Swedish face surrounded by pubic hair, legs to either side, coming down at her. Mouth opening. Quivering from inside that mouth, veinily tumesced, his cock, plunging toward Candy's mouth...

Suck, something commanded, and she did, and choked, and then Pearldoll pushed closer and began to chew off Candy's lips, and it all took a long time, and it was funny how little it hurt to be eaten alive...

"Love to eat Candy," said Pearldoll and Frank.

Before she was drawn in to a puddle of warm blood and liquid flesh, like red candle wax melting, she wondered what part of Frank's body her own face would look out of.

WOODGRAINS

— 1 —

Arlene Toland and William Hargrove. They sat together on his bed, not too close, sipping sherry. It was a warm September evening, and the air was tepid in Hargrove's little apartment. "It smells twice as much like New York City inside as it does outside," Hargrove said, wrinkling his stubby nose. It was a pale, pink-tipped nose: Hargrove was an albino. He got up, opened a window, admitted a breeze and traffic callings. He returned to the bed and automatically filled the ceramic cups. Cups he'd made: one a caricature of Reagan's head, the other of Bush. Hargrove could afford to be free with the sherry, Arlene had paid for it. Hargrove received room and board for managing this dingy apartment building, sold the occasional sculpture for a pittance, got by on almost nothing. He liked living simply. And he liked living alone. He had grown to dislike physical affection. It was intrusive, and it bullied his self esteem, because he wasn't very good at it.

Replacing the bottle and plucking up the cup, he glanced toward his studio. It was the living room, really, closed off with old fashioned sliding wooden double-doors. The door was shut. Good. Fine.

Hargrove sat on the bed, sipped the sherry, hardly tasting it. "You're brooding again," said Arlene. "Depression, self-pity."

Hargrove shrugged. There was no point in denying it; he was enjoying the role, pitying himself, The Suffering Artist. It really hurt, yes, he really suffered, yes. And yet he knew he was enjoying it, and he felt like a fool; but there it was.

He took the smudged newspaper clipping from his shirt pocket, and unfolded it. It read:

'...on a more subdued note the back hall of the gallery contains William Hargrove's sculptures, a great many of them, in wood, bronze and marble. On one level, Hargrove is worthy of unstinting admiration: on the level of the technical expertise. His *Homage* series is for this reason impressive. His *Homage to Rodin* could have been carved by Rodin. His *Homage to Arp* is indeed homage to Arp. But Hargrove's own designs are as quotidian and uninspired as his copies are scrupulous. He can carve flawless copies of any piece in marble; he can render in wood, his favorite medium, the styles of the most opaque or intricate of artists. But innovation, or even a distinctly personal style, seem forever beyond his reach...'

"He shouldn't have put it that way, 'forever beyond,'" Arlene said. "But it's true in some ways." She studied him as he re-read the review. She was slumped, pale, gangly, her deep brown eyes ringed with blue shadow; her brown hair was pixie-cut, giving her a Mary Martin or Peter Pan look, but her stylish tweed suit spoiled first impressions of innocence. "Originality *seems* forever 'beyond' your reach. Looks that way. I mean, you have a passion for sculpting and a passion for originality and you're fixated on innovators. But you can't innovate, seemingly. You wouldn't be so obsessed with other people's work if you had confidence in your own—"

"Hey *okay,* Arlene, *huh?* Enough. Jeezus. They're gonna hire you to ah, carve the fucking *epitaph* on my fucking *grave*stone, you know?"

"I'm just trying to be constructive. You're having fun sitting around feeling like a metaphor for martyrdom, I know, but what you need is constructive criticism. I'm just saying that you don't necessarily lack the talent, you lack the confidence to release that talent—"

Hargrove made an impatient gesture with one white-white hand and glanced toward his studio.

She stared at him. Arlene Toland had a tenacious and irrational (and of course unrequited) love for William Hargrove. Perhaps this was because Hargrove was both an albino and a monomaniacal craftsman, and Arlene Toland was insatiably fascinated with unusual people. Her last lover had been a legless breakdancer.

Beside sculpting, Hargrove had another skill; an ability he had developed solely to accommodate his platonic but precarious relationship with Arlene. He had learned to absolutely and reflexively ignore her when she advanced proposals of intimacy. He blanked these suggestions from his mind with such consummate skill that he no longer heard them at all. His hearing clicked OFF when she discussed romance—no appeal was too subtle for his defenses—and clicked ON when she referred to what Hargrove conceived to be his central problem.

Hargrove rewarded her with a look of avid attention when she said: "So you want to find the inspiration which we are generous enough to assume is latent in you, right Billy-guy? Hell, you'll have to do more than brood, friend. Humm, I mean, you'll have to take *steps* of some kind. Something tough but simple. Decisive. I don't think you really need full-scale therapy. Because this—this *reticence* of yours is more like a phobia than a complex. Maybe, um, obsession with influences has sort of burned you out, left you creatively sterile. You know what I mean? So that all that remains is plagiarism. A vicious circle. And maybe it's time to stare it in the gimlet eye and defy it. You're doing this homage series, the Arps and this 'Rodin in Post-Modern mode' and blah blah blah—but that's just a strategy for getting away from the people who really influenced you. The NeoSomatics. Powell, Arlington—"

"Shut up, will you?"

"They're so much alike they're almost the same artist."

"Yes all *right*," he said savagely. "They're always with me. So what? Could I have a cigarette, I'm out of—thanks. My stuff is a variation of you-name-him in the NeoSomatics and what's the *point,* Arlene? Don't mention them. Okay?"

"Right, you're going to get rid of their influence by not mentioning them? Joey thought you were a real asshole when you tried that stuff on him at the Mall. And avoiding their exhibits and—that's just lumping neurosis on top of neurosis. It's denial."

"I'm clay, Arlene. When I think about them, they intrude on my consciousness, it stamps their style on my clay. That's just the way I'm put together."

"Avoidance hasn't been working, has it? Try something else. The opposite. Deliberately keep them with you. To absorb and overcome them. Maybe some really powerful device—something that's an art statement itself maybe. Tattoo them on you, or—"

He made a face, and snorted. "You bet, ah yeah. Right. Tat*too* them. Oh sure."

"Well, I was just kidding about that. Okay. You don't have to go that far. But carry their pictures around with you and defy them! Put their portraits on the wall! In the face of this constant pressure, this constant confrontation with them— who was it? Arliss?"

He winced.

She went on mercilessly: "Powell?" (He groaned) "Marquette?" (He scowled) "Arlington?"

"Cut it out."

"Hochstedder?"

"Enough."

"Rutledge, Farmer, Beaumont?"

He sighed. "Yes."

"Those. Haunting you. Confront them and the lock on your inspiration will break, hopefully, under the pressure."

"I dunno. Sounds too easy, too simple. But maybe…" His mothwing brows fluttered. His eyes, the color of dilute blood, opened wide and fixed on a lampshade. It was a small, rotating lampshade with a Budweiser advertisement printed above a faded mountain stream which the light, combined with the heat-propelled whirling of the lampshade, was intended to animate into watery rippling. He had purchased the lamp at the Salvation Army Store because Hochstedder had suggested that many artists use bright, hypnotic objects for a sort of mesmeric meditation. A meditation of inspiration. So far, it hadn't worked, except that at times a steady contemplation of the whirling lamp inspired him to drink a Budweiser.

"Pictures of them," murmured Hargrove in his honking alto voice, "pictures of the eight." He drained his cup, set it down with a decisive clack. "It's the only thing I haven't tried. Jeez, resorting to this sort of thing I feel like a bed-wetting kid with, ah, a bell to wake him when he—Yeah but what the Hell, what else to do?"

"But the more I consider the problem," said Arlene cautiously, "the firmer becomes my suspicion that your, um, obsessions have a traceable source, and this source—" she swallowed, watching him sidelong, "—results from unconscious despair at starvation for affection—" click! But while she knew Hargrove was no longer listening she proceeded obstinately, raising her voice. "You presently deny that you desire touching, love, intimacy; Bill, in some part of yourself, repressed, is that desire for affection—it finds outlet in your hang-up with these eight sculptors. Your sculpture is your most intimate connection with the world, Bill—listen to me! *Listen to me.*" And these last words she shrieked, with a sweep of her arm flinging his cup and the half-empty sherry bottle into the air; they bounced one after the other off the opposite wall, staining the pink of his eyes. Arlene was standing, fists clenched, staring at him, her mouth working soundlessly. Hargrove sat complacently, staring at the floorboards between his legs.

Tremulous, she raised her right hand high over her head, preparing to bring it down hard across his face his blank white face. "Don't ignore me like I'm a TV commercial *goddamnit—*"

She stopped. She dropped her hand to her side. She stared. He had entirely forgotten she was there. His eyes were vacant and he was openly yawning. Smitten, she took deep breaths. "Okay, then," she said softly to herself. If Hargrove had been listening he would have heard a lethal edge in her voice. "Bill—I know just how to do it. To rid yourself of them," she said, watching him. Click! His eyes lit up. He turned to her and nodded.

"Go on, Arlene."

"Tattoos. I was joking before, but—I've been thinking. You're extremely talented—you live in extremes, you have a problem that is extreme, therefore you should take extreme measures—"

He laughed. "Come *on*. Be serious. Tattoos. Oh my God. I pity your patients at the—"

"You're nothing!" she said, in a carefully modulated hiss: a voice of authority.

He shrank back. "Hey, do you think—"

"You were right, you're a lump of clay with other people's fingerprints all over it. It's time to take extreme measures, while you still have some recognizable form, lump—" She smiled, suppressed it, noting his increasing depression. He could be driven to anything, now. She said smoothly, "Find an expert tattoo artist, Bill. I know it seems absurd, but trust me. It will be an art statement, and a declaration of independence. Trust me. Arrange for those eight people to be reproduced in great detail on your body. Large as you have room for. It's an art statement; you absorb your progenitors this way, see? And this way you will never, *ever* be able to hide from them. Because they will be with you, in graphic illustration, at every instant of your life, forever."

She knew. She knew he was desperate and she knew he was gullible and she knew that after he realized the tattoos were there for good, really *realized* it, he would fall ill from seeing them, day after day. And, maybe, suicide, if she had read him right.

Arlene Toland: an educated woman, a registered therapist, cultured and traveled. She took pride in living up-to-date, in feeling utterly egalitarian, thoroughly modern. Not for a moment would she have believed that what she had done to Hargrove was anything as primitive, as base as vengeance.

2

He found the tattoo artist in the backpage ads of the *Village Voice*.

HOLOGRAPHIX TATTOO PARLOR, STARTINGLY REALISTIC IMAGES, SHOCK YOUR FRIENDS! BECOME A LIVING WORK OF ART, CHANGE YOUR LIFE! That and a PO Box number.

It had all been arranged by mail. For some unexplained reason they met at a hotel, rather than the tattooist's studio. Hargrove rented the room and waited. There had come a knock at the door...

...But now, after it was done, he could recollect nothing of the appointment. He could not remember the tattoo artist's face. He could remember only that the man had carried a leather satchel. Hargrove had accepted a drink from the stranger. And then—he had awakened to find himself lying on the rug beside the bed, naked, except for the eight tattoos And they *were* startlingly realistic. He had supposed that fine tattooing for a project of this immensity would take months. The business was completed in a single evening. But he could remember none of the details. Excepting—

He had not paid the man. The stranger had not spoken a word; had not asked for money, nor left a bill.

Hargrove tried for half an hour to recall the man's face. A complete blank.

Immediately on returning home, he had looked again for the ad in the back pages of the *Village Voice*. It was not there. He checked again to insure that he had the right issue. It was the one. He called the magazine's classified ads manager. She insisted that the ad had never run in the *Voice*.

Now, regarding himself in the full-length mirror, he shivered.

It was ten p.m. The only light was from a streetlamp silvering the window, and the bathroom light throwing a plank of mucous-yellow across the floorboards. The room was consumed by sharp-edged blocks of light and shadow. Hargrove's rooms were almost bare of furniture or decoration. There was a bone-white stove and a white refrigerator; a yellow foam mattress with white sheets and rough brown blankets. A few black leatherette beanbag chairs in the corners completed the furnishings. In his studio was an unfinished wood-sculpture, five feet high. A woman roughed out of black walnut, an Oriental woman, nude, head bowed. The sculpture stood with her bare feet in wood shavings like a bride on a wedding night with her feet hidden by the gown she had just removed.

Hargrove could see her, now, in his mind's eye, could feel the presence of the wooden lady in the next room. He could not yet go to her. He could not break from his reflection.

He looked at the tattoos, then looked at the room around him, somehow expecting to see the tattoos on the walls, spreading to floor and ceiling like a skin disease. The walls reassured him with blankness.

The apartment's simplicity was owing to Arliss, the man whose face, perfectly reproduced in miniature looked out from Hargrove's pallid right pectoral. Arliss believed that a sculptor should pare the accoutrements of his life-style to a bare minimum, this austerity creating a vacuum which, it was hoped, would attract an esthetic vision to take the place of external stimuli.

Hargrove looked back at the mirror. He wondered what time it was. It was Rutledge who had suggested that sculptors should stroll once a day to "commune with the kinetic anarchy of the city's exposed anatomy." It was time for his prescribed evening ramble. But he could not part from the mirror. He turned his back to the glass and looked over his shoulder. There were Rutledge and Farmer on his back, side by side; Powell and Marquette on the back of his thighs.

He had provided eight photos of which the tattoos were perfect copies. He had obtained the photos from Arlington's Artists Stand Naked portfolio; all eight were full-length photos of the artists, nude and in color...The tattoos were defined in red and black lines, each figure seen face-on, fifteen inches high, touches of blue and brown and pink for eyes and nipples, hair and complexion.

Hargrove slowly shook his head. They didn't look much like tattoos. They looked like tint-retouched photos. Almost three-dimensional. Yet they could almost have grown from within his milky skin, like birthmarks. Or like the faces one discovers in woodgrains. And now, the night after they had been impressed on his skin, he felt nothing. There should be at least a residual stinging from the needle. Nothing.

He licked his lips; they were cracked. He was thirsty. It was Powell who had personally informed Hargrove that a conscientious sculptor *must* become slightly intoxicated in the evening, preferably on sherry. And after his evening stroll Hargrove customarily drank a pint of Harvey's Bristol Cream (which Powell had recommended).

But he could not bring himself to leave the mirror.

This fascination endured for a full hour. Then, he told himself that he should set upon the wooden lady, the *Praying Woman,* whose shoulders evoked so much of that peasant humility familiar to Hochstedder's work—Hochstedder the matronly sculptor portrayed in the space from his right shoulder to elbow. But the self-assured sweep of the *Praying Woman's* back, her chastely-closed legs, resembled the plastic character studies popularized by Beaumont—the young black man tattooed on Hargrove's left biceps. Perhaps he should add to the hollow dignity of her deep-set eyes and parted lips, enhance that martyred complacency common to the gaunt figures Marquette loved to paint; Marquette, engraved on the rear of Hargrove's right thigh.

Hargrove turned to go to the studio, then pivoted again to the mirror. He nodded. He looked at himself and nodded, shook his head, nodded, shook his head.

Hargrove was a true albino, pink at the forearms and above the collar-bone where the sun struck him, ivory elsewhere, with tinctures of ultra-marine and rose. He was squat, with short, meaty legs and almost tubular arms. But he was a good craftsman and the hours of workroom penance showed in the branching blue veins prominent on his hands and arms. His chest was puffy and hairless. The feathery white hair of his head was thinning; he was going bald. There were a few white whiskers of pubic hair framing a groin reminiscent of a Pre-Raphaelite cherub. His canvas-white skin was unblemished and plentiful, ideal for a tattoo artist.

The faces of his influences stared out at him with defiant self-possession. They were meticulously outlined, immaculately detailed, exquisitely shaded.

But he could feel the *Praying Woman* in the next room, and, he felt invoked, compelled to go to her.

He went into his makeshift studio. He selected a cutting wedge from the wooden crate of utensils and approached the statue. He stood stark and naked in the light from the overhead bulb. He glanced down at the tattooed figures with a studied contempt (which he borrowed from Charlton Heston who had used it against a doubting Cardinal in *The Agony And The Ecstasy*); he set to work.

An hour and a half passed.

He stepped back and regarded his emendations of the wistful wooden face. Now, the face showed the emphasis on resignation which had helped to make Arlington's reputation as a humanist photographer. Looking down at the figure of Arlington, immortalized from left pectoral down to ribs, he asked it: "Why did she talk me into doing it?'

3

He went to sleep at midnight. At twelve-thirty he had a dream. He dreamed his arms were arguing with one another over who should rightfully possess the shoulders. And his legs fought over ownership of his hips. But the hips and shoulders protested shrill that they owned their own segments of the anatomy and in fact *they* should have jurisdiction over the legs and arms, and not the other way round. While the arms argued heatedly that they should determine the fate of the shoulders, and the shoulders ranted their claim over the arms, and the legs and hips fought over territory, the stomach and the groin began to quarrel. The groin claimed that the entire body should be given over to him, since reproduction was surely the prime imperative. The stomach angrily protested that Hargrove's person should become entirely stomach, since any fool knew that survival by assuaging appetite has first priority. Only the head was silent.

4

Hargrove woke at two a.m. He was lying on his back. He blinked. He was covered with sweat, yet he felt very cold. Cold and hollow. He was wide awake, rigidly alert. What had awakened him? A movement. Something crawling on his right arm. He swallowed and took three deep breaths. He had

a virulent fear of rodents. Perhaps a mouse was crawling on
his arm. Or worse, a rat. What if it should bite him? Trying to
move only his left arm, he reached out and switched on the
lamp on the floor beside the mattress. He held his breath and
turned to look, raising his left hand to fling the thing away.

There was nothing there. He got up, searched the room.
Nothing. He lay down and reached out with his left hand to
switch off the light. The sense of intrusive movement again,
on his right arm. He turned to look. No rat, no mouse, no
spider. He found himself staring at the tattoo. The light was
shifting, as the heat from the bulb caused warm air to rise
and whirl the vented lampshade balanced on the needle, and
he decided it was that—the shifting light—and the weariness
in his eyes that made the tattoo seem to have taken on greater
depth, as if it were an embossment. A relief. He turned off
the light and fell back on the bed. The rumbling in his right
arm subsided to a tickle, and then muted entirely. It was another
forty five minutes before he found his way back to sleep.

Something woke him at four a.m. He switched on the lamp.
His right arm...in clearly articulated relief: Margaret
Hochstedder, his sculpting instructor at City College. Every
tattoo muscle in the fifteen-inch replica stood out and seemed
to flex itself, independent of his own movements. The arm
felt dead. He reached his left hand to gingerly prod the tattoo's
waist. He could feel the scaled-down musculature, the faint
boss of a tiny hipbone. As if someone had planted a
scale-model of Margaret Hochstedder in his arm, grafted in
so that only the surface contours of the doll showed above
his skin. Like embossments on leatherwork.

He tried hard to operate the arm. It would not move.

He heard himself whimpering. He choked it off. He got
up, staggered, coughing bile, to the bathroom. His limbs were
wobbly, they responded poorly, as if they desired to go
somewhere else entirely. He stumbled to the sink, fumbled
in the cabinet with his left hand for a bottle of sleeping pills.
He took six. He went back to bed, turned out the light.

It will be gone when I wake up, he told himself. He was asleep ten minutes later.

— 6 —

But in spite of the sleeping pills he came awake at six. The sun pushed through the window, screening four rosy quadrangles on the wooden floor. He tried to sit up. He could not move. Not voluntarily. But as he lay there, sodden with barbituates, trying to force himself to move, his right arm began to spasm. It jumped like a dead frog on a live wire. It flopped back and forth, and though he couldn't feel it, he knew it bruised itself on the floor. He looked. The figure was there, almost complete, head and feet outgrowths of his shoulder and forearm like a statuette carved into the leg of an ornate wooden chair.

Lathed from his flesh into three-dimensional roundness, the figure which had taken the place of biceps and bone was struggling, writhing to shake loose from the pinioning elbow and shoulder.

He looked away. He could feel his left leg twitching, its tattoo crawling, molding its shape from his flesh.

The sleeping pills took hold again. Hargrove gurgled and blacked out.

— 7 —

He woke at three p.m. that afternoon. He was foggy from the sleeping pills, and very weak. It took him a long time to realize that he was awake. His mouth was bone dry. It tasted foul. He could smell nothing but the sour of his own sweat. When he turned his head there was an explosion of pins. He winced. He looked for his right arm. At first, he thought it was gone. But it was there, almost out of sight below his ribcage. He could move it now, though it felt odd. It felt aloof. He raised it and grunted, let it fall back. It was no more than six inches long. An exact miniature of the arm that had been there before, without a tattoo. It looked like a doll's arm.

Or the arm of a muscular infant. The biceps was there, whole
and healthy, but only as big as the muscles of his left hand.

Seeing this, Hargrove wanted three things:

First, he wanted to shout. This he could not do.

Second, he wanted to vomit. This he could not do.

Third, he wanted to go back to sleep. This he did, falling
through a cloud of grey resignation.

8

He woke at five p.m. He had been awakened by the
spasming of his leg. It jumped like a fish out of water. It was
a thing apart from him, an ugly carnivore maliciously clamping
his torso. There was no excuse for it. He wanted it to go
away, to be amputated from him. He wished he had a
telephone. He wished he had the strength to crawl to another
apartment for help. He wished his left arm would stop
shivering, and that the figure of Marquette on his left leg
would disengage itself and be done.

He raised his right arm. Somehow it didn't look so small
to him, now. It took him twenty minutes to realize that this
was because his torso was considerably smaller. He wondered
if his head were shrinking.

He wished he had a mirror.

He wished he was drunk.

He wished he was asleep.

He fell into a delirious haze.

He saw, out of the corner of one eye, something scarcely
distinguishable. It was coming toward him.

He stared hard at the ceiling and pretended it was
everything.

9

Detached, tinny voices. Small voices, angry whispers. The
floor of his bedroom was a vast plain. He was a part of the
plateau of mattress in the midst of this vast desert plain. There
were little people moving about down there, below him,
whispering. He looked back at the ceiling. A blue ceiling

fading to grey and teeming, now, with hallucinatory rivulets of his weakness. He swallowed. It hurt to swallow. He swallowed again, winced. His nostrils were dry and caked, they itched. He could not move his left arm or his right leg and his chest was numb. He was very distantly aware of his breathing. He ached, but the pain was like the echoes of a distant thunder rolling to him from afar, across the vast plain of the floor.

He could lift his left leg. He could barely see it. He found he was able to crane his neck so that he could lift his head a few inches. His left leg was shorter than his right by more than twenty-five inches; it was the leg of a dwarf, white and whole and small. He let it drop. He found himself trying to sing a song he had learned as a child.

Do yuh wanna be a pig
A pig is an animal that—

He could not remember how it went. His back was itching, swarming. Insects? He glanced at the window. The sun was going down. He could not feel his heartbeat. And recognizing this, he felt as if he had lost a beloved pet or a dear friend.

 10

It was forty-five minutes before he knew that he was rolling his head back and forth, his eyes taking in the room as mechanically as a radar dish scanning the sky. He was looking but not seeing. He concentrated. What was there? The window, a rectangular darkness, a fan of light in a corner of the pane must be streetlight glow. A finger-smeared face in the grime on that window's outside. A tacky warping and cracking of the glutinous yellow paint on the windowframe. The window seemed to possess the fulsome dimensions of a stained-glass cathedral casement.

The bed, around him: a rumpled brown landscape, wrinkles in the blanket taking on the massive dignity of rolling desert hills. Vague impressions of his infancy returned to him.

He had increasing difficulty distinguishing between himself and objects around him. The bed, the floorboards, the window, the rotating lampshade on the floor—all extensions of his physical person.

No. Someone—Arlene? uh-huh—had once told him that a warning sign of psychosis is the inability to distinguish between oneself and environment. So back off, feel yourself, flex your muscles (he told himself), those muscles remaining, the one at the left shoulder blade—

Something squirmed at his left shoulder blade. It pinched and annoyed him. He tried to roll his body to help the thing escape his weight, but his torso was still numb. Slowly, the squirmer burrowed out from under him. Shortly, he heard its abbreviated footsteps on the floor.

He lost contact, began to roll his head back and forth, like a radar dish.

11

He had been moving about the room for some minutes before he was sure it wasn't a dream, he was actually walking.

The studio door, white and monumental like the marble door of a Pope's tomb, towering over him.

He looked down at himself. Intact, proportionate, the tattoos gone; they had gone, having taken his flesh and blood without spilling any: he was unscarred.

The light from the rotating lampshade wheeled and flickered, drumsticking shadows on the door's glacial panels.

The door stood slightly ajar. He was glad, he was not sure he could have moved it. He certainly could not have reached the knob.

He crept inside, feeling dizzy, weak, but exhilarated. He could move again! The light bulb behind the wooden sculpture made a milky aureole around her bowed head, her head with its semi-cubistic roughness borrowing so much of Farmer. He stood in the inky loch of shadow spilling from the praying giantess, his feet scuffing wood shavings big as shingles.

He discovered an Exacto knife on its side at the base of the sculpture; he scowled at this unprofessional disregard for good tools and, grunting, he picked it up in both hands, hefting it. It would make a pretty fair pike, now. Holding the knife out in front, possessed of a certain exultation, he skulked the wooden base.

He rounded the base, blinking in the full yellow light.

Hochstedder was there, her back to him. She had always been larger than life to Hargrove. Now, she was insignificant, naked, her knobby, wrinkled back to him her mussed hair hanging stringy grey. What was she doing?

Stepping as lightly as possible, Exacto braced, he crept nearer.

She was squatting beside a corpse, a body small as her own. The left arm of the body—now recognizable as Marquette—was torn away, the stump bleeding freely. She had killed him not long ago, and now she was eagerly consuming the flesh, chewing voraciously, as if she could never be full. She'd eaten the arm down to the wrist, had ingested even the bone She knelt close beside the corpse and began to tear strips from the ribs.

Hargrove accepted this. It seemed natural.

He noted that Hochstedder was larger than he.

She was nearly twenty inches tall. He suspected that she had not been larger before she had killed and eaten part of Marquette. As he watched, she grew, almost imperceptibly; the evenly-proportioned swelling was visible like a slow-motion tumescing of a male organ.

Poising the Exacto-pike, he crept nearer. He was suddenly very hungry. He was a jump away from her. He could smell the meat, the good smell of the blood. His stomach growled.

Hochstedder heard. She grunted and spasmodically turned, crouching. A string of dripping meat hung from teeth clenched in her pallid, aristocratic face. But Hargrove had begun to drive the Exacto as she'd turned. Now, it bit her face and she fell, mewling.

— 12 —

After he had dragged the bodies of Hochstedder and Marquette off to the toolbox and eaten them both, he felt immensely better. But he was still hungry. And crawling across the floor, keeping to the shadowed fringes, was Farmer. Naked, white and sagging, Farmer was not an impressive figure. But when he leapt on the sleeping Beaumont he was quite effective. There was an intermingled thrashing of white and negro flesh, and then Beaumont was dead. But before Farmer had finished devouring Beaumont, Rutledge had stabbed him in the back with a ten-penny nail.

Hargrove watched as Rutledge fed. He would permit Rutledge to eat Beaumont and Farmer, to eat them and grow, before he killed him.

Hargrove was sure he could kill him. Rutledge would feel temporarily filled and secure and sleepy, after eating both men, and he would lie down to rest. Hargrove would use this opportunity to jump him.

Hargrove watched for two hours, pausing from his observation only once, to urinate quietly as possible, in a far corner of the wooden crate.

He planned to kill Rutledge quickly and drag him to the toolbox concealment to eat him, so as to guard against ambush.

Abstractedly, he sucked crusted blood from his fingernails.

He had eaten Hochstedder and Marquette, and now he was almost fifty inches high. But he felt nothing of Hochstedder and Marquette inside him. He felt like Bill Hargrove.

Rutledge was almost finished. Hargrove picked up the Exacto knife. It was only a dagger to him, now. He had grown. But the knife would do, it would serve to kill Rutledge. And having eaten Rutledge—and thereby Beaumont and Farmer too—he would grow. He would become large enough to kill Arlington, Arliss and Powell with ease. He would eat, and digest them.

And then he would be large enough to complete his sculpture.

He was looking forward to that.

Idi Amin watched hungrily as they mounted Michael Jackson on the eaves of the castle of Doktur Vreedeez. "Ja ja, Michael," Vreedeez cooed, as P'uzz Leen sprayed the flexible shelac over him. Jackson had been mounted fully stage-dressed and immaculately coifed: alive, trapped, projecting from the side of the building from the waist up, supported by transparent struts, arms bound to his sides.

Michael Sterno, watching Vreedeez giving directions to P'uzz Leen—and noticing Amin fingering his crotch as he stared at the desperate, transparently sheathed superstar—experienced that excitement that was also a kind of illness, a kind of sick fretfulness.

"Ov course," Vreedeez was saying, "one can't always get zose media-figures vun could like. I tried to get zese fellows in Oasis, but dot band is very heavily guarded just now, too closely vatched by people...maybe later...und zo I zettled for zumeone a bit how-you-say 'past it': Mr. Jackson. Und across from Mr. Jackson ve haff Mr. Paul McCartney...very necessary I haff one of der Beatles...but unfortunately Mr.

McCartney died in the zustainable-taxidermy prozess, zo we do full dead-taxidermy on him..."

"He's dead? McCartney looks more or less the same as last time he was on tour," Sterno remarked.

In the forested foothills of Mt. Feldberg, in the southern reaches of the Schwarzwald mountain range; above the realm of ancient oaks and within the shadowy recesses of the dark pine forests; on the melting cusp between dusk and sunset: they stood on the broad porch of the Black Forest schloss. So someone had called it, but what was this architectural grotesquerie? A confabulation of dark whimsy, this place, with its absurdly clashing mixture of medieval castle and German-gingerbread country house, its four-story volcano-glass facades and dark wooden turrets, its crockets and louvers, its multifoiled panes and quatrefoils and lancet windows, its ornamental moldings that seemed as Tantric as Germanic—

Hell, Sterno thought, the place had all the architectural integrity of miniature golf.

And then of course there were the living gargoyles, mounted on the eaves of stained-glass windows above the encircling porch. The "mountings", Vreedeez called them.

"Please," Michael Jackson sobbed. "Please."

"Ja, mein King of Pop," Vreedeez murmured soothingly. "Ja ja."

The forest around the contorted edifice seemed to engorge with shadows as the sun sank; the trees becoming fuller and grimmer as they became darker; the mountains deepening their blues and the snowy peaks soaking up sunset oranges and pinks and tincturing blood-red...

Sterno couldn't suppress a shudder.

Sterno had only arrived that morning, on assignment for the *Stark Fist of Removal Magazine*, replete with the usual First Class accommodations on the Concorde, the almost intrusively comfortable five-star hotels, but he wasn't sure he wanted to be here, amusing though it was to see the erstwhile popstar in this predicament.

Sterno hadn't known Idi Amin would be here and Amin made him particularly nervous. He'd always wondered how the transcendently brutal, notoriously syphilitic Amin had survived so long. Amin's hair had gone white, the whites of his eyes yellow as eggyolk. Most of his teeth were gone; his hands trembled. But the dictator, the monster who'd butchered tens of thousands of his Ugandan subjects for his own amusement, was still alive, still feverishly vibrant in that decaying flesh.

And what could Sterno say? Amin had departed his sanctuary in Arabia, was the permanent houseguest of the so-called Doktur Vreedeez. The story was, Amin had financed the Doktur's investments in Microsoft and certain other key companies that were the source of the Doktur's billionaire status, and the Doktur felt obliged to entertain Amin, despite the fact that, now and then, the Doktur's house servants would go missing.

Vreedeez's majordomo, factotum and chief sustainable-taxidermist, P'uzz Leen, was presumably in no danger from Amin, if that could be said of anyone in proximity to the erstwhile dictator, because of Leen's importance to the doctor. P'uzz Leen almost never spoke; he looked very much like someone Sterno had known in the States, one moment black Irish, the next the Arab he pretended to be now.

"Please," Jackson piped, in his Mickey Mouse voice. "I'm a very rich man. Let me go and you can have it all."

"Ach, I love it when zay say dot," Vreedeez chuckled, as P'uzz Leen sprayed the oxygen permeable flexishellac over Jackson's mouth. Jackson's piping cries became muted, barely audible squeaks.

"This is authentic Michael Jackson?" asked Amin.

"Ja ja, zat es der Michael, not an impersonator. Seventeen million dollars for der kidnap, seven dead bodyguards we left behind, ja, vus vort it. Worth it fer sure."

Hmmm, Sterno thought: "Worth it fer sure", Vreedeez had said. Vreedeez affected a burlesque Bavarian accent—like Mel Brooks doing a Nazi—but almost flaunted his lapses into a Western American accent. Sterno suspected Vreedeez of actually being an American and, despite the German accent, Vreedeez was not trying very hard to conceal it. And like P'uzz Leen, Vreedeez looked eerily familiar though he was sure they'd never met before.

Vreedeez was stocky, dressed in black, mustachioed, curly haired, dark eyed, late thirties—though some say that his apparent age was fifty years behind his real age, thanks to growth hormone treatments and despite his chainsmoking the slim brown Sherman's cigarettes. Now he turned to Sterno and said, "You vould like to see der other mountings?"

"Does a damn prairie squid lie in wait fer a face-fuckin' bat? You bet your ass."

"My donkey? I haff no donkey for gambling."

"Come on, man, I don't believe you're not familiar with that expression, we're a global shit-culture now, and this veneer of—"

"Speaking of veneers," Vreedeez said, interrupting him calmly but with a distinct note of warning, "haff you seen our complete collection? Mr. Jackson is of course only der newest..."

"No, I haven't. I have to ask—are these the real thing? Or are they...I don't know, plastic-surgery-altered impersonators?"

"Mm ruh meee...!" Michael Jackson whined.

"You haff not read the papers?"

"Yeah, sure, man, but...okay, all those people disappeared, sure 'nuff, but you might've taken advantage of that disappearance trend—I mean, everyone assumes it's some kind of massive publicity stunt—and you might've just, you know, made the mockups...maybe it's part of the publicity stunt put on by the real Michael Jackson and whoever...I mean, otherwise why would you invite me here? I mean, shit, if I report on this...of course it's a so-called underground magazine but it's read by all the key World Leaders anyway...and you'd have cops swarming here from every damn country missing its celebrities?"

"As for taking a chance on dot, vell, it is important for me dot a representative of der media see what I haff here, but not necessarily dot it is, finally, reported in der media..."

"It's enough I just...see it?"

"Ja. To ask vhy, consult mit der Carl Jung books."

Sterno's shudder, then, had a different quality to it; less frisson and more fear. How was Vreedeez going to prevent it from being reported 'in der media'?

"Und now...I present, around und ziss side uff der schloss, as you zee..." They strolled around a corner, Sterno and Idi Amin and P'uzz Leen.

"Whoa!" Sterno burst out.

Lit from beneath by the soft floodlights that had come on when the ambient light dropped, were four slightly wriggling, transparently sheathed, gargoyle-mounted internationally known...figures. Cindy Crawford, Kate Moss, Naomi Campbell and—

"Madonna! Bitchin'!"

"Melph meeeee!" Madonna whined, from within the sheath of oxygen permeable shellac. Under the shellac she wore a bit of filmy black lingerie and a lot of jewelry.

"That's got to be her for real," Sterno breathed appreciatively. He wondered at his own lack of sympathy for the kidnap victims; but then they'd long ago voluntarily abdicated their own humanity, so it all seemed very natural somehow...naturally unnatural...

"Zis spot over here is being prepared for Alanis Morisette," Vreedeez said, losing his accent halfway through the sentence.

Madonna quivered within her sheath of semiflexible shellac...

"She looks sick, poor Madonna," Amin observed. "Maybe you take her out a while, give her to me, I keep her a pet."

"We discussed that before, Idi," Vreedeez gently chided. "You'd only kill her, and it's too hard to get them sheathed and unsheathed..." He'd discarded the "German" accent entirely for the moment. "...if they die we simply open up the abdominal zipper and complete the taxidermization...But you are right: She does look under the...under der wezzer...a bit zick...P'uzz Leen, are der intravenous and extravenous tubes functional for Miss Madonna?"

P'uzz Leen stroked his black mustache thoughtfully as he opened the Sustainability Panel and checked the various feeder tubes. Then he nodded. Said only, "Yes."

"Gut, gut...Vell, monitor her clozely..."

They paused for refreshments, brought by a mute (literally tongueless) tuxedo-dressed waiter. There was, Sterno noted, an electronic monitor anklet locked onto the waiter's right ankle. Eyes deadened by despair, he offered them brandy and canapés on a silver platter.

"Now over here, ve haff zuh Array uf Writerz...As you see ve haff Tom Robbins and across from him, in rather, may I zay, very uncomfortable proxzzzzzimity, Mr. William Gibson..."

"Hiya Bill," Sterno said.

Gibson—replete with his glasses and Arrow shirt—regarded him owlishly, but didn't try to reply. He at least had the dignity not to beg for a release that would never be forthcoming. Robbins by contrast whined piteously, making Amin laugh.

"I vanted ve get William S. Burroughs or Thomas Pynchon, instead of Mr. Gibson, frankly, but Mr. Burroughs would have died before we complete zuh sustainable taxidermy process, ve suspected, und Mr. Pynchon...well, we went through four zeparate kidnapees zupposed to be Mr. Pynchon, but none of zem were really him..."

"Over here looks like a kind of mixed bag..."

"Ja, ve haff Bono, und Faith Popcorn, und Jesse Helms und Jean le Pen, und Lady Sarah Ferguson der Duchess of York—ve vanted Chelsea Clinton but she vas just too closely guarded, dot Secret Service, always der problem—und here ess Richard Gere und over here Richard Simmons...it's very funny, even in zuh sheath he tries to make der aerobics, very cute...und here ess David Letterman..."

"No shit! Dave! Love this here 'Stupid human trick', Dave!"

"...und Gerard Depardieu, Michael Stipes, Uri Geller, Liz Taylor, Arnold Schwarzanegger—he cry for a very long time, begging us much, Mr. Schwarzanegger...Milosovec...Henry Kissinger...mixed bag as you zay...but over here ve haff a theme, high fashion mit der Calvin Klein, Georgio Armani...und here please meet zuh 'magician' Mr. David Copperfield..."

Sterno had to laugh. "David Copperfield! Hey my man! David! Work out that Houdini escape thing yet?"

"Here zuh fake guroos, Elizabeth Clare Prophet, Scott Peck, Deepak Chopra...Ah, observe..."

Vreedeez reached out and unzipped the sealant over Chopra's mouth. Chopra responded predictably, "You...you have my body, but my soul roams free..."

"Bullshit," P'uzz Leen said, surprising Sterno.

"...and I am sending vibrations into the quantum-uncertainty realm which will miraculously cause the destruction of this abomination...look to your Karma my friend..."

P'uzz Leen reached up to zip Chopra's mouth shut again and just before it closed Chopra burst out, "I am a very rich man! I will give you anything if..." Zip. "...Mumph merf yuff!"

"Now that don't break my heart," Sterno said, chuckling.

But something was bothering him...

It bothered him increasingly, despite his mental rationales...that none of this bothered him.

Just Assholes? Maybe. But these were people, after all.

Vreedeez was smiling at him as he took him around to the rear of the house; the porch ran all the way around. "I veel you are..."

"Could you, seriously, dispense with the fake accent?"

"If you like. You have your own...veneers. Sterno is not your real name and you are not nearly the bad-ass you pretend to be. You're a family man. And as for my accent—we've already taken a psyche-impression of me as the 'Herr Doktur' so it's not necessary to continue it—we'll edit out everything after that..."

"What the hell are you talking about, man?"

Vreedeez ignored the question. "You're from Arkansas, by the way, aren't you?"

"Gotta problem with that?"

"No, not at all, Mr., ah, 'Sterno'. It's just data. As I started to say, a minute ago...you are having doubts about your own reactions to what you see here. It is written quite clearly in your face. You play-act, like so many fringe artists, like The Reverend Shirley and friends, like Survival Research and their cronies, at enjoying the suffering of fools, but real, high-intensity suffering, right here, in-your-face, is more than unsettling. And yet you are not as unsettled as some fragment of conscience in you tells you that you ought to be. And is that really any surprise? You're an American. You take part in all sorts of butchery and cruelty routinely. In media, in your action movies; and in so-called 'reality': There was 'Desert Storm'—you rather enjoyed those smart bomb raids—and there was the Congress that took away all those social services for impoverished children—"

"Hey man that wasn't my doing, none of it."

"No, no it wasn't your doing, not directly. But you are a cell of the organism that did it although you and your friends

pretend otherwise. And what did you do to stop it? Oh but I
forgot: it's hopeless, no? It's all hopeless. And hopelessness
is every cynic's excuse for his enjoyment of his nation's
cruelty..."

"Whoa, whoa, hold on there, old pard—"

"Don't take offense. It's just talk. More brandy? Good
brandy, isn't it? I see you're wearing Nike tennis shoes?"

"What? What the fuck difference does it make what tennis
shoes I'm wearing?"

"Adidas, like Spaulding, like many other American
companies, subcontract the manufacture of their products to
sweatshops staffed by starved, enslaved, badly mistreated
children. Small children." He sounded more entertained by
this fact than outraged. "Sometimes—surprisingly often—the
children are tortured to get more production out of them:
this happens in South America, in India, in Pakistan, in
Malaysia, in other places. The American companies who
subcontract to these foreign sweatshops, they of course know
full well what is going on, and they make their excuses, but
they really don't give a rat's ass."

"I heard something about it but..."

"But you didn't bother to find out more. You are insulated
from the issue by your convenient sense of 'hopelessness',
by the cynical posturing that makes it easy for you to numb
yourself...and hence you can look at my exquisite little
atrocities here and feel more or less nothing. It is enough to
take part in the organism, the big machine, that feeds you,
that sustains you, on the backs of the Third World—"

"Now waitaminnut, when did you, a fuckin' billionaire,
suddenly turn into a Marxist?"

"Marxist? Who said I was a Marxist? I see what is, I take
note, it becomes data I use or discard. I am untouched by it.
I advocate no political ideology. I simply notice hypocrisy
because hypocrisy is blindness, the buffered are blind, and
blindness is exploitable, you see. I am quite above politics.
We all are."

"We? Who's 'we'? Sounds like there's...an organization back
of all this, somewhere.."

"But of course there is...You may call us the Masters of
True Will. That is not our True Name but you are not to

know that. We are those who use the chaotic magic of the world's uncontrolled, blind outpouring of psychic bile, and what you call suffering, and through a kind of ritualization you cannot comprehend—as for example, this time, by turning internationally known figures into living gargoyles—we transform it all...into energy; and the energy we turn into...whatever we wish. For example, you have noticed that I somewhat resemble a friend of yours. But this is not my true appearance at all. Or is it? Was I that person all the time undercover, so to speak, arranging deeper and more subtle levels of hypocrisy in the so-called 'fringe art underground'? Who knows? I will say this: the 'underground' art scene has much more impact on the zeitgeist than it realizes...It is a back door into the collective unconscious—we find it quite useful."

"I...uh..." He looked at P'uzz Leen, who only shrugged, and then at Idi Amin.

"Don't look at me for answer," Amin said. He had inexplicably pulled his penis from his pants and was absent-mindedly massaging it. "I don't understand him when he talk like this..."

"Many are the rituals of mass chaos magic," Vreedeez was saying. "Sometimes, for example, we arrange a small war, so we can transmute the massive outpouring of hypocrisy around the war...as well as, of course, take our part of the financial profits. I myself am a major stockholder in a company that is one of the world's foremost manufacturers of landmines. Did you know that there are more functional, deployed landmines in Cambodia than there are people? Did you know that most landmine victims are civilians and a large number are children? I adore that! These are matters of personal pride to me. And of course the manufacture of landmines and armaments is very important to the American economy—in which you take part. And you see some part of you knows this. Hence you must become numb to suffering, even when you see it in front of you, as you have today...some suffering though is easier than other sorts to ignore, wouldn't you agree? For example...how do you feel about—these?"

So saying he gestured grandly at the new 'array' of living gargoyles at the rear of the castle, in the deep shadow of the dark-forested mountain.

They were "conjoined gargoyles", two people, two celebs, in one sheath: here was Arafat and a certain famous right-wing Israeli rabbi, whose name Sterno couldn't remember—compressed into the same tight envelope of flexible, unbreakable shellac, the rabbi brutally clasping Arafat, above him, the two of them facing one another, projecting from an eave a few feet overhead; blood was pooling, squeezing into flattened pockets of the transparent film over them like blood in a supermarket meat package. Blood from their gnawing; blood from their clawing; blood and spittle and sweat and an effluvium of despair, unseen but palpably felt. Arafat was missing both his eyes.

"G'Broagh Fram buggered by Dobbs!" Sterno swore.

They'd reached a point of near paralysis, the two international political celebrities in the sheath, so contorted and entangled were they; now and then they moved like dying embryos, twitching their last.

Amin was sniggering.

"They don't of course last very long in this position," Vreedeez said. "...after they die we draw out their blood, replace them with a preservative and hardener—like Louis Farrakhan here and—"

"Jesse fuckin' Helms!"

"Precisely."

Farrakhan and Helms had died in one another's arms; Farrakhan had chewed away most of Helms' throat: the old man had definitely taken the worst of it.

Sterno's stomach lurched.

"But," Vreedeez said, "this is the sort of thing you always wanted to see—right...'Sterno'? You and Reverend Shirley and Janor and the New York 'fringe' scene? But you haven't really got, as they say in Mexico, the *cojones* for it. You identify with the suffering of these...temporary creatures. That is the famous and relentless irony: these are nonentities, all these 'stars' of the world stage, they are, as Lou Reed said, a 'temporary thing', quite ephemeral, as in the famous Ozymandias poem, but in this case we can savor their significance in the media overmind, which is one layer of the energy structure that we manipulate through what is both art and ritual, to create a—"

"You're telling me way too much, man," Sterno interrupted. He was looking at the forest, wondering if he could sprint into it before..

Before what? P'uzz Leen didn't look armed but probably was. He had the look of quiescent lethality about him.

"Too much, Mr. Sterno? Too much what?"

"I mean—you are planning on letting me go?"

"You will go as free as a man ever does. Now then...Here you see—"

"I don't know if I want to see any more.."

"Don't be rude, Mr. 'Sterno'. Here you see—"

"And listen, there are lots of people who know I came here."

"To be sure. As I was trying to say, here you see Tom Cruise and Stephen King—combined into one living-gargoyle-sheath, and if you'll step closer...you see they're still alive...Just a little closer, Mr. Sterno, look here—"

Sterno stepped close—caught up by curiosity. Was it really Cruise? Tormented, half crushed, sallow, quite insane, the side of his face chewed away by Stephen King, but yes—

As he was looking at Cruise and King he was vaguely aware that P'uzz Leen was doing something—

Something seen from the corner of his eye—

Unzipping the—

Tom Cruise's finely-muscled arm drooped down, and twined 'round Sterno's neck and pulled him up, off his feet; one of King's arms was free now, too, grabbing Sterno by the jacket collar; Sterno struggled and screamed.

Amin had grabbed Sterno's arms, held them pinned. Was giggling into his ear.

Another unzipping. Stinking, rotting mouths began to chew at him...Tom Cruise's stinking mouth...Stephen King's...began to chew at him...to chew at his face...

"Death is, after all, the only true freedom, Mr. 'Sterno'..." Vreedeez was saying, lighting a cigarette. "As for the people who know where you are—we'll either have them killed by 'suicide' or we'll buy them off. It's surprisingly easy to buy off 'underground' artists. Just offer them a major record contract or a movie deal..."

The pain was—

But they broke Sterno's neck, and the pain was gone and buzzing blackness sucked him in.

——— ◆ ———

"No no no no, Idi," Vreedeez said. "You may not eat the man's testicles. I wish to...Idi...Stop that!"

Vreedeez sighed. He'd finally had enough.

He signaled P'uzz Leen, who drew the dart gun from his pocket and fired it neatly into Amin's neck. Idi Amin fell, paralyzed.

"We'll mount Idi here on the new array...maybe with the Archbishop of Canterbury...Now, P'uzz, see that Mr. Sterno's remains are fed to all the living gargoyles; a little bit, at least, for each, except of course for the brain—I'll be taking that with me for big-interface downloading. We should get a significant charge from this juxtaposition; events will tilt in our favor once more...Perhaps we should take advantage of it and foment a war...Oh and buy more stock in Adidas and Spaulding..."

FLAMING TELEPATHS

He saw them, that first time, because they were invisible. Spaced noticed holes in the crowd. Places, in the packed nightclub, where no one seemed to be standing—yet people moved around those places as if someone were there. Something on the floor no one wanted to step on, maybe. He could imagine that all right. But there seemed to be a lot of those empty spaces. And they were weirdly...symmetrical. So he pushed his way over to check it out. That was Spaced: He was an investigator. A questioner. A looker as much as a participator. That's what set him apart from the rest of the scene—and what endeared him to the others.

Saturday night had packed the Black Glass. The place was dimly lit, walls glittering with a constellation of chrome, covered with studded black leather (they'd spent all their money on that, which was why they had only one functional bathroom; just one of many flagrant violations of city codes). As gum-chewing roadies put the guitars in place on their racks by the Marshall stacks and laid out the cables, getting the medium-small stage ready for the first band, the deejay spun a cut from Motorhead's *Orgasmatron*, speedmetal shaking the floor, walls, and ceiling like the monstrous amplification of a steel foundry, the sounds of some sinister and sentient factory aglow with molten metal.

A cauldron spouting sparks—Incandescent arcs—went the lyric Spaced made up in his head. He wrote lyrics for people, but made his paltry living writing rock reviews and performance art crit for *Ear Spear* magazine. He wasn't a musician himself; he didn't like being onstage. He didn't like anyone to look at him that closely. "The shamans of the rock stage act out our psychodramas for us, exorcising our demons," he'd written the previous week. And Velcro Cunt, reading that, had said, "Spaced, you're too intellectual about it to enjoy it. Or maybe, like, you're—I mean, no offense, but— maybe you're like too old to really get into it. The scene."

Thirty-one? Too old? "I get into it, my way."

"You're too...I dunno...too *Warhol,* man."

"No, uh-uh, Warhol was a drone. You wanta come home with me, I'll prove I'm not a fuckin' drone."

"One of these days I'm gonna take you up on it and you'll be scared shitless."

That was last week. This week, it was a hot September in Los Angeles—hot in the Black Glass, too, because it was crowded. The Iron-Ons were headlining, with a Texas band called the Strokers opening. The Iron-Ons had a following that was almost bloodthirsty in the intensity of its devotion. Working his way across the room, Spaced sniffed the air, sifted impressions, getting the tone of the scene tonight. Like a coyote sniffing the air at a water hole. Tonight was a screwed-down steel spring, tensility precariously in check. The air was heavy with tobacco smoke and dusted pot; you had to be careful where you breathed if you didn't want a PCP buzz. Spaced stood well out of the way as a bouncer rousted an ice smoker, shoving him ahead by the collar, the guy dropping his glass pipe to shatter on the floor as he tottered out the door, his eyes jumping like riffled cards— buzzed on ice, smokable methedrine. That and crack weren't tolerated here. Acid was back, though, and Spaced picked up LSD and MDA vibes in the giddy animation of the faces around the edge of the crowd, the kinetic excess of the dancers moving on the dance floor. He watched a tall, anorexic girl in a neoprene bikini moving like the hand of a Wild West show performer trying to get some serious snap into a bullwhip.

But most of the crowd was simply drunk, or trying to get there.

And there was, as ever, the C and S crowd. Clean and Sober. Over by the open exit door where the freshest air was, dancing together. A growing contingent, the C and S— like Spaced and like Velcro Cunt, Gigger, and Benny—they took no drugs, nor drank. Their rock trancing was inwardly induced.

More than once Spaced had found himself wondering how he could thrive so in this hot, dark, and claustrophobic miasma of posturing. And he'd answered himself: It was like asking how you could enjoy being in a woman's vagina, a place that was also hot, moist, and swollen with self-declaration.

He edged on through the crowd, and got to one of the holes, the place where no one had been, where everyone stepped around—and there was someone there. Twenty feet away you couldn't see the guy, though he wasn't particularly short. Up close, he was suddenly *there*. The first of them. Conspicuous for his lack of movement, like a concrete piling in a surging sea.

He was a pasty-faced man with thin hair. The hair was pattern-balding in an odd way; like shrubbery on a veldt, it wisped here and there. For some reason, the odd hair really struck Spaced, though the club was a showplace for odd hairstyles. *This* hair just grew like that. It was like the guy had a disease. And then the pasty guy looked over at Spaced— looked from his fixed niche in the crowd like an oppossum Spaced had once seen in the park, watching him from inside an overturned garbage can. The dude's eyes bugged a little; his lips were slightly too red. He wore a suit.

The suit, in itself, wasn't so strange. You might find any sartorial style at the Black Glass. There was punk—now in the form of thrash and speed-metal, Metallica modalities—and there were head-bangers and there were neopsychedelics and there were people who affected the austere look that might fit into a really anal, severe sort of suit—the Eurotechni look.

But this guy's dull white suit fitted him badly, and not the kind of David Byrne bad fit that was deliberate. So Spaced thought: Must be from the Liquor Control Commission, maybe watching to see if they serve underage here. I oughta warn Alfredo.

The deejay was playing The Pixies' "Wave of Mutilation" as Spaced went to find the Black Glass's owner and warn him that some sort of bureaucratic dweeb was going to hassle him. But then, thirty elbow jabs and grunting pushes later, he came on another hole in the crowd. With a woman in it, a woman with a scarf on her head, who could have been the twin sister of the first dweeb. And moving between a couple of bodyguards, pushing through to join her, Spaced saw The Reverend Carlyle.

No, really. Reverend Carlyle, king of Channel 47.

Carlyle was scarier than Swaggart, scarier than Jim Bakker, because he was smarter and slicker and didn't make mistakes. He wore the same kind of vaguely western three-piece suits the usual televangelists wore, the requisite slick of oil pulling back his widow's peak, the sparkling smile and those deep-set eyes that gave out reassurance like a keg, pumping beer. He had, too, the slight southern accent, a folksy way about him, a big gold Rolex, and a wife who had hair as fixed and calcified as a snail's shell. He had that televangelist's avuncular earnestness; he had the televangelist's Pentecostal strut when he was working the stage. He had all of it. But he *didn't fuck up*. He was never caught buggering choirboys, or skimming money. Every investigative reporter in the state had tried to dig up some dirt on him, and aside from the conspicuous consumption of his lifestyle—which seemed to be a necessary part of his image, a sign that God was rewarding His Beloved— they came up with zilch. Even the IRS sheepishly admitted Carlyle was legally clean.

And here he was right smack in the middle of the Black Glass. Like a crucifix laid in a vampire's coffin.

"Van Helsing was a fucking killjoy," Spaced muttered staring at Carlyle, forgetting about warning Alfredo, the owner.

That's when the first band started. The Strokers were flailing out a southern boogie with a hard metal edge, fueled by speed and Jack Daniels. It was hard and fast enough; it went over okay.

Spaced watched Carlyle, who watched the band and the crowd. After a while, Spaced felt someone watching *him*. He looked around and saw the hairless dweebs, their eyes fixed on him. A smell like rotting dog food gusted through his head—and a pain that was like a sentient migraine, coming in waves from two directions.

He staggered away and shoved toward stage right. The music was so loud here near the speakers he felt like he was pushing through the amplified sonic medium as well as through people. And then he was backstage, behind the stacks. Gary, one of the skinhead bouncers, glared, then relaxed when he recognized him. He waved Spaced on through, and went back to doing a homemade tattoo on his arm with a small knife, a bottle of ink, and a bottle of alcohol. Puncturing in the pattern, some kind of crude zombie face; dabbing the ink onto the stipples in his skin; wiping with the alcohol.

Spaced felt his head clear as he moved through the warren backstage, past the stammering scribbles of graffitied pressboard walls, thinking, What the fuck was that? That thing I felt out there...Drug flashback? He'd been clean for years....

He found Velcro Cunt, Benny, and Alfredo sitting around with the drummer of the Iron-Ons in the cramped dressing room; the drummer and Alfredo, on the couch, were nursing bottles of Dos Equis from a Styrofoam cooler. The room smelled of stale beer, sweat, old smoke, and pee, much of the stench from the slumped, legless, and colorless couch that barely fit between the walls. A broken, much spray-painted mirror leaned against one wall. A naked light bulb, spray-painted pink and blue, on the ceiling, gave the air a carnival tinge. Benny and Velcro were, of course, drinking mineral water. Spaced accepted one gratefully and squatted on the floor next to them. The Strokers throbbed in the walls like a poltergeist presence, but it took only a little shouting to be heard in here. "You won't fucking believe who's out there!" Spaced said. "Did you see him? Carlyle?"

Alfredo squinted at him as if that would help him hear better. He was a tubby Hispanic dude about forty, with flat-topped black hair and little designs shaven into the sides of his head over his ears—guns crossed with dollar signs. "Whatchoosay? Who?"

"The fucking Reverend Carlyle! From TV!"

"Shit!" Velcro Cunt let her mouth drop open and stay that way. "Bullshit!"

"No way bullshit. It's the man."

She shook her head. She was a white girl, but she had her hair cornrowed, each row a different color. Her face was made up livid, lips black, her clothing more or less like Minnie Pearl's. She lacked only the hat with the tag. And she had big, battered motorcycle boots which looked oversize on her long, skinny legs. She'd met Spaced at a meeting—Narcotics Anonymous—and got him into the Black Glass scene because of the sizable contingent of Clean and Sobers here. They insulated one another from the drugs and booze.

But they believed in rock and roll.

"Carlyle from TV?" she asked, incredulous. "You mean rock-'n'-roll-is-the-Devil's-drillbit Carlyle? You mean every-performer-in-every-rock-band-is-a-living-demon-disguised-as-a-man Carlyle? *Here?*"

"You got it."

The drummer was drunk and skinny, his pimply chest bare; he had two mohawks that were grown extra long at the front to droop over his face, clear down to his chin—moth antennae. He giggled and shouted, "All right! Fucking Carlyle! I'll give him some fuckin' Devil's music, ma-a-an!"

Alfredo groaned. "Oh God, no. It's not a joke. He's picked us for some reason—he'll have parents picketing us, police in here, narcs—" He said some more in morose Spanish.

Benny frowned thoughtfully. Everyone waited to see what he would say. Whatever Benny said mattered. Benny had waist-length hair, half dead white, the other half jet black. A beard bifurcated in the same colors. Weathered cheeks from working at the docks. Sleeveless black leather jacket, rotting Levi's, and disintegrating tennis shoes. Fading biker tattoos. He also had a master of fine arts from Stanford.

"Motherfucker," he muttered. "Carlyle. It's funny, but it's not. Alfredo's right. He's gonna fuck with us. And some of us are going to die."

He said it in that weird, offhand way of his. Like he wasn't guessing. Like he'd seen it, somehow. Now and then he said something like that, and it always came true.

That's when Gary burst in. "They got TV cameras out there!"

The doormen hadn't recognized Carlyle, had naturally assumed that Alfredo would be happy with any TV publicity. And Carlyle's crew was already set up. Nerdy, mustachioed camera- and soundmen wearing earphones and carrying portable cameras. Expensive ones.

Carlyle had a mild-mannered but immovable-looking quartet of bodyguards standing around him, big beefy guys with sweet smiles and T-shirts that said. GOD LOVES YOU AND THE DEVIL HATES YOU. TAKE YOUR PICK!—REV. CARLYLE

Spaced and Velcro stood to one side, staring, as Alfredo argued with Carlyle over the shoulders of a wall of beef. They couldn't hear a lot of the argument through the heavy sonic weather generated by the band, but Spaced could make out that Alfredo was saying he had the legal right to oust anybody he liked, and Carlyle replied, "If you've got nothing to hide, why forbid the cameras?"

Alfredo returned to his friends, looking defeated. "No matter what I do, he'll make it look bad. Let 'em see, fuck it. Let 'em take their pictures. Let 'em see it's just dancing and a little drinking. Mostly." He turned to Gary, who'd stayed at his elbow. "Check the dressing room, make sure nobody starts fucking back there. No one gives head in the bathrooms. And no drugs anywhere. Have the bartenders check everybody's ID, even if they got gray hair and no teeth."

"I know some eighteen-year-old ice-smokers fit that description anyway," Velcro said.

Spaced was watching Carlyle and his crew. The cameramen were getting shots here and there, but only in a token, sporadic way, and Spaced had a sense that Carlyle was waiting for something specific to come down. What did they think was going to happen? The days of slam-dance riots had passed. Mostly. The crowd was too polyglot for that now. The scene in the early nineties was a confluence of countercultures. All of it lumped into alternative music, alternative performance. You could see an Irish radical folk band opening for a CountryWestern-punk band opening for a speed-metal group. Mope rockers opening for rap. There were some clubs on the Strip that specialized in pure head-banger heavy metal, with all the trappings of comic-bookish diabolism—so why had Carlyle chosen the Black Glass?

Must be the Iron-Ons. The lead singer had told a newspaper recently that he thought Carlyle was the reincarnation of Adolf Hitler. And the guitar player had said the band was paganist, worshiped "The Goddess." Which was a *white* magic thing, but not to Carlyle....

All of this flashing like rock-video shots through Spaced's head as he watched the televangelist. Carlyle was taking notes, smiling with celestial smugness, charged even now with the charisma that had made him God's Sole Rep for this planetary franchise—for, anyway, millions of viewers. He was cornball to look at, but gave off something appealing, Spaced decided. Like some Disney hero playing Daniel Boone. And maybe something more. A translucent numinosity....

They watched each other from their two camps. Alfredo's contingent and Carlyle's. There was some mugging for the cameras, of course. First among those was, naturally, Bulb.

He called himself Bulb, but Velcro and Spaced called him Dimbulb. A gaunt, heavy-metal rocker with a flaking Motley Crüe T-shirt and ancient black leather pants beginning to rip at the seams, long, desiccated black hair with a white lightning-bolt streak, six earrings on each ear, a skull nose-stud, and teeth that should have been growing at the base of some swamp cypress. Tattoos Carlyle was certain to take an interest in. Dimbulb lived next door to the club and had decided it was his true home. He had spurts of intelligence and long, dry wastes of vacuity. Lately, he had attached himself to Spaced and Velcro Cunt.

"Hi, Cunt!" he said, jogging up from the dance floor, reeking of sweat and venous smokes. "Got a butt?" He was completely oblivious to the annoying congruity in his use of "cunt" and "butt."

"Only the one I sit on," she said. "And don't call me 'Cunt.' I told you. It's Velcro Cunt, or Velcro. Show some respect."

"Oh yeah, yeah, sorry. You don't smoke either, huh, Spaced? No. Hey, what you think of this moron Carlyle shit, huh, you guys?"

Velcro shrugged. Spaced stared at Dimbulb, sadly, thinking about cliques, and belonging, and not belonging.

Theoretically, Spaced deplored cliques—and yet he had drifted
into one. And true to cliquishness, he really didn't want
Dimbulb in on it. The guy was a social abscess. He was the
kind of guy who'd adopted head-banger rock, easy heavy
metal form, with its charge of adolescent symbolism, as a
replacement for having a genuine self-image, a sort of oily,
toxic repellent against the swarming mosquitoes of self-dislike.

On the other hand, the Black Glass was a place for outsiders
to come in from the cold. Even Dimbulb. And when there
was a band bringing down something they could all connect
with, Dimbulb, dancing in the melee, would briefly be on
the same wavelength as Spaced and Benny and Velcro...

Velcro, now. Velcro was a painter, with a ramshackle loft
on the ragged edges of downtown L.A.; she knew who she
was, and her gear, her look, were an amusement for her, and
nothing more. And the music was a way to get into the trance,
the true high that the Clean and Sobers talked about. She
was a complex person, with an intricate mesh of light and
dark places in her, all interlaced with humor. Quietly, Spaced
adored her.

"Look," Spaced said, pointing, talking quietly to Velcro.
"You see the hole in the crowd? Go check out who's in there."

"Somebody sitting on the floor? Or a midget? A punk
leprechaun?"

Spaced laughed at the idea of a punk leprechaun. He
attempted a brogue. "Faith, and the IRA'll bring anarchy to
the U.K. on this fine spring marnin'!" They laughed and
Dimbulb did, too, blinking in confusion. Spaced went on,
"No, really—check it out."

She went. And came back. "Who was *that?* It's like if you
looked up 'dweeb' in the dictionary and they had a picture—
it'd be that guy! He looked at me so weird! God! I felt kind of
sick, too..."

"Yeah, did you get a feeling like—"

But just then Carlyle started his own show. The band had
just finished its encore—a strained encore that they'd done
on the provocation of only a smattering of applause—and
the deejay'd put on some John Hiatt folk rock to give the
ears a rest when Carlyle took his opportunity to do some
kind of broadcasting preamble.

The makeup lady was dabbing at his face, but he waved her away and pointed at the camera. The smile came on like someone had thrown a switch. "Thanks, Joey," he said into his hand-mike, gazing benevolently into the camera.

"Huh?" Velcro began. "Joey?"

Spaced figured it out. "They're going to tape a big intro for him later, someone saying, 'And here he is, the Salvation of the Nation—the Reverend Jimmy Carlyle! Live from a remote location at...blah-blah-blah.'"

"At a 'den of satanic worshipers,'" Velcro said.

"Yeah, all *riiiiight!*" Dimbulb crowed. "Satanic wor—"

The rest was lost when Alfredo came up from behind and clapped his hand over Dimbulb's mouth.

"Shut up, *cabrón*. Things are bad enough."

Not that Dimbulb would know real satanic worship if it bit him in the ass....

Carlyle was saying something about his show, *God's Country*, coming to you remote from a nightclub in a very, very dark corner of Los Angeles. "It's funny how things as they will be in the next world," Carlyle said gravely, his sad we're-talking-about-lost-souls expression drooping on his face, "are sometimes foreshadowed in this world. Look around me at this nightclub. The red lights, the darkness of the place, the faces painted to look like creatures out of nightmare— friends, have you ever seen anything that looked more like Hell?"

Groans, jeers, catcalls from the listening crowd. Some applause. Velcro yelled, "Yeah, Alabama man! Now, *that's* Hell!" More laughter: Alabama was Carlyle's home state.

He went on, looking around at them pityingly. "The truth is painful, and they cry out against it, in their own way. This is a rock and roll club—that's right, the Reverend Jimmy Carlyle has gone to a rock and roll club! God brought me here tonight to witness. I have had a vision, a dream—like something out of Ezekiel, it came to me. God, my friends, is going to show Himself to us tonight, as He showed Himself at Sodom; as He showed Himself to the Romans when he struck down their empire. I know this as surely as I know that I will and must pray for every soul in this...well, they call this place the Black Glass. Very appropriate. Black glass, like the blindness of sin...." He began to pace between his bodyguards, back and forth, loosening his tie, working himself up a little. "I don't know what the sign will be...but it comes tonight, friends, and it comes here...and it comes to signal a new epoch, a new era. Brothers and sisters, if you have someone you care about who may not be watching tonight, call them up, cry out to them that a miracle is readying itself, is about to be shown to everyone who chooses to tune in to Channel 47....Get them in front of that TV, because what they are going to see tonight will change their lives—and confirm their faith!"

Alfredo was flat-out gaping at Carlyle. "What the fuck is this man babbling about?"

Carlyle was reading from the Bible now. From Timothy 4:1. "...in the latter times some shall depart from the faith, giving heed to seducing spirits—'" He paused to look meaningfully at a girl in a leather miniskirt and extravagantly cleavaged chain-mail halter top. "'—And doctrines of devils....'" And he looked up from the Bible, raising a hand as if to exorcise demons, showboating onward, churning up a mighty wake as he told his well-worn tales of rock 'n' roll debauchery and debasement. He cited teenagers who'd killed themselves while listening to heavy metal rock 'n' roll. He referred to heavy metal bands with diabolic symbols on their album covers. He spoke, without a trace of humor, about playing records backward to hear satanic messages subliminally imprinted. He mentioned so-called sociological studies from Christian universities linking rock and roll to rape, pornography, teenage pregnancy, and drugs.

He explained simply and clearly that rock and roll was a favorite tool employed by Satan's demons.

Dimbulb could hardly contain his glee, Alfredo was about to have Dimbulb thrown out.

And then Benny walked up to Alfredo, and the little group of people—Alfredo, Velcro, Spaced, and Dimbulb—turned to listen. Benny brought people into alignment like iron filings on a magnet.

"There's violence in the air here," Benny said.

Alfredo looked around. "A riot? I don't think anybody's taking the guy seriously, they're all making fun of him—"

"No. I meant *literally* in the air. You'd better stop the show, close the place down. There are—"

He was drowned out by a slow-motion explosion: a single earthshaking chord struck by the lead guitarist of the Iron-Ons. They were a white band except for the black lead singer, who was shooting for a place in the new black/white hard-rock crossover niche "Living Colour" had carved out. But with a harder edge, a Bad Brains vibe. They had their share of black leather, they draped long black silk scarves from their wrists. Just because Carlyle was out there, the lead singer had mockingly painted diabolic makeup on his face. And just because Carlyle was out there, the crowd, mocking Carlyle's down-home mythology, now erupted into their best imitation of damned souls dancing in Hell. Carlyle smirked with secret knowledge, and his cameramen grinned, getting it all.

Alfredo slapped his forehead and groaned.

The tune steamrolled right into another, even fiercer rocker, the lead singer shrieking that he was going to butt-fuck each and every member of Congress personally because that's what they'd been doing to the rest of the country for years...Carlyle's soundmen getting all this tinder for Moral Majority outrage....

Benny was looking around with fierce concentration. At those holes in the crowd.

That's when Dimbulb jumped up onto the stage, in rock frenzy's own spontaneous audience participation, bounding awkwardly around up there, ignored by the band, dodging the roadies, making the...oh, shit...making the sign of the Devil with his hands...looking like a rock 'n' roll Richard Ramirez....

Fuck! Spaced thought.

The camera pushing through to get a better shot of Dimbulb. Bulb leaping off the stage at the camera. The crowd laughing, opening up around him, giving him room to dance, as the band did a cover of the old Iggy tune "TV Eye."

And there was a TV monitor Carlyle's crew was using, to one side, Dimbulb babbling in fake-demonic tongues and leering and shoving his face right up the camera lens, looking like a real jackass, playing right into Carlyle's hands; another camera zooming in for a closeup of Bulb's biceps tattoo of the down-pointed pentagram with the Devil's head.

And over it all, Carlyle shouting a reading from Revelation: "...And the beast was taken...and them that had received the mark of the beast, and them that worshiped his image. These both were cast alive into a lake of fire burning with brimstone..."

There was something in the air...something more than dope smoke and tobacco and sweat steam...

A pressure. A certain suppression, a distancing of sound. A transparent weight. A sentient and minatory heaviness. The thunder of the band became impossibly muffled by the sheer denseness of this presence. Until it focused...on Dimbulb. Closing in on him like an invisible spotlight.

And he burst into flames.

As Carlyle read from Revelation: "'...and fire came down from God out of heaven and devoured them...'"

There were screams. The band stopped playing. Spaced pushed through to Dimbulb, who was writhing in the flame, clawing himself on the floor, enveloped in blue and red fire.

Spaced's first thought was that someone, some agent of Carlyle's, had doused Dimbulb with gas. But there was no gas or kerosene smell, and anyway...

Anyway, the burning was coming from within Dimbulb's flesh. He was burning *around* his clothes, at first, his skin giving out little tongues of flame like the holes on a gas-stove burner, his own flesh consuming itself—reddening, blackening, bubbling, breaking into tarry flakes edged in oozing red, the Devil's-head tango distinctly marked out with lines of red flame....

A cameraman shoved in close to suck all this into his thirsty lens.

People ran for the doors, screaming, while others tried to douse the flame with pitchers of water. Alfredo grabbed a coat and threw it over Dimbulb.

Dimbulb's eyes...Walter's eyes...That was his real name, Spaced knew—Walter. Dimbulb was Walter Duffe. Walter Duffe was looking out from eyes that were about to boil out of his skull. Just one look of bone-deep imploring escaped from those eyes, and then—they boiled over.

Nothing would put out the fire. It came from inside him— it had, anyway, been seeded inside him—and there was no escaping it. It consumed him like an ant under a magnifying glass's concentrated sunlight, in less than a minute.

The lead singer shrieking into the mike, accusing Carlyle of having set Dimbulb on fire, yelling to the crowd to get Carlyle, hold him down, throw his ass in jail, send him to the fucking gas chamber—

And then the lead singer of the Iron-Ons burst into flames.

Fell screaming onto the stage. The other members of the band threw down their instruments—the guitars and bass making an amplified clangor and thrum and whine, as if the instruments were wailing out an inarticulate electronic fear—took off their coats and ran to the singer. And when they extended their hands to put the coats on him, to try to smother the flame, their hands under the coats burst into flames. A chorus of screaming that could have been rehearsed...

They drew back—and the flames in their hands went out. They stood there with red, blistered claws, shaking and gagging and staring helplessly at the lead singer, who burned from within. He seemed to be trying to crawl away from the flames in some way—as if they were concentrated in his lower half, and his upper half was writhing to escape them. No one could get close enough to help him.

The pockets in the crowd that held the dweebs from Hell had bellied outward, everyone pressed back from the two...forced back by a growing intensity of the same psychic pressure that had pervaded the room just before the attack....

Oh, for sure: Spaced knew it was an attack. Knew where it was coming from. And when panic spread through the crowd, driving them toward the exits, leaving the dance floor empty but for Carlyle and crew and the wasted chiaroscuro of Dimbulb who was now just more of the dance-floor litter—Dimbulb lying there, shriveled charman glimmering with receding flames amid the beer bottles and cracked plastic cups and suspect puddles—Spaced was not at all surprised to see the dweebs remaining also, near the walls, staring at the stage. Symmetrical to one another, as if at two of the points of a pentagram. With Carlyle and crew in the middle of the dance floor—in the center of the huge, unseen pentagram. What unseen presences stood at the other points?

The makeup lady and the bodyguards had fled, too. Out of primal terror, Spaced supposed. They hadn't signed up for this. And maybe they were afraid God would look into their souls and see a certain damning hypocrisy....The cameramen stayed. As if held by some will beyond their own, a telltale glaze on their eyes....

The lead singer was clawing at himself on the stage; his movements became weaker. Burning out, in an accelerated parody of what rockers were supposed to do anyway. Exuding suffering like a scream of guitar feedback.

Alfredo and Velcro were somewhere in the background, shrieking at bartenders to get fire extinguishers and ambulances, and the bartenders were yelling back that the phones weren't working...

Benny was stepping up onto the stage.

The cameramen working feverishly to record it all, God's punishment of sinners through his Chosen One, the Reverend Carlyle...

Until Carlyle saw Benny. "Turn off the cameras," Carlyle said softly.

Benny knelt beside the lead singer. Put his hand through the flames. The flames sucked away, back into the singer— were gone. He stopped writhing, relaxed. Relieved, freed. "I'm sorry I didn't quite wake to myself until you were gone," Benny said to the dying man. "But you will be well received. I've asked Jimi to receive you. Go, then...."

A rasp from the guitar player. "Hey...my man..." Recognition in his voice. And then he was dead.

Benny stood, and went to the musicians. Touched them one by one. They gaped at their hands—which became whole. Healed. Then Benny turned, strode to the microphone. Carlyle looking at him white-faced, his mouth working soundlessly.

"Cease your invocations, Devil," Benny told him. Not the usual way Benny talked.

What the hell do we know about Benny, anyway? Spaced thought. Supposedly an ex-biker, rode in from New Orleans with some biker club. But Alfredo had asked the prez of that MC about it once, and the guy had refused to talk about Benny. Would say nothing, nothing at all. Just turned around and walked away, like he was trying not to look scared.

And Benny just hung around, made soft jokes, drank only the occasional glass of wine, jammed on bass and drums with people sometimes...

And gave advice. People just found themselves asking for his advice, and it always came out all right if you took his advice, too. Spaced remembered a time he—

Whoa. Wait-a-minnut.

The dweebs were pointing their hands, extended before them, at Benny. Benny was smiling distantly, his deep-set eyes unseen except for the occasional glimpse of two evanescent points of light needling from far back within the sockets.

The cameramen, working under the direction of an entirely different will now, had begun filming again. The soundmen had begun recording.

Moving like sleepwalkers, the band, the surviving Iron-Ons, picked up their instruments and began to play an R & B thing in four-four.

Spaced recognized it. From an early ZZ Top album.

And Benny began to sing, with understated, bluesy authority.

The lyrics were something about how Jesus just left Chicago; he goes to New Orleans, turning the Mississippi into wine—and then he heads for California. The next line was blotted out as another sound erupted from another part of the room. The dweebs. Their mouths opened wider than any human being could open them, repudiating, with howls sirening from them, their heads spinning on their necks as if on turntables....

Not howling inarticulately. It was a word. One word: *"Down!"*

As in—hold it down. Keep them down. As in suppression. "DOOOWWNNNNNN!"

A black-light radiance issued from their pointing arms, the variety of energy that manifests itself as intrusion and rape and the hammer of repression, translated into its essence—

Striking at the stage.

Flames licked up around the stage. The stage caught fire—

The bass player screamed—

But, in a trance, kept on playing—

Velcro ran up behind Spaced, grabbed his arm and shouted, "Run! Run! Let's get outta here!" But he couldn't, and she clung to him, and they watched the fire growing—

But Benny was dancing. That was all. Dancing, a perfect living manifestation of the sound from the speakers as the band played on. Benny invoking something himself, and a gust of fresh, spring-laden air rolled outward from the stage—instantly snuffing the flames.

The wind pushed on, blowing outward, making Spaced and Velcro stagger...

Blowing on to snuff, also, the illusion that enclosed the dweebs and Carlyle. The wind blowing their camouflage away like smoke. And they were exposed, revealed: The dweebs were repugnant things that fused man and worm, the slick gray boa-sized worms in them slithering greasily in and out of great holes in the manform, their forebrains exposed and protuberant, pulsing.

Carlyle, too, was exposed: He was a hideous creature weirdly contorted in on itself, like a scrambled semihuman Ouroborous—his body protracted and bent, defying bone, stretching down from the upper torso so that the head was *literally* thrust up his ass, pushing up through his body and emerging from a wound under his armpit. It was a snarling, demonic face that Spaced thought he had seen when he'd visited Paris—on one of the gargoyles adorning Notre Dame.

The thing that was once Carlyle shrieked in pain and fear and drew its head back inside its own body like a snail into a shell.

The band ceased playing and Benny spoke into the mike, looking into the cameras, pointing at Carlyle. And Benny recited from the Bible: "'And if any man shall say to you, Lo, here is Christ or lo, he is there, believe him not: for False Christs and False prophets shall rise and shall shew signs and wonders, to seduce...'" A verse from the book of Mark, Spaced remembered, quoting Jesus.

Then the dweebs, the flaming telepaths, ran and slithered to the creature that had been Carlyle, frightened children scurrying to their parent—leaving nasty wormtrails on the ground behind them—and Carlyle and the dweebs embraced, began to claw into one another...tearing into each other, as if tunneling to escape in one another...

Until Benny made a gesture, and spoke a Name, and Carlyle and his minions imploded in flame. Flame that looked like a film of a fire running backward, sucking in on itself, vanishing, taking Carlyle and the dweebs with it. Imploding them. A flash of light, and they were gone—vanished but for a black grease-spot on the floor.

Benny turned to a camera. Looking into it gravely, he said, "The Devil—the true Devil—hates rock 'n' roll. Strives to suppress it through his false prophets. The Devil hates rock 'n' roll because the Devil hates freedom, and freedom of expression and anything that unifies men. And God...God loves music. All kinds of music. God thinks with music. And when God chooses..." He paused—then grinned, and shouted: *"God knows how to rock 'n' roll!"*

Acting on some inner prompting, a divine instinct, tears streaming from their eyes, the band suddenly thundered into a rock 'n' roll tune of its own construction, improvised and immaculate: an immaculate conception.

Some hidden fog machine billowed silvery smoke from backstage. The smoke rose up into a cloud around the band, hiding them for a moment, cloaking Benny—and then it receded...the band left glistening, still playing...

And Benny was gone.

Of course, there never was a fog machine backstage at the Black Glass.

All the courage that Spaced never knew he'd lacked was suddenly there when Velcro gave him a ride home in her old Dodge Dart. So he asked her what he'd always wanted to ask her.

And she said, "Goddammit, Spaced, I thought you'd never ask. I've been waiting two years, man."

"I asked lots of times."

"No. It wasn't the same. You never asked like you cared about me before. It was a jokey come-on, before. Let's go to my place. Your bed's too small."

She swerved the car into a U-turn.

And on the car radio, with the synchronicity that was never quite really accidental, came a song by the Call. It was called "Let the Day Begin." It was a song about love, about God and about hope. And it had a rock-steady beat.

HOW DEEP THE TASTE OF LOVE

Sid Drexel was just totally into it. He was so fucking happy it stank from him. Just coincidentally, his wife was dead.

He was sitting in the bar of Tuffy's, the "Hottest Little Singles Bar in the Bay Area," and the place was jiggly with women. Some already had men talking to them, but there were women sitting in twos and threes who were only marking time with each other while they waited for a Sid Drexel to make his move.

Drexel could barely keep himself glued to his barstool. He bobbed his head to the MTV stuff coming from the hidden speakers near the big-screen TV, he chewed handfuls of twiglike pretzel sticks, and he made rude noises with his straw in the soupy dregs of his second strawberry daiquiri. He had to talk to somebody. He tried the bartender, an almost unnaturally good-looking guy with a golden tan, wearing an odd, sleeveless tuxedo. The bartender had pumped-up arms, and he moved with no wasted motion as he poured things, shook things, gave things, accepted things, wiped things; Drexel admired the way one smooth action became another.

"Tom Cruise's got nothing on you," Drexel said.

The bartender glanced at him as he opened a glass-washing machine. The look seemed to ask if Drexel was in the wrong kind of bar.

"I mean," Drexel hastened to explain, "that movie *Cocktail*—Tom Cruise played this slick bartender—"

"Oh. Yeah. Thanks." The bartender did a sort of glissade to the Jack Daniels bottle, sweeping it off its rack and pouring, all in the same motion.

"My wife's dead," Drexel announced, beaming at him. "I mean, it's a shame and all. But, tell you the truth—"

"Oh, I understand," the bartender said. He took someone's money for the Jack Daniels. There was a small tattoo of a star inside a toothy mouth on the bartender's tanned forearm, Drexel saw.

"You understand? You know what I mean? Twenty-one and a half years, my friend. You know what else?" But Drexel decided not to say it: that he had once considered killing Helen. Not too long ago, either. But it was risky. And divorce? Jeez, with his contracting business and California's community-property laws, she'd take him for half of everything. But *this* way…Boom! A car accident! And none of his doing! It was so sweet that the cops had checked her car to see he hadn't messed with the brakes or something. But he hadn't, he really hadn't; he'd just been lucky. And he still felt lucky.

"Maybe it's the dance training," the bartender said, with narcissism glazing his eyes. He looked at Drexel. "The reason I can do the Tom Cruise behind the bar."

"You're a dancer?"

"Why you think so many ladies are here? To see you?" A crooked grin said he meant no offense. He nodded toward the small, circular, tinsel-curtained stage. "Male dancers for the ladies. My bar shift ends in twenty minutes. Five dancers in all."

"Oh." Thud. There it was. The ladies were here to see guys undulating their muscle tone on the stage. "And I got to leave?"

"In twenty minutes it becomes ladies only. But come back after showtime." He winked. "At eleven." He drifted over to talk to a tall, busty blond woman with skin that looked faintly blue in this light. The bartender looked directly at Drexel, then back at the blonde.

Eleven, he'd said. Eleven? Drexel'd be half in the bag by then, or half asleep. He had to get something *going* with someone. Helen was in the ground a month now, he had given himself a week's vacation, he had plenty of money, he had that pricey Mercedes convertible that Helen had bitched about, and he had his looks. Okay, sure, his face was sagging around the edges, and he had that pattern-baldness thing, but he was still a good-looking guy...Maybe he should have had his teeth cleaned.

Don't worry about it, he told himself. Just—*go for it*. Life is short. And Helen had been very particular. Everything had to be just so when she did it. Except for a couple of whores watching the clock the whole time, and Billy Jane Dotts in her parents' garage, Helen had a corner on Drexel's sexual experience. And Helen was not into...exploring. You read those magazines—*Forum*, things like that; people wrote in all kinds of letters about every damn kinky thing in the book. Like there was nothing weird about it, in particular. Like it was okay. But Helen wouldn't even talk about it, let alone...

"Excuse me. Is this seat taken?" It was the blonde.

No, came the reply in Drexel's head, is yours? But he was savvy enough to say, instead, "Nope. Have a seat." She was damn good-looking. Smooth skin—still looking blue-black—beautifully Asiatic eyes, the shape of her face maybe Hispanic, some kind of foxy crossbreed. The hair looked like a wig, but so what? And those *tits*. God. She sat with her shoulders thrown back, chest jutting in her tight cream-colored sweater. It was sewn with black beads in an odd pattern he almost recognized but knew he'd never seen. He didn't spend much time looking at the beads. Her breasts were almost too magnificent to be real. Then, too, she had that wig. And she was tall. Maybe...

He looked at her closer. Some kind of transsexual?

He looked at her neck, her lips, her cheekbones. No way: This was a woman.

She looked frankly back at him. "Aren't you going to offer? I mean, here's the first guy I've met all night I'd like to buy me a drink, and he's the only one not offering."

"Oh—well, shit, I-mean—yeah! Bartender! Hey, pal, anything this lady wants…I'll have another…right."

She said her name was Sindra. She had some kind of slight accent he couldn't place, maybe Middle Eastern. She sat very quietly, but he had a feeling she was just bursting with something inside, like him. *We're two of a kind.*

He prided himself on his sense of humor, so he tried telling her a joke. The bartender listened in, wiping the bar. The only one that'd come to mind was: "So this guy comes into a bar with a frog growing out of his forehead! A whole, live frog! And the bartender says, 'Hey buddy, how'd the hell that happen?' And *the frog* says, 'I dunno, it started out as a wart on my butt.'" She stared at him for a moment; he seemed to have startled her, somehow. She and the bartender exchanged looks.

Then she laughed politely. "Do you believe in omens, Sid?"

"Hm?" Drexel shrugged. "Sure. I hope it's a lucky omen, whatever it is. Say, pal, can I get another? Right."

He got only halfway through the daiquiri before an amplified voice interrupted the MTV T&A to announce that the men had to leave in five minutes for the ladies only show. The ladies clapped and whooped.

"Well hell. I guess you're waiting for the show, huh, Sindra?" Drexel asked. He thought that was a pretty smooth segue.

"Actually, no," Sindra said, adding gravely, "no, I'm…waiting for you, I think. I need someone to live out some dreams with. Tonight."

He felt his groin churn with blood. "Yeah? Man, I've been waiting for someone like you for…" And it all came tumbling out. She listened, nodding, as they put on their coats and—without ever having to discuss it—walked out to the parking lot to his car. On the way out, Drexel absently noticed the bartender up onstage, half nude, throwing his muscles suggestively around, and she didn't even glance at the guy, *not once*, and the bartender gave them a long look that might have been a kind of resentment.

"I understand exactly what you've been going through," she told Drexel, holding his gaze with hers as they stood by the white convertible, in the monoxide velvet of the warm Indian summer night.

He hadn't noticed, in the bar, how golden her eyes were. Golden—or almost lemon-colored.

"I was in the same position—in more ways than one—with my husband of many years," Sindra said. "He would try nothing new. And sex is like a continent. A tropical continent It must be explored to be appreciated. Don't you agree?"

"Hey, listen, I...okay, maybe it sounds like one of those things that's just...that everyone...that's...what's the word?"

"Trite? Cliché?"

"Right! Trite, like, but Sindra, I couldn't agree more. I am just totally there with you."

He hadn't gotten to his forties without knowing when something was too good to be true. If some guy wanted to pay you three times the rate to build something that was too easy to build, it was always too good to be true. The mob was covering up something, or there was some other hassle behind it.

And he knew Sindra was too good to be true. Women like her just didn't come at you this easily.

"Don't they?" Sindra said.

"What?" He did a double take.

"I can see it in your expression. You don't trust me. 'People don't do this sort of thing.' There are some one-night stands, but women who...well..."

"Women as good-looking as you don't offer to, you know, uh..."

"Fulfill a man's every fantasy within minutes of meeting him?" She smiled. "I didn't offer that."

"Oh. Right. I, uh—"

"But you're right: I was going to. I still am."

"Uh, is there, I mean—"

"No charge. Unless you cost something."

He laughed. "Hey—for you, it's free."

They both enjoyed that. He was having one motherfucker of a good time. He really was.

"How would you know if things like this never happen?" Sindra asked. "Living with your Helen, you'd be out of circulation. But you must have heard about it happening to other people." She was slightly hunched down in her seat to keep her wig out of the wind streaming over the open top of the convertible.

They were tooling down the 580 toward the turn-off that'd take them into the Berkeley Hills, where Sindra lived. Drexel replied, "I've heard of people having encounters like that, but you always figure those stories are bullshit."

"No. It's simply...rare. Rare that it comes true. See, it only comes true for special people, who are into special things. And those people are rare. They're *select*. A kind of sexual elite. And they're carefully selected."

"You *selected* me? Like you've been watching me?"

She hesitated. "No. No, but—I have a special instinct for these things. That's why they send me."

His hands got sweaty on the steering wheel. "They?"

"Here's the exit..."

He took it, mechanically. "You said *they?*"

"Perhaps I should have said we. You did say you wanted to experiment. To really live. Go into some new directions. Why don't we talk about it frankly? You can tell me: What sorts of things did you want to try?"

"Uh...well..." Could he really tell her?

"Tell you what: I'll go first. Turn right at the next light. Best get in the right lane. That's it. I'm into being tied up with my own panties, given golden showers, then covered in fragrant oil and gang-fucked. Among other things."

If he'd been in a cartoon, his lower jaw would have bounced on his lap. Which would have been kinky itself, considering his hard-on.

"Jesus," he said, shaking his head in admiration. "'Among other things'? I really—I admire that. How you can just come out and talk about that and...and not only talk about it. This is great. I always wanted to...well, lots of stuff. Two girls. And being...being spanked by two girls. And they make me do things. Then I spank them. And make them do things."

"Turn right again. Up the hill here. Turn left at the corner."

"Up near the big burn-out, huh?" They were driving through the hills charred by the Berkeley-Oakland fire of '91. The black ash had seeped away in the rains, except along the concrete foundation lines of the burned houses most of the

ground was gray and muddy and erosion-raked. Chimneys
jutted here and there like those termite towers you see in
pictures of arid African plains.

He drove onto her cul-de-sac. The fire had been a windfall
for Drexel's contracting business, but he hadn't been on this
particular street. All the houses were burned away except
one, with thick brush around it. Brush that should have
burned, he would have thought.

"Yes, we were lucky in the fire. The neighbors were
crowding us." She smiled distantly. "'Make people do things,'
you said. What sort of things? In your fantasies?"

"Hm? Oh, God."

"Come on. I told you mine."

"Right. Chewing on people. Chewing on feet. Clean feet,
of course. Chewing on private parts. Not…not hurting anything
but…sucking and chewing on fingers and toes and nipples,
really *chewing*…God, it feels good to just…" He shifted in
his seat. He hadn't been this hard since his teens.

He parked in front of her house. Drexel had flirted with
architecture in his one year of community college; he
recognized the house as an old Maybeck, heavy on the dark
wood, the intricate levels, the big windows. The yard was
overgrown; he didn't recognize most of the plants. There were
pines encircling the place and more pine and fir, singed
survivors of the fire, marching down the hill behind it. The
Bay. Berkeley, much of Oakland would be visible on the
other side of the house, maybe even San Francisco.

They went up the mossy flagstones; brown pine needles
fringed the stones, and stiff silvery-green brush pressed in
from both sides of the winding path. Sindra stepped over
something on the porch—something that made Drexel
backpedal a few steps. A large gray tarantula. It made tentative,
feathery movements, like the fingers of an anxious piano
player, and slipped into the succulents lining the porch. "It's
that time of year in the East Bay hills," Sindra said, noticing
his reaction. "It gets warm and they come out and mate."

She unlocked the door and they went in. It was cool and
moist here and smelled of mildew. They passed along a dim
hallway to a living room. There were picture windows that

should have looked down on Berkeley and the Bay—but they were covered with red cellophane. There were large, shapeless cushions on the hardwood floor. Nothing else to sit on.

He stood awkwardly in the flushed light by the window as Sindra went to the built-in bar. There were paintings on the walls, but standing here he couldn't quite make them out.

Sindra knelt beside a small refrigerator—the movement tightened the skirt around her ass. She took out a Mason jar of dark liquid and poured some into two cups with a little cola. "I make a mind-fuck of a cocktail," she said. "I keep it premixed."

She brought the glasses back to him, and they each drank. The stuff was both sweet and acrid. He couldn't quite...

"What is it?"

"Tarantula venom, partly," she said, as he began to twitch.

Even in his toxic delirium, he thought passingly: They must be silicone. Too perfect, too firm.

She was on her back, nude, legs spread, her whole body beckoning. Her breasts looked violet in this light, with purple-brown nipples. They were vast, jutting, round, perfect, and just impossible.

But they weren't silicone. One of the whores had been silicone-enhanced that time. Kneeling between her legs exploring with his hands, he knew: This wasn't the same. This was...

They were meaty. They were *big* breasts, not like enhanced pectorals, and she had a real pussy; it wasn't as if she were some kind of transsexual, no. But these things were filled, he assumed, with muscle. Which was impossible, wasn't it?

He thought about all of this for maybe two and a half drugged seconds. Then the convulsions hit him.

After a while he stopped noticing. The convulsions stopped scaring him. And not long after that they stopped entirely.

It was all the same to Drexel: He had gone through the panic and sickness stage, and now, with the psychedelic effects of the high-dose venom, he was riding waves of psychotic exultation through a storm of light. The storm's colors were sultry shades of the primaries, and neon variants of violet and emerald and gold, whipping past him in arching, interweaving wires, like lasers gone rubbery. The wires of light dove into him and careened down his spine, each color a different sensation; other lights arched over him like the buttresses of some infinitely refined cathedral, where even the building stones were of stained glass. And occupying completely the floor of the cathedral was the naked Sindra and her impossibly perfect breasts.

He'd twitched his clothes off, and his cock was hard as teak. She took him immediately, all in one embrace, cock into yielding, slick pussy, his face into her cleavage.

There was a delightful scent off her that was like venison and gardenias with just a touch of frying trout. It translated into taste as he thrust his tongue into her meaty cleavage; he rocked back from her a little with the intensity of the feeling, a sexual sensation as palpable as the heat waves you felt rolling off the tarmac when you stepped off a plane in hot-season Florida. "Jezzusya...Jezzusya..." His heart felt like a molten lump. He couldn't quite talk. "Jezzusya fuggincredibuh...Yuh incredibuh..."

"Why thank you, Sid," she said quite clearly, her voice chiming against the incandescent glass of the air.

He shoved up into her and he seemed to go farther than physically possible—as if the cleft of her kept parting, wider and wider, as if he were wading into her, as a man might wade into a swamp.

And her nipple in his mouth—it moved, the nipple *probed* in his mouth....

"Bite it, sweetheart," she said, sweetly and lucidly.

"Yuh ruhlly wahmuh?"

"I really do. Bite it hard."

He bit down, and forty years of frustration came rollicking out of him, singing. A lifelong weight he'd taken for granted simply curtsied and left him. This was *way* better than he'd hoped for.

"Bite harder, much harder. Yes. Now harder still." Her voice was quite clear and insistent, there was no mistaking it, but it was hard to believe she wanted...

"Harder."

"Yuh sure?"

"Oh yes."

He bit down as hard as he could, and if he hadn't been in unspeakable ecstasy he would have screamed in revulsion as her skin parted under his teeth. As his teeth sank into the meat of her.

"Now chew it up."

Oh no. But he could no more spit it out than a two-year-old boy could spit out his first taste of real candy. Maybe he'd be sorry later, maybe he'd be explaining it to the police and the *National Star* and specialists in criminal psychiatry, but right now was Right Now more than it ever had been, and this was the most delicious bite he'd ever taken; it was the most satisfying oral sensation he'd ever felt. Her flesh was drugged. It was cocaine and heroin and quaaludes, oozing velvety fingers of electric delight into his brain. As he chewed, he waited, rather abstractedly, for her to scream and push him away. But after he swallowed—that itself a deeply satisfying act, awakening unheard-of erogenous zones in his esophagus—she demanded, *"Take another bite. A big one."* When he hesitated, she said, "Bite and chew it up and swallow! It *doesn't hurt me!"*

He ate most of her right breast and was working on the left before he began to feel full. And even then he could feel the bitten-off breast *melting* in his stomach...dissolving into him, more rapidly than with anything so banal as digestion. The taste was of meat, almost a sausage but more delicately flavored, and some sort of exotic fruit pie, and just a *faint* touch of blood, hardly any at all, and a faint underflavor of something he'd had at a Japanese restaurant. Roe? Sea-urchin eggs?

And the texture: wonderfully creamy, but with just the right meaty resistance to his mastication.

He could hardly breathe, with his sticky face thrust deeply into the rind of her left breast. But he couldn't get enough; he was infinitely hungry, endlessly consumed by lust. His hips thrusting, cock working almost incidentally in her pussy (orgasm was not an issue, so to speak—he was far beyond that), he devoured the pulpy wet blue-violet glory, working his way greedily down into the breast, down to a sort of root...Like the little nubbin one finds at the inside bottom of a pumpkin, a kind of internal stalk. He gnawed at the stalk, sucking away the last of the drugged flesh around it—and she said, "That's about right, I'd say."

The stalk opened and took hold of his tongue.

Someone in the background said, "Are you in full contact?" A man's voice.

"Yes," she said. "I have his tongue and his cock."

He tried to pull free, of course; both extensions of him were pinned, and pain warned him not to try again. The pain was as intense as the pleasure. It commanded him to stillness.

He was still drunk on her, the high had programmed a profoundly somatic trust in him. He was hers.

A man squatted behind Drexel and thrust something in Drexel's ass.

But he knew from the shape of it—it hadn't been a penis. It was a rounder, more truncated shape. It dissolved, like the stuff in his stomach, and seeped into him.

He saw someone else out of the corner of his eye—another man, kneeling by Sindra's head. Bending, thrusting his hips toward her face.

She bit off the man's penis and chewed it up, her smile droopy with euphoria.

The man arched his back, but not in pain. This wasn't something masochistic. There was no blood at the bitten-off root of the man's cock. Only the same bluish pulp at the stub.

Drexel couldn't see the man's face clearly from this awkward angle. But he recognized the tattoo on the muscular arm: the bartender.

He felt something flush into him through his tongue; tingling, interpenetrating. Something else warmly *hissing into* his trapped cock, like a backward ejaculation. Some secretion, entering him, from her. He sensed that the seeming cock that Sindra had bitten off, the flesh of the bartender, had been *processed through her* somehow and was now entering Drexel, fertilizing the meaty secrets he'd swallowed.

Most of the time he would lie passively in the low, bowl-shaped bed. Squirming only occasionally, when the internal sensations unsettled him. Now he reposed dreamily, listening to her soothings. Sindra was standing over him, telling him a few things just to keep him quiet, so it would all seem natural. So he wouldn't struggle, though there was little struggle left in him. His limbs had merged arm into arm, leg to leg. There wasn't much he could do. The inhabited flesh he'd swallowed, with the secretions that she and the men of her peculiar species had mixed into it, were changing him; were guiding him, on a cellular level, along some metamorphic byway of synergenesis.

She remained nude when she was in the house; so did the "bartender." So did the others: the women with the slightly blue skin; their heads, when they'd removed their wigs, furred with the faintly waving blue polyps; the men had golden polyps on their craniums, and their skin was softly gold. It was not a tan.

The bartender's cock was growing back.

As Sindra stood beside Drexel, gazing at his changing body, smiling beatifically, he could see that her breasts were already rapidly growing back as well; the little stalks were covered over, the rinds of the old breasts fallen neatly away At this rate she'd be back up to size in a week.

A little boy came to the incubator bed; a boy of about five, nude and golden-skinned but without the quivery polyps on his scalp the others had. More than once he'd come to look at Drexel with some unspoken personal fascination.

Sindra shooed the boy away with a murmur, then turned to the bed, reached in, and stroked Drexel as she spoke. "It's all a cycle, a natural, beautiful cycle, Sidney. We have a pact with them—we call them the Guests. They are the brethren of the Akishra. Their world intertwines ours, in places; we've always had a sort of overlapping ecology with it, with their dimension. A lot of the old Nature gods were just people altered by the Guests, Siddy." She cocked her head thoughtfully, looking for the most calming way to explain it. "Some of us are suitable to be hosts to the Guests—and others are to be incubators, for their young. It's to do with your DNA, I suppose, and your spiritual type. It's something we can sense. Carl and I sensed you were perfect incubator material—and so you are! Not everyone is suitable, so it's fortunate the Guests only need to lay once or twice a year.

The Guests use us as hosts—people like me, and Carl, your 'bartender'—and they change us and give us life. A very, very long life with many pleasures. They pass through us to you incubators, and we feel no pain, and our lives are sweet and varied." She paused to stroke his swelling belly.

"They've passed fully into you, Sidney; *you* brought the layings of the Guests in, hungrily, and willingly. I used the venom of our pets to make it faster. And because I enjoy it. But we didn't really need the drug. *You wanted me that way, Sidney*—and now you're fulfilled!"

She crouched beside the incubator bed, letting him try out his feeble protest, which came out as unintelligible mutterings. She stroked him, and pinched one of her own nascent nipples thoughtfully, as she went on.

"Hush, hush and lay still, Sid. The real miracle is still to come. We fertilized that which you devoured from me; from my breasts; it's growing in you. You won't be one of us; they need you differently. But you'll have your own rewards..."

She bent near him with a sponge of nutrients, sweet and syrup-thick, blowing kisses at his muted lips.

At the Feedtime, the time of reconfiguration, they no longer had to soothe him. The unneeded part of him was gone. It was displaced when the one who'd grown in his belly moved up, through the passages within, and entered his skull for its first feeding.

Sindra and Carl and the boy and the others knelt beside the incubation bed. Hugging one another in excitement, they watched as the transformation achieved its penultimate stage.

The Guest had moved into Drexel's head like a hermit crab into a seashell. Now the onlookers gasped in wonder and joy, like anyone privileged to watch a birth, as Drexel's head detached itself from his neck and crawled—*the head crawled*—on its gastropodic underside, down the length of Drexel's body. It began to graze contentedly, nourishing itself on his flesh. It would fill itself thus until the Growtime should come, and then the bonding with a host: the little boy who watched eagerly and happily beside his parents, Carl and Sindra. The boy had been instructed in what to expect; he would not become an incubator like Drexel—he would become a carrier for a Guest, like Carl and Sindra, immortal and perfect. He watched rapturously as the Guest in Drexel's head fed on the body it had quit; he watched in a glow of anticipation, eager for the day the Guest should be ready to join with him, to bring him into the manhood of his people...

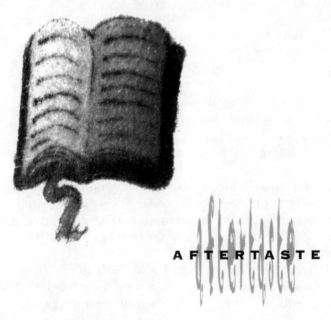

A F T E R T A S T E

Saturday Night, 8:45 P.M.
West Oakland, California

Dwayne was sick of hearing Uncle Garland talk. The old man would talk about Essy and he would talk about the dope and he would talk about grindin', about everything but his own goddamn drinking. Sitting in that busted wheelchair at the kitchen table, talking and sipping that Early Times. Talking shit about his angeldreams, too. One more word about the dope...

But Dwayne tolerated more than just one more word, because he needed Uncle Garland. He needed a place to stay and some place to run to. So he just sat and listened while he waited for Essy to get up, waited for Essy to get them started again. Essy in the next room, had to crash for awhile, been two hours already. Fuck it. Dwayne could taste rock at the back of his tongue; smell it high in his nostrils. All in the imagination.

The TV was on, with the sound turned off. A rerun of a show with that guy used to be in *Taxi*. Tony something.

"You listening to me, Dwayne?" Uncle Garland demanded, scratching his bald pate with yellowed fingers. His rheumy eyes looking at Dwayne and not seeing him. Moving with less life than the TV screen. Blind. The old man was blind, but that was easy to forget, somehow.

"Can't hardly not listen, you talking all the time," Dwayne said.

"The dope killing this town, it be killing our people," Garland was saying. "Killing the black man. I'm fixin' to go the Next World, and I'm glad to be goin', Praise Jesus, with the devil eating this world like a pie..." Didn't pause to take a breath.

Uncle Garland's place was an apartment in the Projects, in the shadow of the freeway that collapsed in the '89 earthquake. Used to be you heard the freeway booming and rushing all night. Now it was eerie quiet. Or quiet as it ever got in the Projects.

"Tell you some true now," Uncle Garland said, using the expression that always prefaced a long, long lecture. "These are the end times, that the Lord's truth. In my angeldreams, they come to me and tell me it's so. And it's on the news, about the dead people rising. It's in the Bible, son, when the dead rise it's a Sign that the Lord is coming for Judgment—"

"That's complete shit," Dwayne snorted. Why didn't fucking Essy get up? Maybe he wouldn't help him, get him started on the rock today. Cousin Essy think he's a big Grinder now, selling dope, stylin' like a B Boy, but he got nothing to show for it. Not like he paying the rent here. Some grinders they put their family in a nice house, buy them cars. Essy don't give the old man shit, so don't tell me you're the big Fly. Of course, the old man wouldn't accept the money, he'd know it was dope money...

"It's the dark wave, the night wave that sweeps over things, son. It changing the world, readying for the end times. People, they do evil to each other and it opens the door for more evil. Evil deeds call up evil spirit and its hunger enters the dead, it's a sickness on the land..."

Dwayne couldn't stand it anymore. Fuck Essy. He'd get his materials, one way or another.

He stood up abruptly and headed for the door. Put his hand on the knob. Said, over his shoulder, "Uncle you tell Essy I got tired of waiting. I going to—"

"No p'int in telling Essy shit. He dead."

Dwayne felt a cold wave, like that wave of darkness the old man gabbled about, ripping through his gut. "Bullshit."

"I feel it. He died, maybe an hour ago. Got some p'ison in him."

"Shit," Dwayne said again, and opened the door. He wasn't going to go in and check on Essy. Wake him up when he's crashing, he'd go off on you. Anyway the old man was full of shit.

But as he walked down the hallway he felt like Essy was dead, too.

In the kitchen, Garland sat up straighter on his wheelchair: he heard Essy stirring. Heard the creak of the bedsprings Garland had been blind so long he scarcely noticed the darkness anymore. But now, it seemed to take on density and weight; his blindness seemed to thicken about him and chill him like a cloud covering the sun.

Heard the shuffling steps coming. Knew for certain what it was. The dream angels had left him in no doubt.

He reached out, found his cane, forced himself to his feet. He rarely stood anymore, but this time the danger of it, of fracturing one of his porous old bones, didn't matter. He crossed to the broom closet by the old, whirring refrigerator. Moving only a little more slowly than the footsteps coming up behind him from the next room. He felt for the knob, found it, pulled the closet open. Found the old pistol where he kept it under the oily rags on the top shelf and drew it out, his hands shaking.

Then thought: What if the dark wave brings me back too?

It wouldn't be Garland, not really him, but...

He heard a dream angel whisper: Not you, nor your old body.

He heard the shuffling nearer. Heard no breathing with it. No breathing, not any.

He raised the gun. Raised it to his mouth, pressed the barrel up against the palate, pulled the trigger.

His last thought was: Leaving a kind of gift for it.
Light.

9:57 P.M.
Downtown Oakland

Dwayne knew. He knew even before the white guy got
out of his car. You could see it by the way he drove up, the
car moving almost spastically, and the way he parked, the
sedan slung across two parking spaces outside the liquor
store, and the way his head moved around like one of those
little dashboard dolls that's got a head wobbling on a spring.
The white guy was fucked up, really fucked up, and probably
on base. Crack cocaine.

He was opportunity on the hoof.

The white guy had longish red-brown hair, bright blue
eyes, and a little reddish mustache. He was driving a tan
Acura, maybe a '95, and he had a gold watch on his right
wrist. This was looking better and better.

Hobey saw him too. But Hobey was across the parking
lot, trotting up real slow. Hobey was too old, too fat. Didn't
smoke, drank Night Train instead.

Dwayne was leaning into the white guy's passenger side
window by the time Hobey got there. "Whus'up," Dwayne
said, "What you need, tell me, I help,"

The white guy's mouth was hanging open a little. His eyes
dilating, shrinking, dilating, shrinking. A tongue so dry you
could almost hear the rasp of it as he licked his lips.

"Rock," the guy said. "Crack," Things white guys called
base cocaine.

"How much?"

"Uh—sixty bucks worth."

Man, he was fucked up. Not supposed to make a deal that
way, people rip you off. They sure do.

Dwayne almost laughed. But he said, "Okay, I take you
there."

"Get in."

Hobey was coming around to the guy's driver side, "What
you need, chief? I get it for you, I find the best—"

"I got it," Dwayne snapped. "I taking care of it." He gestured briskly to the white guy. "Hobey's a rip-off artist. He gafflin' people all the time. Let's go."

The guy changed gears like a robot and they backed out, nearly plowing into the brick wall on the other side of the lot. Then they were careening down the street, Dwayne hissing, "Yo, chill this thing down, man, you get the cops on us."

The white guy slowed down to a crawl.

10:15 P.M.

This part of San Pablo Avenue was mostly liquor stores; flyblown bars with the light bulbs burnt out in their signs; adult video stores where fag hustlers cruised the video galleries.

"There it is," Dwayne said, now. "That hotel."

It was an old white wedge of a building, tall and narrow, on a sort of island where three streets almost intersected. The rest of the block was abandoned office space, rickety old buildings. Doc was standing in the doorway of the hotel, all in white as usual. A white suit, with a pink carnation. His black Jag was parked just a few feet from him where he could keep an eye on it.

"Thas the dude," Dwayne said. "Got a Jaguar XKE, doing this shit." Dwayne couldn't keep the admiration out of his voice. That Doc had it together.

"Pull up over there," Dwayne said. "No, fuck, don't—shit!"

The guy cut across two lanes with a screeching right angle turn.

"Shit!" Dwayne looked around as the guy parked. No cops. Lucked out again.

"What's your name?" the white guy asked. Dwayne.

"I'm Jim. Okay...uh..." He looked through the window at Doc. Knew he couldn't go over and buy the shit himself. Or thought he couldn't, anyway. Probably could have.

But Dwayne was banking on Jim White Guy not knowing that. And, in fact, Dwayne could feel he was going to connect good here. Fuck Essy. Dwayne could grind his own business.

Essy could come asking Dwayne for a start. (No way Essy was dead, that old man was getting brain damaged from drinking...Drinking kill you...)

Jim went on, "What you want for this?"

Dwayne said, "A dove."

"Half a dove."

So he knew what a dove was anyway. A forty dollar rock of crack.

"Whatever you wanta do, hey homes, it's okay. I'm not one of these gafflers like Hobey—"

"Yeah, yeah." The guy was getting a weary look as he took a chip of rock out from a jar, broke it in half in his teeth, put one of the halves in a pipe...Shit. The pipe was a *pipe*. It was a motherfucking briar pipe. Lighting it with a Bic. Sucking at it.

Dwayne felt his scalp contract, his mouth go dry as he watched. Smelled the oily perfume and insecticide tang of the smoke. "You oughta get yourself a stem, man. What kind of fucking pipe is that?"

"Only one they had left in the store. I'll get a stem later. Here's sixty. Don't cruise on me, you'll be fucking up a good thing." The guy was involuntarily grinning as he said it.

"Gimme a blast," Dwayne said. The guy handed over the pipe and the Bic. Dwayne took a hit. The pipe worked shitty, but good enough for now, except it burnt his fingers having to hold the Bic upside down over the bowl. The blast feeling blossomed in him. It rushed through him and instantly he began to work on ways to get more. This guy, no telling how much money he had. Probably had a bank card. Maybe—"Go on," Jim said, taking the pipe back.

Dwayne folded the sixty bucks into his palm. "Keep that pipe low, watch for cops." Still shaking a little from the blast, he got out and crossed to Doc, thinking: Play this guy carefully.

10:50 P.M.

Hobey almost went to sleep on the bus. Last time he did that he slept past his stop, took him half the night to get home. He was tired and when he was tired he noticed the creakiness in his bones more. Fuck that damn little nigger, that Dwayne. Someone had left an *Oakland Tribune* on a seat. There were headlines on the metro section that said: THREE MORE CRACK DEATHS *Coroner Doubts OD Cause.*

"Huh," Hobey said. Some bad shit going around. That kind of shit, that's why he didn't smoke. Shit like that.

The night sky was jet black, looking starless over the glaring anti-crime lights on Martin Luther King, Jr. Way when Hobey got off the last bus.

He turned down Winston street. There was action over to the parking lot of the 7-11, but Hobey didn't care, he was too tired to fuck with trying to get in on it. Some of those piped-up motherfuckers shoot you, Uzi your guts out soon as look at you. Don't be fucking with it when you're weary.

He stalked past a dirt lot where an old crackerbox house was almost demolished. Hobey used to work in demolition, before he got kicked out of the union, and this mess made him shake his head. The demolition had been subcontracted to some damn non-union crew! Just went after it with crowbars and a rented plow. It looked like a tornado had flattened the house at random, a scattered pile of plasterboard and timbers like a crazy snail shell for the slug of a rotten old mattress...

Hobey stopped and stared.

The mattress had moved. Had humped up, a little. By itself. Humping up so there was a dark little cave under it. Fringe of wet, mildewed mattress stuffing hanging down over the mattress cave. Like a gooey wig over the face that was coming into the light, showing, now, in the little cave. Something crawling out...

Just some homeless nigger, Hobey thought.

The fella was about forty feet away, coming out on his hands and knees. All raggedy. Looked beat up, like he'd been tossed in there and stuff dumped on him. Maybe that mattress got dragged from somewhere else to cover him. The man ditched because they thought he was dead, most likely. Hobey had seen it before. Somebody ODs, the rockhouse doesn't want the body around so they drag it to the nearest river or vacant lot, dump it, cover it up, let the bugs chew it up so nobody knows who it is...

Only they thought this guy was dead and he wasn't.

Should stay out of this. But he was feeling kind of low about himself, felt like doing for somebody, give him a lift. This man was lower down than he was...

"You need some help, man. You lookin, poorly," Hobey said, picking his way through the debris toward the man. Didn't recognize him. Black man, maybe was a teenager, not much older. Not standing up straight yet, hunched over. Something hanging off his head, maybe mattress stuff..

Ten feet away. Hobey stopped. The man took a shaky step, bringing him into a streak of streetlight shine. Lifting his face toward Hobey.

He had eye sockets full of ants.

Ants in the empty sockets, the ants moving all squiggling and searchingly the way ants do. Seeking and chewing, shiny and restless. No eyes. Ants.

"My Lord, man..." Hobey breathed. "What they done to you..."

Then he saw the spike. Big rusty metal spike from some concrete support of the house. Bent and blunt. Right through the man's chest.

Right through the motherfucker's heart.

10:55 P.M.

White guy on a binge, that's what he was. Didn't smoke most days, but tonight he got mad at his wife or something, he go out on a binge, Dwayne thought. Not used to it, puts him farther out of his head. He's righteous tweakin'.

Dwayne watched Jim White Guy crossing the street. Walking to the bank machine. A little island of light in the dim street: a little high tech sweetness in the concrete and fake marble.

Leaving the keys in the car. Leaving the keys with *Dwayne*. A complete stranger.

Got to be tweaked to do that.

Now Jim White Guy was standing at the machine, swaying, twitching a little, trying to figure out the buttons in that state. Probably end up leaving his card in the machine. Better check.

When Jim Pale come back, they going to need that card. They'd already burned through the dove, and another one, and the guy was making his second run to the bank machine, and he'd left the keys in his Acura, and...

The high was buzzing in Dwayne, but the buzz was fading. Time for another hit. He lit up some of the base he'd palmed when Jim White Guy wasn't looking, sucked it up in the stem, the glass pipe he'd picked up on Telegraph Avenue.

There. There it is. Spreading out in him, expanding through his nervous system. The blast. The rush spreading its wings. Wings made of flash-paper on fire. Going up, gone.

Blasts were getting shorter, weaker. Need bigger hits. Maybe some black tar to go with it, ease the landing. Maybe take the car now.

But then Jim White Guy was back, sliding in. "I got some money for that pussy, too," the guy said. Thinking he was real street smart talking about pussy that way.

They made a stop at Doc's dope house, Dwayne breaking some of the dove off with a thumbnail, sliding it into his change pocket while he was walking around behind the Acura. Then Dwayne said, "Okay. Left at the corner. If you want ho's."

It was coming together in Dwayne's head. He knew a whore, Joleen, used an empty building up on Martin Luther King and Winston.

They found Joleen easy. She was a floppy titted bitch with skinny legs, not getting much work, walking up and down the sidewalk in front of the condemned house. Across the street from the demolition lot where Samson Ramirez had dumped that OD case out of his rockhouse. Joleen, clutching a fake patent leather purse, was moving back and forth like a wind-up toy, marching on broken-down white Adidas gone gray from the street.

Jim White Guy was so high anything with tits looked good to him. Two minutes, and Dwayne had him out of his car, across the sidewalk, making a quick deal for Joleen. Acting like Joleen was going to do them both. Joleen was cheap. Didn't work out of a house or a motel or anything, she couldn't handle the overhead. Bitch just do it right there in your car or wherever was handy. Forty dollars for two. Another time, if he was trying to get some pussy from a toss up, he'd trade some smoke for it. But now he didn't want to waste time in negotiations.

"I got a place back here," Joleen said, leading them up a walkway used for storing garbage cans. The side door had been knocked off its hinges long ago. They stepped through it, went down a stairs, into a furnace room. There was a pile of dirty blankets in the corner; gray light coming through a grimy window from the street.

"Shit," Jim White Guy said, whirling on Dwayne. "You setting me up to rob me? I got some friends, I'll fucking have you killed—anything happens to me, they—"

"We here for some pussy. Look, I got my dick out. I usin' my dick to rob you?" Dwayne pulled out his dick, wagged it at Joleen, who dutifully went to her knees. Started sucking. Wouldn't be able to get it hard, after all the base. Not Jim White Guy's dick either. But the man was too piped-up to care.

"I'll take her from behind while she does you," Jim White Guy said. But what he was doing was firing up his pipe.

"All right, I hear you!" Dwayne said, and slapped Jim's side in a companionable way; taking the Acura's car keys from Jim White Guy's jacket pocket as the white guy got his blast.

"Suck the man's dick, Joleen, he payin' for this shit," Dwayne said.

Joleen silently shifted over to the white guy, unzipping his pants, taking his pasty, shriveled thing out in her hands.

"You gonna give me a blast, honey?" she said, playing with his dick.

The guy took out the pipe, put it in her mouth, flicked the Bic onto the glass bowl. Not noticing Dwayne moving off behind him.

"Got to pee," Dwayne muttered.

Then he slipped out the door, out to the car. With luck, the white guy be distracted for a few minutes, long enough for Dwayne to get away with the Acura.

And it worked okay, as far as it went.

Tuesday, 2:05 P.M.
Fremont, California

"Are you?" Patty said. Her tone matched her expression.
Brittle.

"Yeah," Jim Diggins said, "I am. I'm sure." Feeling like it
was the truth. He was sure he'd never do cocaine again. How
could he do cocaine again after all *this?* (But, yeah, he'd said
the same thing before the last binge...)

She was angrily taking clothes out of the dryer, putting
them directly into her suitcase, hardly bothering to fold them.
Jim wouldn't have thought that you could take clothes out of
a dryer angrily, but Patty could do anything angrily. She could
brush her teeth angrily.

"You're passive-aggressive, you know," she was saying.
"This is just another way to express hostility. Getting stoned,
getting robbed."

"That's a pretty solipsistic idea of things," Diggins said.
Jim Diggins. Jim White Guy. Jim Pale.

He was leaning against the concrete sink next to the
washer. A cobweb hung down from one of the old
two-by-fours that held up the kitchen floor, feather tickling
the back of Diggins' neck. He didn't have the energy to move
away from it. He felt like the core had been dug out of him.
He might collapse inward, any second. His head fall into his
chest. Fold up like the Scarecrow of Oz without straw.

"Jim," his wife was saying, "I heard this crap three times
before. You were sure, this time. No more, you said." She
was a thin woman, with long straight brown hair hanging to
her bony ass. She had violet blue eyes that everyone thought
were her best feature. She wore shorts, which maybe her
legs were too skinny for. She looked especially pinched and
taut when she was angry.

"This time I'll get counseling."

"You *got* counseling, Jim."

"I mean, therapy, serious therapy. Maybe even Schick
Center or something."

"How about a car? Are they going to give you a car at the
Schick center?"

"We got insurance."

"We'll still lose money and it'll take a month to get the insurance payoff."

"Look—" He was near tears, crushed by humiliation. "I know I'm a screw-up sometimes but most of the time I work hard for you and Donna..."

"I don't want to hear that speech either." She carried the suitcase out of the laundry room to the stairs.

Ten minutes later she was gone. She'd taken Donna, their four year old and she'd gone, her sister coming all the way from San Jose to pick her up. Jim doubted this was intended to be permanent. It was like making him stand in a corner. More humiliation. What really hurt was not being able to hold it against her. Who could blame her? He'd had a drug relapse, and he'd done cocaine again—crack this time, for God's sake. Crack. Which had a nasty street smell about it, the taint of crazies and thieves and whores. And he'd wallowed with all of those—with a thief, with the sleaziest kind of whore (could she have given him AIDS from an unfinished blowjob? could he say for sure she hadn't?), and a crazy. He was the crazy. He'd been totally out of his head. A miracle he'd only had his car stolen. Could have been robbed of his credit cards. Could have been murdered. Could have been killed, driving under the influence of the stuff.

That fucker Dwayne.

Jim thought about it as he got himself a Corona and walked through the house from the kitchen, through the dining room and the parlor, to the front room they never used except as a kind of showplace for the furniture Patty'd picked out. His footsteps sounded loud in the house. Lot of creaking boards he'd never noticed before. He could hear water trickling in the sink of the front bathroom where his little girl had left it running, as usual. He couldn't bring himself to turn it off. He crossed to the window, his hand tight on the beer bottle. Looked between the white curtains at the big, wind-blown oaks in the Barton's front yard, across the street. On the ground beneath the trees, tangled shadows of branches and leaves moved like dark seaweed in a translucent ocean.

That fucker Dwayne had seen him coming. Seen a stoned stupid middle class white dumbshit.

He drank half the bottle of beer down all at once. The beer was like running cold water on a burn. For a moment it smoothed over some of the pain. The depression.

"You knew it was going to make you depressed afterwards," Patty had said. *"When you go on one of these stupid binges you always feel like total shit for a week afterwards. How come you don't think about that before you—?"*

"I don't know, hell, I don't know," he'd said. *"I just get too stressed out or something and it's like somebody throws a switch, I just turn into a fucking drug robot and I go find it. I mean—I've got it down so it only happens once or twice a year now—"*

"Once a decade is too damn much," she'd said. Snapping it.

"I know. I know."

"Christ, don't you think about afterwards at all, Jim?"

"All I can think about is how I'm scared to crash. As long as I keep the drug coming I don't think about it." And he snorted derisively at himself, mumbling, *"It's like skydiving with a busted parachute. It's a great ride till you hit the ground."*

No sympathy at all from her this time. He couldn't blame her. That came sneering back at him again. Could. Not. Blame. her.

For about the five hundredth time since he'd gotten out of the Crisis Ward of the hospital Sunday afternoon, he thought about killing himself. Get a gun. Blam. Brains on the wall.

He thought about killing Dwayne, too.

My car. How dare he touch my car.

The phone rang. He walked in a dream to it. It took an effort of will just to pick it up and say, "Hello?"

"This is the Oakland police department calling for Mr. James Diggins—"

"That's me."

"You reported a stolen car..." He read out the license number, the other specs.

"That's my car."

"The car was found by a patrolman yesterday morning. It's been towed to a lot at..."

3:30 P.M.

Why had they taken only three wheels? he wondered numbly.

The Acura was tilted onto its right side wheel rims and the left rear tire. The car's hood was standing open. Dwayne must have gotten spooked or burnt out, Jim decided, after taking three tires. Anything that could easily be detached from the engine was missing. The front seats were missing, too. The trunk had been cleaned out, tools, tire and jack were missing. The headlights were missing. The radio was gone, pried from the dashboard like a rotten tooth.

And the windshield was smashed out by vandals.

The insurance company would want to have the car repaired. It would be expensive, but still cheaper than a new car. It'd take weeks. Then he'd get to drive around in this reminder of the night he'd had a nasty fight with Patty, gone out and gotten blown away on coke and fucked up royal. Maybe even got AIDS for all he knew.

He stared at the hulk of his car.

Shit. He couldn't believe it. He'd let this happen to the family car. It was a ton or so of pure, raw, undiluted *symbol.* Sitting on the hardened dirt of a towaway lot.

That fucker Dwayne. It wasn't Dwayne's fault, ultimately, he knew that. It was his own fault. Dwayne was just a drug addict who'd seen an opportunity that Jim Diggins had stupidly dropped in his lap. But, nevertheless, Dwayne had preyed on him. It was like stealing from a blind man. A retarded blind man. Dwayne was raw, undiluted symbol, too.

And Jim wanted to kill him.

Thursday Night, 10:07 P.M.
Oakland

A sultry night at Winston Street and Martin Luther King, Jr. Way. Lots of goods going around. Joleen and Binda turning toss-up tricks to get their blasts. Dwayne pacing in front of the rockhouse. Thinking: two hundred forty-five dollars. For all that stuff I got out of that Acura. Could have gone to the joint for stealing a car. Nobody wanted to buy a hot car. All that risk for a hour's worth of rock...

Then here came Samson Ramirez in a new BMW that looked carved out of a single block of snow and ice. So new it didn't have the plates on it, just a sticker in the windshield.

Samson was half white, half Mexican, but he'd been on the street so long Dwayne thought of him as just another homeboy. He was a hard motherfucker, and getting harder as his biz got bigger. He was supposed to he pulling down even more money than Doc now, which was what his white BMW was about, Dwayne figured, to advertise that.

Samson was pulling up in the white BMW, parking across the street and a ways down, not wanting to associate the car too obviously with the rockhouse. He had long, wavy brown hair in a fancy unisex perm, a brown leather jacket and brown leather pants with just a touch of a Latin flare about them. He had his Mexican Daddy's perfect white teeth. Perfect, but he'd had an incisor replaced with a gold tooth, to go with his thick gold chains.

Raiders came out of the rockhouse to meet Samson on the sidewalk. Raiders was a tall black man in a red jogging sweatsuit that he never changed or washed, a gold Raiders' medallion around his neck and a blue waistpack slung around his hips. The pack hung like a scrotum because of the snub-nosed pistol in it. They called him Raiders because when his talk wasn't about grinding it was always about the Oakland Raiders; he held the team in reverence like they were gods.

Dwayne thought: Maybe I do it now. I could walk up to Samson when he's talking to Raiders and ask for the delivery work, talk him up good.

But he didn't have the nerve yet. The man didn't know him.

Dwayne stepped back into a doorway, where he wouldn't be noticed, He waited, listening in.

"'nother one died," Raiders was telling Samson, "and 'nother one killed with his head busted in."

"Same as old Hobey?" Samson asked.

"Same as Hobey. Head busted in like a melon."

Dwayne felt a strange contraction in his stomach. Hobey was dead? He hadn't heard. It was never a surprise to hear that someone he knew had died. He'd seen his father beat his mother with piece of pipe and he wasn't surprised when she died in the hospital. And he had an aunt was a whore, died of pneumonia that was probably from AIDS. But Hobey had seemed like a survivor.

"They think dogs are gettin' into them," Raiders was saying. "Somebody bust their heads in, then wild dogs come along..."

"You making me sick, I don't need to hear this," Samson said, grimacing. "What makes you think it was the silver cap that did the other ones?"

"I sold it to them both half hour before. One of them went right here, died in the house, other one out in the alley."

"You get rid of them?"

"What you think?"

"So what you want me to do about this shit?"

"Maybe it's the bug spray."

"Everybody uses bug spray for bonding."

"Not this industrial shit we been getting. They use Black Flag or something. We oughta go back to it, maybe it's this stuff that's been—"

"Shut up. It's not us, *pendajo*. Okay? This bug spray I got makes the stuff go farther, people like it, they come back for more.

"Reporters was hanging around, 'safternoon. Asking shit."

"They connect it to us?"

"Not yet."

"Then fuck 'em. It's not us anyway." Samson made a dismissive motion, a hummingbird blur of his hand, and started toward the front steps that led up to the old two bedroom stucco place that was the neighborhood rockhouse.

Dwayne started to go after Samson. Froze when he saw Raiders glare at him. They'd already had a run-in. Come back when you got the green, Raiders had said, we not hiring. You come around with money or we hammer your whole fucking body.

Samson was going into the house. Opportunity walking away. Dwayne rubbed his Bic-thumb calloused with a forefinger, could almost feel a rock there, between his fingers. Could picture putting the dove in a pipe, firing up. Could almost taste it.

Once Samson was in his "office" there'd be no getting to see him. Not from where Dwayne was at in the pecking order.

Dwayne smelled base, someone smoking somewhere. Turned and saw Joleen in the front seat of a beat-up van, her head bobbing over some guy's lap. The guy firing a blast in a broken-off stem, the glow pulsing, lighting up a little blue skull tattoo on the guy's cheek, and showing his face. He was a big, dirty yellow-haired white guy, a biker type, with an overgrown beard and matted hair; a biker who'd had to sell his bike for crack.

Dwayne smelled the burning base. Watched the flare of pipe. Heard the biker grunt as the blast rocked him.

Fuck it. Dwayne couldn't stand it. He started up the stairs, after Samson. "Yo, Samson—!" he called after him. "Yo, my bro, wait up—"

But then Jim White Guy stepped out of the bushes with a gun. A .45 automatic. He was grinning. Motherfucker was real proud of himself.

10:15 P.M.

"You fucking with me, right?" Samson said.

Raiders shook his head. "While I was out. Ramon told me. Three more dead, just all in the last half hour, right here in this fucking house."

Samson and Raiders were in the pipe room, which had once been someone's living room. Now it was a big box, just a place to sit and smoke crack with a couple of burn-pocked mattresses on the floor and a smell like a shitty diaper from the plugged-up toilet in the bathroom off to one side. Naked bulb, windows double boarded over, linoleum curling up off the sagging wooden floor. Intricately calligraphed posse graffiti on the walls next to the mattresses. One broken stem in a corner.

Samson swore in Spanish. "What you do with them?"

"Some of the posse taking them to the dumpster behind the Pioneer Chicken place. I fucking don't know. I ain't smoking none of that silver cap."

"You don't be smoking at all around here. I go off on you, I catch you. Don't smoke at work." But he was thinking about something else.

"We use up this batch, then maybe we switch to Black Flag for the bonding agent in the stuff—who's making it up?"

"The base? Ramon."

"He get sick?"

"Hard to tell with Ramon."

"Okay, we get rid of the Bug Deth now, but we use up this batch of the cooking. That's forty, fifty thousand dollars, Raiders."

Raiders looked like he was about to argue when Ramon and Buzzy came running in, yelling, and Ramon was missing half his face.

10:18 P.M.

Jim stared at Dwayne. Jim wasn't sure how he was going to do this. Or what exactly he was going to do. Should he really do it, go ahead and kill him? Or maybe just kneecap him? Bust his knees open with a bullet. Fucking change his life for him. Ruin *his* transportation.

"How much you get for that shit you took off my car, Dwayne? More'n four hundred bucks? Probably less. Pretty pathetic, asshole."

Dwayne just stared back at him. "You got me confused with somebody, man." Maybe if he kept saying it, the guy'd buy it. Just keep saying it, make him doubt himself.

"No. Uh-uh. I was fucked up but I remember you vividly, Dwayne. And Joleen. I found her, see I figured she wasn't in on it, so I didn't shoot her, and she told me you'd be here eventually."

They were standing in the thick shadows by the dark green bushes, standing amidst dog crap in the balding front yard at an angle where nobody could see them but they could see most everybody. Jim White Guy had picked the spot carefully.

Inside the house. Ramon on his knees clutching his face, blood runneling down his arm, and twining through the links

of the gold chain on his chest. Sobbing. Samson trying to get
a coherent story from him.

"The bodies in the dumpster *what?*"

And then the naked, filthy guys came stinking and
stumbling into the piperoom and when Ramon saw them he
screamed and scurried away on his hands and knees. Samson
thought they were some kind of homeless lunatics until he
saw that one of them was dragging his guts behind him on
the floor.

Outside, Dwayne saying, "You mixed up, man, you piped
up or something, got me mixed up wid somebody. It dark
out here, too. Let's go in the light, over there, you see if it
really me. Come on, put your gun in your pocket." All of this
was halfhearted. Dwayne realized he was hoping Jim White
Guy would shoot him. Put a hole in the hole.

"You lying sack of shit," Jim Diggins said.

Dwayne took a step back, into the streetlight shine. Jim
took a step toward him. Aimed the gun.

Then they heard the screaming from the house, and the
gunshots. Three seconds of Dwayne and Jim gaping at the
house. Another thirty seconds of uncertainty, staring at one
another. Dwayne saying, "We better get the fuck—" That's
when the naked, coughing man with brains on his fingers
came staggering out of the darkness by the bushes, coming
from the back door. Coming at them.

Dwayne knew it was brains on the naked man's fingers,
because of the head the dude was carrying under his arm. It
was a handsome head with a lot of hair that waved like a
jacket fringe as the naked guy moved. A big gouge taken out
of the skull. It was Samson's head.

"Oh fuck," Dwayne said. Recognizing Samson's
still-twitching face on the severed head. Seeing that the naked
motherfucker lunatic had one nasty, filth-caked hand in the
hole in Samson's head, was scooping out the brains, eating
them, using his fingers like a kid eating the frosting left over
in a bowl...

Jim and Dwayne stared at the naked guy. A white guy
with a bloated stomach and snaggly brown teeth. The naked
guy was staring back without blinking, his milky eyes not

moving. Standing there, swaying like he might fall over any
second.

Jim was making a choking sound down in his throat.

The naked guy dropped Samson's head. Thump. It rolled
a little, in the grass. The naked dude thrust his head out a
little on his neck, like a cat, and sniffed at them. Sniff. Sniff
again. Then he made a croaking sound, his mouth exuding a
stink that made Dwayne want to puke. He took a step toward
Dwayne. Sniffing. Made another sound. A word this time.

"Base."

He reached his hands up toward Dwayne's head.

Dwayne backed away and fell over. The guy dropped to
his knees beside Dwayne and gnashed his teeth at him,
reached for his head and...

Dwayne hoarsely yelling, "Jim, help me, man!" This wasn't
the way to die. Not this way. Uh-uh, no.

Jim hesitated. Then he fired the .45 at the naked guy.
Blam. The flash strobe lighting up the yard for a tenth of a
second, a flame licking out, the dead man staggering...

Oh yes, Dwayne knew it was a dead man.

Staggering, turning toward Jim, all his movements like
flinches. The dead man with a hole right through its heart.

Jim felt unreal, looking at the walking dead man. Like he
should lean back in his chair and reach for the popcorn and
just let things happen on a screen. He fought the feeling,
thinking: *this is happening to me.* Aiming at the dead man's
head. Blam, flash, right between the eyes. It went down like
a puppet with its strings cut.

Then it started thrashing, kind of floppy-sideways on the
ground, like a landed fish.

"Base," it rasped. "Crack. Rock. Silver top. Base."

There were three more coming around the other corner of
the house. Two more on the street, coming down the sidewalk.
Mostly naked. One of them didn't have any eyes, and it had
a rusty piece of metal through its middle, its head moving
hurky-jerky. All of them coming toward Jim and Dwayne.

One of them was carrying Joleen's head. Her head raggedly
torn off at the neck. Holding her head up to its face, biting
into Joleen's forehead. The naked men coming at them
sniffing, snuffling...

Dwayne and Jim ran up the stairs, into the house.

Both of them yelling the same thing so much in synch it sounded rehearsed: "FUCK FUCK FUCK FUCK FUCK FUUUUUUCK!"

10:35 P.M.

They found two freshly killed women in the front hall, one with her head missing, the other one with her head only half attached. The top gone from that head. Scooped out. Part of the brain. Just part of it. They only wanted...

Jim threw up in the pipe room. Samson's body was curled up in one corner, a puddle still spreading out from it, Ramon dead beside it, face down. The back of his head gone. One of the naked guys was scraping like a cat at the closet door, and they could hear someone sobbing in the dark closet.

The naked bulb lit the room brightly, every corner of it. Stark and sharp.

Jim straightened up, feeling like he was going to hyperventilate and walked over to the crawling thing at the closet door (thinking about what it was, with quiet amazement: a human being gone literally rotten, dead meat dragged around by hunger like an empty cart dragged by a rabid horse. It was entropy that could feel hunger; scraping at the door in a tape loop of robotic stupidity, a thing that had once been a person, someone whose picture had appeared in some high school year book...) and shot it twice in the back of the head, near the spine. It twitched and slumped, then started moving again—but weak now, like a dying roach. Probably have to incinerate the son of a bitch to really kill him, Jim thought.

Feeling numb, Jim dragged it away by the ankle and shoved it in the bathroom, crammed a board under the doorknob to lock the thing in. It made faint scrabbling sounds behind the door.

Jim went back to the closet. It was a long way across the little room. "Come on out, man, I shot the fucking thing," Jim said to the guy in the closet. He wanted living people around him.

Dwayne was pushing bodies up against the door to the hall. Samson's headless body, Ramon's body. Dwayne was crying without tears, his face contorted like a little kid's. Jim looked at him and thought: He's no more criminal than I am. Just another guy on a street corner. Used to be a kid watching Saturday morning cartoons.

Dragging mattresses up against the door, dumping them on the bodies, now. That wouldn't work for long. Those things could pull people's heads off. They were strong.

Jim opened the closet door. A black dude in a grimy jogging outfit was crouched in there, hugging his knees, shaking. There was a little snub-nosed gun on the floor between his feet. Probably used up all the rounds in it.

"Raiders, thas Raiders," Dwayne said.

"There a phone here?" Jim asked Raiders. Jim tasting vomit in his mouth.

"They gone?"

"No. They're outside," Jim said. Fighting panic. Fighting the urge to shove the guy out of the closet and get in it himself. "I said, 'Is there a phone here?'" *Don't lose it don't lose it don't lose it...*

"In the office."

"Where's that?"

"Behind the steel door, down the hall. Give me that fucking gun."

"No way." Jim turned his back on Raiders. Stepped over the corpse. The dead thing made a movement with its whole body like a worm on a hot sidewalk, and then lay still again.

Jim stopped in the middle of the room, his gun in his hand, wanting to scream but not having the energy, still sick to his stomach, thinking that all this should feel dreamlike, but it didn't now, not anymore.

That was because there was a smooth and ordinary continuity between being strung out, crashing on crack, perceiving himself as human vermin...and being here, with the dying and the dead who moved around.

The hall door heaved inward, cracking down the middle. A black woman's face with milky eyes in the break. *Big* black woman wearing bloodstained designer jeans, but naked above the waist. She had one enormous pendulous breast, the other

mostly chewed away. Her upper lip raggedly absent so that
her teeth showed in permanent feral baring. She was pushing
through the blocked doorway, pressing the broken wood
aside.

Climbing over the dead. The dead climbing over the dead.

"Base," she said, in a croak. "Crack. Rock. Silver top. Base."

"Some kind of poison in the base," Dwayne whispered to
himself. He was standing with his back to the wall opposite
the door, just looking at her. "Kills them and the dark wave
brings them back."

"The dark what?" Jim asked.

"Garland...Uncle Garland said—" He shook his head. "It's
just too much greed, he said one time. Spills over and changes
things..."

Dwayne and Jim stared at the woman, and then at the two
dead men coming in behind her. They weren't cooperating
with her consciously, but shoving in beside her like impatient
commuters forcing their way onto a BART train. Two walking
dead men, one white, an aging punk rocker, and the other
black. Their faces peeling away, one of them missing his eyes.

The light flickered. Jim thought the bulb was going to go
out and they'd be in here, in the dark with these things sniffing
after them. The light flickered again, but didn't quite go out.
The shadows distorting the faces on those two living dead
men in the hall. Jim thought, in the flickering light, that their
faces had changed. Their faces become Dwayne's face, Jim
Diggins' face. Mouthing, "Base, Rock. Silver Top. Base."

Jim raised his gun

Raiders stepped up from behind, clouted Jim on the side
of the head with the empty snubnose. Jim went to his knees,
skull tolling like a cracked bell, and Raiders yanked the gun
from Jim's hand, ran at the big dead black woman shrieking
"FUCKING FREAK BITCH CUNT!" Firing the gun into her face.
She threw her arms around him like a loving mother, then
fell backwards, pulling him onto her. The two hungry dead
men behind her lunged onto him, biting down on his head.
Sharing it, biting into Raiders' skull from both sides. Jim could
hear the sound of it, of their teeth in the bone of Raiders'
cranium. A squeaking grating sound that seemed somehow
louder than Raiders' scream.

Then Raiders was quiet, and there were wet, crunching noises. Dwayne said, "Fuck this," and was dragging a mattress up, holding it like a shield. Jim got up, got behind the mattress with him, and helped him shove it onto the mass of feeding dead blocking the doorway, using the mattress to keep the dead down so Jim and Dwayne could scramble over it and out into the hall. Two more of the dead were swaying in the front door. Dwayne and Jim dodged to the right, down the hall. The office. Through the open steel door.

A kitchen. An AK47, without a magazine in it, lay on an old, ornate wooden kitchen table. Next to it was a freezer bag full of base crystal, half spilled onto the table top. On a sink to the back was a big, five gallon steel pot crusted with crack cocaine residue. A gallon can of something called BUG DETH *All New! Industrial Strength for Big Jobs!* stood on the counter next to the sink. The Hispanic boy in the corner, eating something. He had been about twelve. He was eating raw crack from another freezer bag, a sack with blood and brains dripped into it; chewing bloody crack cocaine up like a mouth full of rock candy.

There was a dead man on the floor; missing his head, too. Near the dead man, also on the floor, was a phone off the hook with a mechanical voice coming out of it, small and foolish, saying, *"If you are not going to make a call, please hang up the telephone..."*

Jim almost dove for the phone. Crouched in blood, by the stump of a neck, with an effort of will he made his hands work the touchtone buttons. His heart going off like one of those obnoxious car alarms.

The dead were coming down the hall. Scuffling. Making sniffing sounds. Dwayne scooped up a handful of the base fallen on the table, a big handful of crystals, couple thousand dollars worth. Stared at it hungrily. Jim watched the boy in the corner eating bloody rock cocaine, while he told 911 that there were murders happening here. Not trying to explain more than that. (Thinking, in some twitchy corner of his mind, that it would be easy to get a handful or two of the rock for himself, hide it somewhere, come back after the cops and the things were gone, fuck it, it wasn't like anything mattered anymore—and then he had a flash vision of himself chewing a hole in his own kid's head.) Jim told Dwayne, as he hung up the phone, "The shit's poisonous, Dwayne, even more than usual."

Dwayne looked at the double handful of rock cocaine. Then bent over, dipped the base in a puddle of blood and brains and tossed the whole double-handful through the door, into the hall. Scrabbling, clawing sounds as the dead went for it.

Jim Diggins carried the phone across the small room, and smashed the head of the dead boy eating the cocaine, twice, crushed his skull, very thoroughly, with a corner of the phone, each blow making the phone ring a little.

The boy slumped, twitching, bloody cocaine dribbling from his mouth...not dead, you couldn't kill them that easy.

11:30 P.M.

A lot of cops milling around.

The Detective in charge was named Johnson, a tall, mild-eyed black guy, a uniformed lieutenant with a college cadence to his talk. Jim had ditched the .45. Didn't tell the cops the background to the story. Johnson listened to the story, as Jim told it, then went to his cruiser, his face flashing in and out of red with the cherry-top light. He spoke into a microphone, something about cocaine-overdose hallucinations and mass murder and hysteria, as the paramedics carted the truly-dead away. Paramedics shaking their heads in weary amazement.

Carrying the *dead* dead. The others, the ambulatory dead, had crawled out back, when the cops had come. Hid themselves. Still functioning, instinctively, to protect themselves. Still out there, in the city, somewhere, sniffing around. Settling for any kind of living flesh they could find, now, Jim supposed.

But then again, it wouldn't take them long to find more crack heads.

Dwayne and Jim stood to one side. They'd been told to wait, put on the back burner for the moment. Johnson was convinced they were bystanders, not the killers. Jim said,

"Shit like this doesn't happen by accident, Dwayne. Something's talking to us. All of us."

Dwayne said nothing. He stared at light on the cop car. The headless bodies being hoisted into the ambulance.

Jim said, "What your Uncle said about a sickness in the air, the dark wave thing...Well, shit. I don't know. I mean, I don't know if there's a God, man, but I think we ought to act as if there is one, you know?"

Dwayne still said nothing.

"Dwayne?"

Dwayne said, softly, "I gettin' the fuck out of here."

"Where you going to go?"

"Way different neighborhood."

"Is that right? Hey, Lieutenant Johnson!"

The cop said something more into the mike, then walked over to them. "Yeah?"

"This man here stole my car. A few days ago. I went to talk to him about it when all this happened."

Dwayne said, "He's full of shit."

Jim said, "They dusted the car for prints. I insisted on it. They got your prints, Dwayne. They got evidence of that. Not of anything else." Meaning: no evidence that Jim had been buying drugs.

Dwayne looked at Jim like he was going to bite through Jim's skull himself. "You pale motherfucker."

"Just what I need," Johnson was saying, wearily putting cuffs on Dwayne. "As if I don't have enough to deal with. You have the right to remain silent..." He went through the whole thing.

"You don't know what I do for a living, Dwayne," Jim said, later, talking through the half-open window of the car; Johnson had put Dwayne in the back of a cruiser. "I'm a lawyer. I've gotta lot of connections. I can get you remanded to my custody, set you up in drug rehab. Both of us in drug rehab."

"Fuck you, you pale bullshit motherfucker."

"You better hold onto that attitude, you're gonna need it sometime, Dwayne. I'm doing this to help, man. Because I had a choice and you didn't."

"You think you on a Mission? *Fuck* you, you kneejerk liberal cocksucker!" Dwayne shouted out the car window as Johnson started the cruiser and drove off.

Jim was taken to the precinct in another cop car. After awhile all the rest of the police cars drove off into the night, vanishing into the darkness where the hungry dead were shuffling, sniffing the air.

BLACK HOLE SUN, WON'T YOU COME?

He could not rid himself of the feeling that the old shaman was playing with him—with Primut himself!—even though this toothless Indian, this bag of bones, was bound with rawhide thongs, staked out helplessly writhing under the hot coals, under the salt, the urine in his wounds. Totally contained, trapped in his own lodge on this wind-wracked Yukon ridge, tortured—yet in command? It was not possible.

"They say you are five hundred years old. I have reason to believe this is so," Primut told him. "They say you accomplish this with human sacrifice. There are hints it is a tradition older than the shamanism of the North American Indians. It sounds as if they're talking about Atlantis. But human sacrifice was practiced amongst the Aztecs—perhaps it came from there?"

The old shaman could not be drawn into discourse. He merely glowered and smirked through his suffering.

"Your methods," Primut went on, "are a combination of psychic displacement and human sacrifice—are they not? Speak. There is no good reason for you to prolong your suffering."

The old man did not answer, but only laughed with the rasping of a dull saw. Had he somehow taken a drug that buried the pain?

"I will let you languish now, perhaps to die, perhaps to live and contemplate the torture to come," Primut said, "and if—" He stopped, frowning, seeing the old man laugh again; though now the shaman was so weak the sound could not be heard.

Then the shaman spoke.

"I am going to die, you fool, and in seconds. I have no reason, by your lights, to tell you anything. So now I will tell you what you want to know—now that I cannot be forced to speak. Human sacrifice you call it. No. It must be done in face to face conflict with someone who can fight back, although it does not matter if they have a weapon, nor does it matter if they do fight back. They must be standing and unrestrained. Then you take the knife in your hand; you sense the knife with the whole of your attention; and you will focus another part of your attention in a certain part of your brain, and look at them with the other seeing, so..."

And in a few words he told the secret. Primut understood. He was not unfamiliar with the fundamental techniques of the esoteric world. It was, black magic and white, all work with the power that men call *the attention of the mind*.

"Now," said the old man, "you are wondering—" He paused to cough, and shudder. "...wondering why I have not renewed my power. That I will not tell you. I will tell you only that I learned that I had accrued a terrible debt, and would not make its payment any worse. I have chosen to call Death to my lodge and to give him meat and drink. Now Death, like any good guest, has brought me...also...a gift. And to you I have given only a—"

But the shaman said no more; death took him.

———— ◆ ————

That first morning of the Day of Halcyon Slaughtering, Primut stood on a high ledge of a deserted skyscraper in a deserted Manhattan, enjoying the autumn wind's futile efforts to dislodge him; he stood gazing down at the gathering in

Central Park, unable to believe his luck. Here the radically diminished population of the Earth had gathered, passively awaiting his rapacity. Ten thousand or so, in ragged concentricity around a circular mirror three stories high. People in their late teens—or seemingly so—through old age. No children. All races, all types, dressed in no special uniformity and with no special distinction.

Most of them waited with exasperating patience in the fields and woods around the clearing where the mirror stood. They calmly waited their turn to filter through the labyrinth, which was marked on the bare packed ground in white chalk before the high circular mirror, on four sides. It was something like the medieval labyrinths found on the floors of cathedrals. He had no notion what the ritual portended; he was well over a century out of touch with the remnants of Earth culture.

With a hunger for lives, he had descended from his Yukon caves, where he had holed up for more than a century, only to learn that a certain scientist, driven mad by the world's purulent overpopulation, promulgated a virus that would inexorably render humanity sterile. Social chaos followed, derailing efforts to create children in lab settings; only a few were born and after a time, no one tried anymore. The great Depopulation was seen to be the will of God. He gathered some sort of spiritual consensus had flowered and changed priorities. He knew nothing more and cared less.

How many of these ten thousand—the last human beings on Earth—would he have the pleasure of dispatching?

Each victim's life, consumed in his personal fire, was like the fuel that burned to fill the hot air balloon of his ascension. And knowing that, how could he not come to delight in it? Indeed, he concluded that it was merely his due. Was he not the center of all creation?

He knew perfectly well how relative this notion could be. Certainly everyone thought of themselves (or so he assumed) as the center of the universe. And so they were—so long as they succeeded in asserting that centeredness. It was a war of personal solipsisms. And if a man could be immortal— why not kill all sentient beings? What if it took a few hundred trillion years? How better to pass the time?

What were they doing, below, now? They'd ceased to mill through the labyrinths, had begun some sort of sheeplike group meditation, around the great circular mirror. Were they worshipping vanity, gazing at themselves in rapture? But no. He could feel it: it was something subtler.

Primut gazed down on the gathering in the park, and decided that the sheep had come to him to be shorn; the lambs to be slaughtered, and he would no longer keep them waiting. There was no point in being rude.

Down many flights of stairs he went, planning all the while, till he came to the street and the large rebuilt 20th century recreational vehicle he used for travel, and for the array of his tools.

Because of the rules of the ritual, he would have to use the blades. Bullets would have been so much more expedient. But with the blades, it was like a reaving, if you thought of it in the Druidic way, he supposed, though in the American Indian tradition it was more like skinning an animal properly hunted down.

———— ◆ ————

Twilight. Primut watched the last people on Earth from the forest.

Central Park was almost entirely overgrown; it had gone almost ostentatiously wild. Only two paths were maintained, both leading to the earthen clearing near the middle, where once rock concerts had throbbed and political rallies had resonated with cheering. Now the fields and forests were absent of amplified sound; even of rollerbladers and babies in strollers: there were only the multifarious calls of song-birds, the ratchet-racketing of insects and sometimes the crack of elk clashing antlers; a family of leopards, and a pack of wolves, released when the Central Park Zoo was liberated, decades ago, were said to roam the park, feeding on the peacocks who poked through the grasses, the pheasants that whirred from copse to copse, the darting rabbits, and leaving the remains for the turkey vultures wheeling like shadows of the One Cross against the sky. Primut himself planned to leave gorgings for the glossy-black vultures.

Once more the last people were milling, in a steady line,
through the labyrinth painted on the ground; tracing the
labyrinth's weave from a mazy exterior to its heart, the void
at its center, which brought them face to face with the mirror.

Through binoculars, he watched as one by one the
followers of the labyrinth, on reaching its center, approached
the mirror. Here, they capered grotesquely, groping themselves
in parodies of sexual abandon, or preening as in mockery of
pride, or flailing in an aping of anger, of violence, of grasping
and gluttony, of mindless sin; and as they did this, they
watched their reflection in the mirror. And then, after but a
minute or two of this, they ceased this demonstration, and
stood silently, watching, as the reflection continued to cycle
through its mockery. It carried on the japing without the japer.
Was what seemed a mirror some highly refined video computer
technology? Was it magic? Primut only wondered at it idly.

Each of the labyrinth wenders watched himself or herself
mocked by the mirror; and then watched as the image
vanished entirely. It faded and was gone and there was only
blankness; the mirror reflected everything in the park but the
one standing directly before it. And then the vanished image
reappeared—this image quiet, serene, present, like the one
reflected. It duplicated the sleek, economic movements of
the man or woman before it, as they turned away and walked
off the labyrinth to the crowd waiting in the field, where they
were given food.

And so it went, as the hours passed; a little light seemed
to glimmer from the mirror, just enough to continue.
Sometimes there was music, but it was music that, somehow,
Primut could barely hear. Sometimes there was dancing;
sometimes not. Sometimes food and drink were passed.
Sometimes not. But always the lines wound quietly through
the labyrinth.

Large predators will pursue a herd of antelope discreetly;
usually hanging back, watching, following at a distance,
waiting for a straggler, an animal sick or lame to pick off, the
predator doing its bit for natural selection. Primut flattered

himself that he was one of these; though in his heart, in some squamous chamber sealed with scar tissue, he knew it was not so; that he was not in harmony with nature, the way a hunter might be. But buffering away such knowledge is just what scar tissue is for.

So he felt the exhilaration of a hunter as he stalked the edges of the crowd, that evening, seeking stragglers. He saw no one stupid or lame or sick; but they all had to relieve themselves, in holes dug and re-filled after use, from time to time. And some would take walks, to appreciate the woods of an evening. A few made languid love at a little distance from the others. These were his targets, at first, as he probed at this temporary organism of consensual parts, this, the Final Crowd.

The first few—a man alone, then two women strolling together—he killed purely for sustenance, to restore his charge of provisional immortality. They seemed only faintly surprised and utterly unafraid as he braced them and gave them a moment to respond—as ritually required—as he drew the S-curved blade from the long strip of blades dangling from his stained leather apron, and then hissed the blade out in a single deft motion to open his victim from stem to stern. They cried out and looked at him in something like astonishment and pity and with another look which he could not quite identify and then expired with truly surprising expedience. There was no writhing and groaning, and no look of horror as life drained away. He drew the life force from them, and was revitalized, but never quite satisfied.

He expected them to try to disperse, when the bodies were found, or to send policing parties after him, but neither thing happened; he saw not even a hubbub of response to the murders. They simply buried the bodies, said a prayer, and went about their business: the same business as before.

"What tiresome, boring people," he muttered, frustrated.

After the next series of murders he tried to stir them up a bit, just for fun, leaving messages written in blood on the white paths to the labyrinth, beside the corpses. His favorite message was:

NO APOLOGIES TO NIETSZCHE
(THE SYPHILITIC MOTHERFUCKING WIMP)

and, second to that:

AYN RAND WAS A GUTLESS OLD DYKE

...though he knew the allusions were probably lost on them.

He tried leaving bloody swastikas, pentagrams, goat-heads, the usual inflammatory symbols. No reaction beyond a mild bemusement.

After a few hundred victims, as the autumn wore on, fraying toward winter, he tired of cryptic messages and decided on direct interrogation. He felt a kind of perverse, whimsical impulse to understand these people. Something to think about once they were gone. Perhaps he could write it up—for himself to read in a few hundred years.

He fully intended to kill them all. He believed he would reach a kind of critical mass when he killed nine or ten thousand, that would give him so much vital energy he would need no more renewal; he would be immortal forever.

One day Primut caught a celebrant—so they called themselves—in a snare. He dragged the fellow—about 45, a tired-eyed blond—off the trail and into the woods. The man didn't try to resist, but only watched Primut curiously.

"Now," said Primut, "you will answer some questions for me."

"Certainly," the fellow said. "My name is Wenj, by the way."

"My name is Not Legion. There's only one of me. That's the point. Tell me this: do you not know who I am?"

"You're the gentleman who kills."

"Do you know why?"

"Something ritualistic. Probably involving sacrifice, maybe the endowment of power, or longevity. The usual sort of thing."

Wenj was sitting up, with the snare around his ankle, one knee cocked, leaning against a tree, watching Primut with an exasperating confidence.

"So do not your people intend to do something about me?"

"We already have. We have decided to love you."

"Oh, gag. I mean, really, have a sense of proportion. Couldn't you try to restrain me and then love me?"

"Do you enjoy being restrained?"

"No."

"Wouldn't be very loving to restrain you then."

"But don't you love one another? After all, if you don't try to kill or capture me, I'll kill more of your friends. Not very loving of you to fail to protect them from torture and murder."

"When you've hurt them—have they seemed really hurt?"

Primut could not answer, not definitely. He had seen physical pain in them, but no matter what he did there was always that maddening sense of pity from them. They seemed to always have a kind of detached acceptance, a way of being part of the suffering but apart from it too. At last he said, "There's some sort of...self hypnotism going on. Or maybe drugs."

"None of that, no. It's just the state we're in...is fixed in the ground and in the void, and we are absolutely present and absolutely not-here at the same time. You can only hurt our false selves. When you hurt us you hurt the capering, primitive thing, the shadow thing, the trickster ape you see in the first stage of the mirror ritual. Not our actual selves."

"Horseshit. You're brainwashed religious zealots."

"If you like."

"Who's your leader? The charismatic guru type."

"There is none. We've quite consumed our teachers."

"Well, you can't possibly love me. You can strike New Age poses of 'giving love back for hate' or whatever, but that treacly crap aside—even the great philosophers don't prescribe endless blind love. It's about balance, even for you humanistic types."

"We have our own balance. You know perfectly well I love you, Primut. But in a sense I cannot, as you say, love you: only with God's help can I love you. God loves you through me."

"Bull-fucking-shit. And how do you know my name?"

"Look at me and know..."

Primut looked at him for a moment. There was no sappiness, no cloying falseness about Wenj. Just a steady gaze of maddeningly bottomless compassion—

Primut looked away. "Some sort of mind control, telepathy, something of the sort. I will not allow you to do this to me."

"Whatever you like."

"You remind me of those little creatures in the Al Capp comic strip...'Kill me, fry me, eat me!'"

"I'm afraid that was before my time."

"You disgust me."

So saying he drew his number seven blade. It was double-bladed, shaped like the letter Y, with the stem of the Y being the grip. He glowered down at Wenj who looked up at him without a trace of fear. With a single stroke of two blades, Primut sliced Wenj's head from his shoulders. The celebrant made not a sound.

The next morning he began the long reaving. He stepped out of the woods, and walked up to the crowd.

No one ran.

He began to cut. People fell. Still no one ran. In fact, after a time, those on the edge of the crowd nearest him began to move toward him, stepping over the dead, pausing to say goodbye to the dying, coming up for their turn.

He gutted and sliced and tore till he was head to foot dripping in red muck and was up to his ankles in filleted humanity and still they came. They all gave him the same look. They didn't actually say, "I love you." But it was in the look.

"I defy your mind control!" he bellowed, slicing.

He shouted himself hoarse and sliced his blade dull. He went away to rest, and bathe, and sharpen his blade. No one followed. They cleared away the bodies and the next morning they were there waiting. *I love you.* They continued their ritual at the labyrinth, the mirror. He tried to break the mirror and couldn't; he tried to blot out the labyrinth but they didn't seem to need to actually see the lines to know where it was. He turned to blotting out humanity instead. He whetted his blades and he hewed a forest of humanity down. The wolves and the vultures came when the bodies became more than could be quickly buried. Still he continued his endless wet work.

And so it went. He cut a swathe through them, and they seemed neither eager to receive it nor to escape. They approached him out of sheer generosity—or so, he thought, they'd have him believe.

I love you.

He tried eating their flesh to shock them. No particular reaction. Just the pity; the love. He tried torturing one before the others, but after about an hour the light went out in the victim's eyes. She simply died, though she really shouldn't have: he'd been very careful.

What's happened?" he demanded. "How has she died? I have not permitted her to bleed to death."

"The others who already died came and took her," said one of the older men. "Spirit to spirit."

He recommenced reaving, furious and frustrated. I love you. He forgot about his own ritual; his own imbibing.

This time he cut a furious swathe, his limbs moving so fast, so hard, he was like a human harvester, a lawnmower of flesh, and he collapsed of exhaustion, at the end of the day, and slept among seeping corpses.

The next day he took up his work with grim determination, finding a rhythm, moving with an almost supernatural economy of motion, like a Taoist butcher, his blade whispering their bodies asunder.

Weeks passed. The winter winds began to nose into the city like Yukon wolves. He put on gloves and his breath steamed as he worked; wounds steamed into the sky. He had long ceased his own immortality ritual. He sensed he was long past needing it. What he did now was purely philosophical.

He harvested, he reaved, he cut them down...

At last there was only one left. One in a seemingly endless ring of bodies.

"There is no one left to bury your friends," he said.

"The vultures bury them in their way. I love you, Primut."

With a shriek of rage that echoed out of the park and off the crumbling skyscrapers, Primut killed him.

He had killed everyone in the world. Personally. Face to face. And he was alone, and it was an enormous relief. He had

done it; he was the center of the human universe. He'd have
known, psychically, if there were other living humans on the
Earth. They had all come here. There were no space colonies.
There was only...Primut.

He didn't have a problem with it. He thought perhaps
he'd kill an elk, have a steak, forage a brandy, settle down
with his CD player and some Mozart.

I love you, Primut.

"What?"

He looked around. Had someone spoken?

I love you. I love you. We love you. We all love you. God
loves you.

Now he could see them. The power that he had
accumulated over the years opened the window of the spirit
world, and he could see them: the thousands he had
butchered. He could see them all around him. Transparent,
but things of substance, if not biologically substantial. He
snarled, and drew his number 13, a very light machete, and
he sliced through the nearest of them: it was Wenj.

"Hullo, Primut. I love you."

"SHUT UP, WENJ! AND DIE AGAIN!"

Slice—the blade went through and of course there was no
effect. I love you. Slice. I love you. Slash. I love you.

He cut and cut and cut no one. None of them were hurt.
Their forms went back together the way water does after
you've run your hand through it. I love you. They were all
around him, radiating love and acceptance.

And he...would live forever.

He thought of suicide. But of course he'd be among them
spiritually and he'd only hear, endlessly...

I love you. I accept you. I love you, Primut.

He ran. But even when he was away from them, they
were always with him. That's how love is. I love you. Love is
Hell, you bet your ass.

Primut dropped his weapons, every one of them, and fell
to the ground, and clutched himself into a fetal position, and
buried his face in his arms and tried not to listen, but it was
all the louder, all the stronger thus, the very thing he feared
most: actual love. And he knew that it would inevitably

consume him, and burn at him till what he had created over the centuries was only ashes; and these devils, these nightmares, these horrors would make him love them back. And he hated them for it.

JOHN SHIRLEY is the author of numerous novels, screenplays (*The Crow*), and short stories. Some of his best known novels include CITY COME A-WALKIN', ECLIPSE, WETBONES, and the recent SILICON EMBRACE. His short fiction has previously been collected in HEATSEEKER, NEW NOIR, and THE EXPLODED HEART. He lives in the San Francisco area with his wife Michelina.

The URL for the official John Shirley Web site is
http://www.darkecho.com/JohnShirley.html